FRANCHISING IN AFRICA 2014

Legal and Business Considerations

KENDAL H. TYRE, JR., EXECUTIVE EDITOR
DIANA VILMENAY-HAMMOND, MANAGING EDITOR
COURTNEY L. LINDSAY II, ASSISTANT EDITOR

LEXNOIR FOUNDATION

LexNoir Foundation is the charitable, educational arm of LexNoir, an international network of lawyers connecting the African Diaspora.

This book, *Franchising in Africa 2014: Legal and Business Considerations*, is published by LexNoir Foundation and reflects the points of view of the authors and editors as of the date of publication and does not necessarily represent the opinions, interpretations, or positions of the law firms or organizations with which they are affiliated, nor the opinions, interpretations or positions of LexNoir Foundation or LexNoir.

www.lexnoir.org

Table of Contents

International Franchising in the African Context

Kendal H. Tyre, Jr. and Diana Vilmenay-Hammond
Nixon Peabody LLP

Financing the African Franchise Venture

Benjamin Gyepi-Garbrah, Jr. and
Manbegrot Shimellis SATIG LLC

Inclusive Business in Africa

John Luiz, Jonathan Goldberg and Lauri E. Elliott
Conceptualee, Inc.

Franchising in Angola

João Afonso Fialho
Miranda Correia Amendoeira & Associados

Franchising in Botswana

Bonzo Makgalemele
Chibanda, Makgalemele & Company

Franchising in Burundi

Gilbert Nyatanyi
ENSafrica | Burundi

Franchising in Cape Verde

João Afonso Fialho
Miranda Correia Amendoeira & Associados

Franchising in Democratic Republic of the Congo

Emery Mukendi Wafwana, Nady Mayifuila Dina, Jonathan van Kempen, Edouard Laddy Tshishimbi Mpamba, Emmanuel Otshudiema Bengu and Dr. Sancy Lenoble Matschinga
Emery Mukendi Wafwana & Associates

Franchising in Egypt

Girgis Abd El-Shahid
Sarwat A. Shahid Law Firm

Franchising in Ethiopia

Yohannes Assefa and Biset Beyene Molla
Pioneer International Legal Consulting

Franchising in Ghana

Divine K.D. Letsa and Elizabeth Ashun
Bentsi-Enchill, Letsa & Ankomah

Franchising in Kenya

John Syekei and Joseph Githaiga
Coulson Harney

Franchising in Mozambique

Diogo Xavier da Cunha
Miranda Correia Amendoeira & Associados

Franchising in Nigeria

Theophilus Emuwa and Tiwalola Okeyinka
ÆLEX

Franchising in Rwanda

Désiré Kamanzi
ENSafrica | Rwanda

Franchising in South Africa

Taswell Papier
ENSafrica

Franchising in Tunisia

Yessine Ferah
FERAH & Associates Law Firm

Franchising in Zambia

Mabvuto Sakala
Corpus Legal Practitioners

Franchising in Zimbabwe

Nellie R.F. Tiyago-Jinjika
Scanlen & Holderness

Appendices

About the Editors

Kendal H. Tyre, Jr.

Kendal is a partner in the Washington, D.C., office of Nixon Peabody LLP. He handles domestic and cross-border transactions, including mergers and acquisitions, joint ventures, strategic alliances, licensing, and franchise matters.

In his franchise and licensing practice, Kendal counsels domestic and international franchisors, franchisees, licensors, licensees, and distributors regarding U.S. state and federal franchise laws as well as foreign franchise legislation in a variety of jurisdictions. Kendal drafts and provides advice with regard to franchise and license agreements, disclosure documents, and area development agreements and has extensive experience drafting and negotiating a variety of other commercial agreements. His client base spans the United States and foreign countries, including South Africa, Kenya, and the United Kingdom.

Kendal is a frequent contributor to franchise publications and a frequent speaker at franchise programs held by the American Bar Association's Forum on Franchising and the International Franchise Association.

Kendal is co-chair of the firm's Diversity Action Committee and its Africa group. Kendal is also the executive director of the LexNoir Foundation.

E-mail address: ktyre@nixonpeabody.com

Diana Vilmenay-Hammond

Diana is an attorney in the Washington, D.C., office of Nixon Peabody LLP. She is a member of the firm's Franchise & Distribution team.

In her franchise practice, Diana works with domestic and international franchisors on transactional and litigation matters. Specifically, she counsels franchisor clients regarding state and federal franchise laws, disclosure, and registration obligations. Diana drafts and negotiates various commercial agreements, including international franchise and development agreements.

Diana has co-authored numerous articles on franchising and frequently co-hosted the Nixon Peabody franchise law webinar series. Recent topics have included:

- "Franchise Case Law Round-Up: Implications for Your Franchise;"
- "Social Media Part II: Best Practices in Protecting Your Brand in the New Media;" and
- "The Awuah Case: Bellwether or Outlier."

Diana received her J.D. from Howard University School of Law and her B.A. from Georgetown University. She is a member of the American Bar Association (Forum on Franchising).

Email address: dvilmenay@nixonpeabody.com

Courtney L. Lindsay II

Courtney L. Lindsay II is an associate in Nixon Peabody's Corporate and Finance practice. In his corporate practice, Courtney assists for-profit and nonprofit entities with transactional matters and corporate governance. In various capacities, Courtney has been involved in multiple merger and acquisition transactions, including drafting and managing due diligence.

Previously, Courtney worked in the legal and business affairs department at a national cable network, where he handled matters related to the network's LLC agreement, including drafting board and member consent agreements.

As a student in the University of Virginia's law program, Courtney served as the Admissions Chair of the Black Law Students Association, where he was responsible for managing and organizing association events, as well as hosting admissions panels at undergraduate institutions throughout the mid-Atlantic region.

Courtney received his J.D. from the University of Virginia School of Law and his B.A. from the University of Virginia. He is admitted to practice in the Commonwealth of Virginia and the District of Columbia.

E-mail address: clindsay@nixonpeabody.com

Dedication

Kendal H. Tyre, Jr.: To Delores Marie and Ken Sr.

Diana Vilmenay-Hammond: To my family with lots of love

Courtney Lindsay: To Mom (Cindy), Dad (Courtney), my siblings, and family

Acknowledgment

This book could not have been written without the hard work and dedication of each of the contributing authors from various parts of the globe who are listed in *About the Authors*. Thank you.

We would like to acknowledge and extend our heartfelt gratitude to Michael Collier, Maria Stallings, Pierce Han, and Keri McWilliams of the Washington, D.C., office of Nixon Peabody LLP for their invaluable assistance in revising, proofing, and editing all the various editions of the manuscript.

To our family, friends, and others throughout the LexNoir community, words alone cannot express what we owe them for their encouragement that enabled us to complete this book—a special thanks to Liz for always going the extra mile with the kind of feedback that put flesh on the bones and to Tim for being there since the beginning and always being ready to assist (and, more often than not, critique).

About the Authors

Elizabeth Ashun—Elizabeth is a Foreign Associate at Bentsi-Enchill Letsa & Ankomah in Accra, Ghana. She relocated to Ghana from the United Kingdom in April 2013 and joined the Construction Infrastructure and Transportation practice group of Bentsi-Enchill Letsa & Ankomah until being called to the Ghana Bar. Elizabeth is a United Kingdom Qualified Commercial Property Solicitor with over nine years of experience in commercial property transactional work with experience in property development, sales and acquisitions, secured lending, corporate assistance, and landlord and tenant transactions in the retail, office, industrial, and new build residential sectors. Elizabeth has worked in various law firms and also the Public Sector in the United Kingdom.

Yohannes Assefa—Yohannes is the Managing Director of Pioneer International Legal Consulting in Addis Ababa, Ethiopia. He is an experienced and distinguished business lawyer with business management experience spanning 17 years in the United States and Africa.

Yohannes worked at the Rochester, New York, law firm of Harris Beach PLLC from 2003 to 2007 and then joined the Washington, D.C., office of Hawkins, Delafield and Wood, where he worked as a municipal securities attorney.

In November 2008, Yohannes moved to Ethiopia to help establish the Ethiopia Commodity Exchange (ECX) under a USAID technical advisory contract. Most recently, he served as the Chief of Party of the USAID Ethiopia WTO Accession Plus Project. Currently, he serves as an Adjunct Professor of Law at Addis Ababa University Faculty of Law.

Yohannes earned his law degree in 2001 from Northeastern University School of Law.

Emmanuel Otshudiema Bengu—Emmanuel is an associate at Emery Mukendi Wafwana & Associates. His areas of practice include contract, land and real estate, corporate, general commercial, labor and social security, mining, hydrocarbon, and OHADA law. Emmanuel received his law degree in economic and social law from the University of Kinshasa in 2006. He speaks French, Lingala, Tshiluba, Otetela, and Swahili.

Diogo Xavier Da Cunha—Diogo is the partner responsible for the Mozambique practice of Miranda Correia Amendoeira & Associados in Lisbon, Portugal. He currently provides legal advice to a number of international companies doing business in Portugal and abroad.

Diogo's practice is predominantly of a corporate/commercial nature, with a strong energy component. He is regularly involved in a wide range of corporate transactions and has advised oil, mining, energy, and other international and Portuguese companies in respect of various legal issues, such as company acquisitions, international commercial arbitration, oil and gas agreements, energy law, contract and company law, and, in general, foreign investment operations.

Diogo is a regular contributor to several newspapers and legal bulletins, and has published articles and studies on several fields of law. He was ranked as an Expert in Corporate and M&A in the 2007, 2008, 2009, and 2010 editions of the European Legal Experts Guide. He is fluent in English, Spanish, and French.

Nady Mayifuila Dina—Nady is an associate and office manager of the New York branch of Emery Mukendi Wafwana & Associates. She joined the firm in 2010. Her practice includes business law (USA, DRC & OHADA), mining, energy and natural resources (DRC & OHADA), corporate law (USA, DRC & OHADA), foreign direct investment in French-speaking Africa as well as U.S. federal and state litigation. She holds a JD in private law and civil procedure and a JD in business law. She also holds a Master's Degree in European business law and an LL.M. degree in banking, corporate, and finance laws from

Fordham University, School of Law. She speaks French, English, Italian, and Lingala.

Lauri E. Elliott—Lauri is CEO of Afribiz Group, Inc. and Executive Director of The Afribiz Foundation. She is considered an expert and leader in developing new pathways in and business models for Africa.

Lauri designs, and leads a team which develops, large-scale system interventions to increase the amount of bi-lateral trade, investment, and business between Africa and the United States. Currently, the Foundation is working on partnership ecosystems to catalyze and accelerate partnerships between foreign and African firms – middle market, SMEs, and startups. The interventions integrate and leverage African Diaspora, women, minority, and community networks, offering economic opportunities to all.

She also is co-owner and Editor-in-Chief of Africa the Good News based in South Africa, as well as Afribiz Media based in the US. She is the lead, or sole, author of four books on Africa and global business – Redefining Business in the New Africa, Grow Rich in the New Africa, Going Global on a Dime, and Export to Explode Cashflow and Profits.

Lauri holds a Master of Arts degree in Education from Regent University.

Girgis Abd El-Shahid—Girgis is an attorney in the Sarwat A. Shahid Law Firm in Cairo, Egypt. He is a former Public Prosecutor. He received an LL.M. in International Legal Studies from Georgetown University Law Center, U.S.A.; an LL.B. from Cairo University, English Section; and a B.A. in Economics and Minor in Business Administration from the American University in Cairo. Since his entry into the private practice of law, Girgis has provided legal services to numerous national and multinational companies operating in the Middle East Region. He specializes in banking and finance, securities offerings, joint venture arrangements, acquisitions, legal due diligence, corporate and commercial agreements, telecommunications, and intellectual property litigation. Girgis speaks Arabic and English.

Theophilus I. Emuwa—Theo is a partner at AELEX in Lagos, Nigeria, focused on commercial law. He is widely acknowledged as one of Nigeria's leading tax practitioners. He regularly advises on Nigerian companies' income and petroleum profits tax issues, corporate structures, shareholder rights, and other corporate governance issues. Theo has provided advice on privatization options and strategies for clients, reviewed business process and procedures for operating in the petroleum sector, led several due diligence reviews, and advised on environmental matters and compensation issues after an oil spill.

Theo is an active member of International Trademark Association (INTA) and is on the editorial board of the *Trademark Reporter*, a journal of the INTA. He is the author of the Nigeria section of the *International Annual Review of Trademark Jurisprudence* (also published by the INTA) and a member of the Intellectual Property Lawyers' Association of Nigeria. Theo is also a member of the section on intellectual property, communications, and technology law of the IBA and the Intellectual Property Law Association of Nigeria. Theo is admitted to practice law in England and Wales, Nigeria, and Ghana.

Yessine Ferah—Yessine is the Managing Director of FERAH & Associates Law Firm in Tunis, Tunisia. He is a tax and corporate lawyer with specialization in large-scale commercial transactions. He has many years of experience representing major multinational companies in private and public domestic and cross-border mergers and acquisitions, joint ventures and alliances, tax strategy, banking and finance, and complex commercial agreements. He has been counsel on a number of transactions within energy (oil, gas, and electricity), telecommunications, banking, and tourism industries.

Yessine obtained the post-graduate qualification (DEA) in law from the University of Legal, Political, and Social Sciences of Tunis-University of Tunis, and is currently working toward a

Ph.D. in law at the University of Paris I Panthéon-Sorbonne. He also attended the 2004 Program of Instruction for Lawyers at Harvard Law School. He is a member of the Association of International Petroleum Negotiators, the Chambre Tuniso-Française de Commerce et d'Industrie, and the Bar Association of Tunisia.

João Afonso Fialho—João is the partner responsible for the Cape Verde practice of Miranda Correia Amendoeira & Associados in Lisbon, Portugal. He started his career in the law office of Tomás Andrade Rocha where his practice was mostly focused on litigation. In his early years of practice, João acted for a variety of clients in the finance sector, including banks, consumer credit companies, aviation companies, oil firms, and automakers. From 1992 to 1997, João was also legal advisor to the Loures and the Lisbon City Halls, having participated in several projects related to the Lisbon 94-European Culture Capital initiative.

After joining Miranda Correia Amendoeira & Associados, João expended his practice considerably. In addition to a litigation practice, he became involved in several large investment projects in Portugal, Angola, and other jurisdictions, in such diverse areas as oil and gas, diamonds and mining, infrastructures, telecommunications, real estate, shipping, and aviation. João is a regular contributor to various legal publications. He was ranked as an Expert in Dispute Resolution in the 2008, 2009 and 2010 editions of the *European Legal Experts Guide*. João is fluent in English.

Joseph Githaiga—Joseph is a senior associate in the Nairobi, Kenya, office of Coulson Harney Advocates. He is an accomplished financial services lawyer with more than 14 years of post-admission experience, including eight years as an in-house counsel for two of Australia's premier financial institutions—Macquarie Bank Limited and Westpac Banking Corporation. Joseph returned to Kenya in late 2009 to take up a position as a senior lawyer with Coulson Harney. He is a member of the Law Society of New South Wales and the Law Society of Kenya.

During his career in Australia and Kenya, Joseph has advised a broad range of clients including fund managers, insurance companies, banks, and private equity investors on a wide variety of commercial legal matters and transactions. Currently, his core practice areas include banking and finance, private equity, regulatory advice, and due diligence investigations.

Notable articles that Joseph has published include:

- "*New Business Vehicle in Kenya — Limited Liability Partnerships*"

- "*Intellectual Property Law and the Protection of Indigenous Folklore & Knowledge*", *E-Law—Murdoch University Electronic Journal of Law*, V5 No.2, June 1998

Jonathan Goldberg—Jonathan is the Joint Chief Executive Officer of Global Business Solutions, a consulting firm based in South Africa. In his professional capacity, Jonathan acts as a consultant, lecturer, attorney, and author on matters relating to Labour Law, Industrial Relations, and Broad-Based Black Economic Empowerment. Jonathan is also an Arbitration and Mediation panelist; former Commissioner of the Commission for Conciliation, Mediation, and Arbitration; and a member of the Tokiso dispute settlement panel. He was also recently appointed as a committee member of the Employment Conditions Commission. Jonathan's broader business leadership and acumen was recognized when he received the Border-Kei Chamber of Business/Daily Dispatch businessman of the year award for 2009. Recently Jonathan was awarded the Business Person—Entrepreneur 2012 award at the annual ABSA Jewish Awards.

Jonathan received his Bachelor in Commerce and Bachelors of Laws from the University of Port Elizabeth, located in Port Elizabeth, South Africa. He received his Master's in Business Administration from the University of Stellenbosch in Cape Town, South Africa.

Benjamin Gyepi-Garbrah, Jr.—Benjamin is a Managing Principal of SATIG LLC. He has over 15 years of experience in finance, project management, and business development gathered from working with some of the world's leading financial institutions. These include the Capital Group Companies, Capital Research and Management, Goldman Sachs, and ING Group.

As Managing Principal at SATIG, Benjamin has built the firm's loan origination and cross border funding practice with proprietary funders and lenders of record. Benjamin provides strategic direction for the firm and establishes in-country teams to source and complete transactions. He also develops project life cycles, from origination to execution and spearheads business development initiatives for institutions seeking new market opportunities. As manager of SATIG's franchising division, he serves as the lead franchise strategist and is responsible for sourcing and mobilizing debt and equity capital for clients.

Benjamin is an alumnus of Middlebury College and has studied at Harvard Business School Summer Venture Program and the University of Ghana.

Désiré Kamanzi—Désiré Kamanzi is the head of ENSafrica | Rwanda and has 15 years of experience practicing as an advocate in business law, including commercial law, contract law, banking and financial law, labor law, intellectual property law, mining law, telecommunication law, and ADR mechanisms. His practice experience includes assisting leading local and international investors in establishing their businesses in Rwanda and he has acted for a number of major listed and unlisted clients in the mining, telecoms, transport, and financial services sectors.

Désiré serves as the Secretary General for the Rwandan Law Society and has advised the Rwandan Government through its Investment and Export Promotion Agency (currently Rwanda Development Board) as the Chief Legal Counsel and Director for Trade & Investment Promotion. He has lectured at the law faculty of the National University of Rwanda and has been intricately involved in the drafting of certain identified key priority areas of the Law in Rwanda.

Désiré received his Bachelor of Law (with honors) and Bachelor of Civil Law from the National University of Rwanda. He received his Master of Laws from the University of Ottawa.

Divine K.D. Letsa—Divine is a partner at Bentsi-Enchill, Letsa & Ankomah in Accra, Ghana. He joined Bentsi-Enchill, Letsa & Ankomah in 1990 and currently leads the firm's Construction, Infrastructure & Transportation practice group. He is active in commercial work for oil companies. His firm has six main practice groups including Construction, Infrastructure and Transportation; Energy and Natural Resources; Litigation and Dispute Resolution; Financial Institutions and Capital Markets; Business and Industry; and Technology, Media and Telecommunications. The firm is the Ghana member of Lex Mundi and Lex Africa.

He received his LL.B from the University of Ghana in 1973 and his law degree from Ghana School of Law in 1975. Prior to joining Bentsi-Enchill, Letsa & Ankomah, Divine was the Assistant Director for Civil Litigation and Legal Advice, Ministry of Justice in Cross River State, Nigeria. Divine was a lecturer for the faculty of law at the University of Cross River State. Divine has also served as a legal officer for the State Insurance Corporation of Ghana.

John Luiz—John Luiz is a professor at the Graduate School of Business (GSB) at the University of Cape Town, specializing in International Business Strategy; Business, Society, and Government; and the Economics of Emerging Markets. In addition, he is Director of International Relations at the GSB. Previously he was a professor at the Wits Business School and served in various capacities including as their Director of International Programs and as Academic Director. He has also been Executive Dean in the Faculty of Management at the University of Johannesburg.

John works as a consultant and has undertaken research for the African Development Bank in Tunisia, Development Bank of Southern Africa, the Industrial Development Corporation, the Department of Trade and Industry, the United States Agency for International Development, the Johannesburg Development Agency, and the Centre for Development and Enterprise amongst others. He is active in management training and executive education at several leading multinational and South African corporations and public entities. He has lectured at various universities and programs including the INSEAD My Globe Program, the Grow Your Business program, and the Management Development Program with Duke University.

René-Claude Madebari—René is an associate advocate at ENSafrica | Burundi. He practices in Burundi and specializes in public procurement, corporate law, banking, and finance law. He has published a number of articles and presentations and was a contributor to *Doing Business 2013*, in association with the International Finance Corporation and the World Bank.

René received a LLB from the Université Lumière de Bujumbura in 2009. He is a member of the Burundian Bar and the East African Law Society and is fluent in English, French, Kirundi, and Swahili.

Bonzo Makgalemele—Bonzo is a senior partner at Chibanda, Makgalemele & Company in Gaborone, Botswana. She heads the Commercial Division of her firm. Her practice area consists mainly of corporate and commercial work including intellectual property, commercial agreements, commercial litigation, procurement, legislative reviews, policy formulation, and privatization. She is admitted to practice in The Supreme Court of South Africa and The High Court of Botswana. Based in Gaborone and founded in 1994, her firm is a multi-practice law firm.

Bonzo received her Bachelor of Laws degree from the University of Botswana in 1990, a post graduate certificate in Advanced Corporate and Securities Law from the University of

South Africa in 2005, and a certificate in Infrastructure Project Finance from the Institute of Public Private Partnership in 2006.

Dr. Sancy Lenoble Matschinga—Sancy is a Juriste International of Emery Mukendi Wafwana & Associates. Prior to joining the law firm in 2013, he worked in several law firms in France, in the French Ministry of Interior (Department of Homeland Security), and the French Council of State. His areas of practice include public business law (public contracts, European public procurement, infrastructures, public-private partnerships). His areas of practice also include mining and hydrocarbon, and natural resources and investment law in French-speaking African countries. Sancy holds a Ph.D. in public law, a Post-Master's degree in public and private law of economics from Evry Val d'Essonne University, a Master's degree in public business law from Paris 1 Panthéon-Sorbonne University, and a Master's degree in law from Marien-Ngouabi University. He also holds the bar certification of attorney-at-law from Paris Bar School. In 2012, he was certified with a Master Series for Distinguished Leaders from Skinner Leadership Institute in Washington, D.C. He is a member of the French-American Bar Association and he speaks French, English, Lingala, and Munukutuba.

Biset Beyene Molla—Biset is an attorney with Pioneer International Legal Consulting in Addis Ababa, Ethiopia. He is an experienced and licensed lawyer with extensive tax and regulatory compliance experience. Biset graduated with an LLB in law from Addis Ababa University, Faculty of Law, in July 2003. Shortly after graduation, he worked for the Ethiopian Federal First Instance Court where he served as an assistant judge until November 2005. He joined Alpha University College as Graduate Assistant II while studying for his master's in Business Law (LLM).

Shortly after he finished his graduate degree, Biset was promoted to the rank of lecturer at Alpha University College. He later joined the Ethiopian Commodity Exchange as Discipline and Enforcement Manager where he also worked as Assistant General Counselor. In 2010, he was admitted to practice law before the Ethiopian Federal Courts and began practicing law as a litigator. Currently, Biset's practice focuses on litigation before the Ethiopian Federal courts and tax and regulatory consultations. He also advises the National Exchange Actors Association at the Ethiopia Commodity Exchange. Biset also lectures at the Faculty of Law, Addis Ababa University

Edouard Laddy Tshishimbi Mpamba—Edouard has been an associate of Emery Mukendi Wafwana & Associates since 2013. His areas of practice include business and corporate, hydrocarbon, public procurement, mining, investment, land and real estate, intellectual property law, and litigation. Edouard received his law degree in private law from the University of Lubumbashi in 2002. He also has a background in international criminal law having worked as law clerk at the office of the prosecutor of the International Criminal Court at The Hague. He speaks English, French, Tshiluba, Lingala, and Swahili.

Gilbert Nyatanyi—Gilbert heads up ENSafrica | Burundi and is an executive at ENSafrica. He has more than 15 years of experience in general legal advice and more than 10 years of solid experience in banking and finance law. He practices in Burundi and specializes in secured transactions, acquisition and corporate finance, syndicated loans, and capital markets. He has acted for several companies, financial institutions, and governments on a wide range of legal matters in Europe and Africa (especially the United Republic of Tanzania, the Democratic Republic of Congo, the Central African Republic, Rwanda, and Burundi), and has an extensive high level network on the African continent. Gilbert's practice experience includes advising several international clients in connection with assets financing, credit transactions, mergers and acquisitions, and secured transactions.

Gilbert has a Masters of Law (1995) from the University of Ghent (Belgium) and is fluent in English, French, Dutch, German, and Kinyarwanda. Gilbert is recognized as a leading lawyer by the following reputable rating agency and its publication: *Chambers and Partners Global Guide to the World's Leading Lawyers 2012 and 2013*—General Business

Law (Burundi) and 2013 General Business Law (Burundi) (South Africa).

Taswell Papier—Taswell is a director at ENSafrica in Cape Town, South Africa. He has 22 years of experience. He currently practices as an attorney in the corporate commercial department. He specializes in black economic empowerment transactions and infrastructural projects and is the lead advisor on one of the country's largest infrastructural development projects. He has extensive experience in mergers and acquisitions, franchising matters, and has advised on one of South Africa's leading and most significant oil and gas initiatives currently underway.

Taswell has also acted as a mediator in a number of high profile commercial disputes. He has acted for international corporations doing business in Africa, South African corporations doing business internationally, and for the country's largest financial institutions, including the Financial Services Board. He also advises on Parliamentary and ministerial matters, and has acted for all spheres of government—local, provincial, and national. Taswell's practice experience includes all aspects of corporate commercial law, such as the drafting of commercial contracts and corporate governance.

Mabvuto Sakala—Mabvuto is a partner at Corpus Legal Practitioners in Lusaka, Zambia, and a lecturer at the University of Zambia Law School. He has been in practice since 1997. Mabvuto handles a wide range of legal matters including those involving alternative dispute resolution, arbitration and mediation, and business and commercial litigation. He heads the Dispute Resolution department and the Employment Law specialty practice group. Mabvuto's firm, formerly known as Corpus, has been a member of Lex Africa, a network of leading law firms on the African continent. It is also a member of the World Services Group.

Mabvuto received his LL.B. in Law in 2000 from the University of Zambia, a practice certificate from Zambia Institute of Advance Legal Education in 2002, and a Masters of Law in 2006 from the University of Nottingham in the United Kingdom.

Manbegrot Shimellis—Manbegrot is an attorney and associate at SATIG, LLC, where he is directly involved in all aspects of the firm's core operations. In this capacity, he co-manages and drives SATIG's Corporate and Project Finance Advisory and International Business Development initiatives. As in-house counsel and finance associate, he is capable of freely moving between the two different areas. Manbegrot's professional background includes strategic and capital advisory for global clients, as well as mergers and acquisitions advisory in the real estate, metals and mining, energy, and financial services sectors. He is well versed in the nuances of the quantitative and legal aspects of the global investment process, including the formation and operation of business entities as well as the implications of investment options in both the fixed income and equity arenas. He is an alumnus of Ohio Wesleyan University, where he earned a B.A. in Economics and American University where he earned his law degree and his MBA. Manbegrot is a member of the New York bar.

John Syekei—John Syekei is a partner in the Nairobi, Kenya, office of Coulson Harney Advocates. He was admitted as an Advocate in 2005. He trained at Daly & Figgis Advocates and Deloitte and headed the Intellectual Property Department at a leading firm as a partner until joining Coulson Harney in March 2010. He was admitted into the Coulson Harney partnership on March 1, 2011.

John advises clients on M&A transactions in the IT, telecommunications, and health care sectors. His practice areas and experience cover commercial intellectual property advice, IP litigation, advertising law and litigation, advice on drafting and/or negotiation of information technology agreements on the seller or buyer side, and advice on the protection and enforcement of trade mark, patent, copyright, and industrial designs. He practices across Africa directly for local clients. He also acts for clients in intellectual property infringement actions, anti-counterfeiting raids, due diligence investigations and reports, drafting of licensing and franchise agreements, trade mark oppositions, trade mark cancellations, and domain name dispute resolutions before WIPO.

Nellie R.F. Tiyago-Jinjika—Nellie is a partner at Scanlen & Holderness. Over the years, she has specialized in corporate and commercial law. She has experience in joint ventures, acquisitions, due diligences, drafting and negotiating commercial contracts, commercial litigation, and registration of intellectual property. In recent years, Nellie has assisted young Zimbabweans in the establishment of businesses and has advised and provided assistance to foreign and local prospective and actual investors in Zimbabwe.

Nellie is registered as a conveyancer, an administrator registered with the Estate Administration Council of Zimbabwe, and is also a member of IBA (International Bar Association). In 2011, the Zimbabwe Institute of Patents and Trademarks Attorneys (ZIPTA) was resuscitated. Nellie served as the Administrator in 2012 and remains a member to date. In addition to being a member of ZIPTA, she is also a member of INTA (International Trademarks Association).

Jonathan van Kempen—Jonathan van Kempen is an associate in the law firm of Emery Mukendi Wafwana & Associates. His areas of practice include corporate law, mining and hydrocarbon law, international mergers and acquisitions, OHADA law, international contracts and project finance in natural resources, and energy and infrastructures in Africa, particularly in Francophone Africa. He holds his law degree from the Catholic University of Louvain (Belgium). He has a master's degree in German and international law from the Georg-August University of Göttingen (Germany) and a post-graduate in business management from the HUB of Brussels (Belgium). He also holds an LL.M. in international business and trade law from Fordham University, School of Law (New York). He speaks French, English, German, and Dutch.

Emery Mukendi Wafwana—Emery is the Founding Partner of Emery Mukendi Wafwana & Associates, created in 1995. His areas of practice include mining and hydrocarbon law, electrical power law, energy law, investment law, corporate law, aviation law, OHADA law, intellectual property law, legal evaluation of projects, and litigation. Emery was awarded by the *International Who's Who Legal of Mining Lawyers 2012* as a legal expert in mining law. He is also founder and Chief Editor of *Juricongo*, a legal website and portal of Congolese Law (www.juricongo.com). Emery holds his law degree in economic and social law from the University of Kinshasa. He speaks French, English, Lingala, and Tshiluba.

About the Book

Franchising in Africa 2014: Legal and Business Considerations is the second edition of this work. It serves as a practical, succinct, easy-to-use reference tool for lawyers, business people, and academics to use in navigating the myriad laws and business issues impacting franchise arrangements in Africa.

There is a gap in the franchise industry literature covering franchise matters on the African continent. This book fills that void. It provides an overview of the franchise industry in Africa and addresses the typical legal issues confronted when expanding a franchise system overseas, and particularly in Africa. It highlights issues encountered when drafting international franchise agreements and provides practical ways in which to finance the African franchise venture. Finally, the book also covers those laws governing franchising in sixteen African countries – Angola, Botswana, Burundi, Cape Verde, Democratic Republic of Congo, Egypt, Ethiopia, Ghana, Kenya, Mozambique, Nigeria, Rwanda, South Africa, Tunisia, Zambia, and Zimbabwe.

In each chapter devoted to a particular country, an author, who is a legal expert in the designated jurisdiction, addresses the basic questions that a franchise lawyer would need to know to competently represent a client in expanding their franchise system to that country.

Each country chapter organizes a discussion of each country's laws under various headings and in a uniform format. Topics were sent to each country's author in the form of a questionnaire attached as *Appendix A*, and each author drafted responses to the questions presented. A general overview relating to the political and economic history of the country at the beginning of each chapter provides an initial context for the regulatory framework.[1]

The authors for each chapter are listed at the beginning of a chapter and their biographical information is listed in the previous section, *About the Authors*.

Counsel should always consult with local counsel in the relevant jurisdiction instead of relying solely on the information contained in this book. The laws governing franchising on the African continent are evolving and local counsel in the various jurisdictions are best positioned to provide timely, relevant advice applying the current law to the particular facts of a case.

---

1 The source of information for these sections is the Central Intelligence Agency, https://www.cia.gov/library/publications/the-world-factbook/ (last visited March 7, 2014).

International Franchising in the African Context

Kendal H. Tyre, Jr. and Diana Vilmenay-Hammond

Nixon Peabody LLP

Washington, D.C.

I. Industry Overview

The burgeoning African economic growth has had a tremendous impact on franchising in Africa and it will likely continue in the future. As of May 2012, African nations comprised seven of the world's ten fastest-growing economies.[2] Wholesale and retail commerce, transportation, telecommunications, and manufacturing are the biggest driving forces on the continent.[3]

By 2030, much of Africa will attain lower-middle to middle class majorities and consumer spending will expand from US$680 billion in 2008 to US$2.2 trillion.[4] According to McKinsey & Company, Africa currently has more middle class consumers than India, which has a larger population.[5]

---

2 Howard French, *Seven of the World's 10 Fastest-Growing Economies Are African*, BUSINESS INSIDER, May 21, 2012, *available at* http://www.businessinsider.com/seven-of-the-worlds-10-fastest-growing-economies-are-african-2012-5.

3 *Id.*

4 *Id.*

5 *Id.*

Recent Expansion into Africa. Against this backdrop, franchising in Africa has experienced phenomenal growth in recent years. The news headlines cite the growth taking place.

Yum Brands, the parent company of KFC, is expanding the fast-food brand and plans to open outlets in Senegal, Ethiopia, and the Democratic Republic of Congo.[6] Baskin-Robbins announced in 2013 its plans to develop in South Africa.[7] Kahala, the parent company of Cold Stone Creamery, debuted on the African continent in Egypt in June 2012 when it signed a 10-year master franchise agreement that included the goal of opening eight stores in the first four years. It expects to continue expanding throughout the continent of Africa and recently entered the South African market.[8]

Subway, the U.S. fast food sandwich franchisor, continues to expand in North Africa. As of October 2010, it had four units in Egypt with plans for further growth.[9] Also, in 2011, Burger King indicated its intent to enter South Africa's already robust fast

---

6 Alex Park, *How Bill Gates Is Helping KFC Take Over Africa*, MOTHER JONES, Jan. 10, 2014, *available at* http://www.motherjones.com/environment/2014/01/kfc-africa-chicken-usaid-gates-foundation?utm_source=feedburner&utm_medium=feed&utm_campaign=Feed%3A+motherjones%2Fmain+(MotherJones.com+Main+Article+Feed).

7 *Baskin-Robbins Announces Plans to Develop Internationally in South Africa and Germany*, June 24, 2013, *available at* http://news.baskinrobbins.com/Press-Releases/BASKIN-ROBBINS-ANNOUNCES-PLANS-TO-DEVELOP-INTERNATIONALLY-IN-SOUTH-AFRICA-AND-GERMANY-434.aspx.

8 *Cold Stone Creamery Enters Continent of Africa with Egypt Expansion Plans*, BUSINESS WIRE, June 5, 2012, *available at* http://www.businesswire.com/news/home/20120605006456/en/Cold-Stone-Creamery-Enters-Continent-Africa-Egypt. *Cold Stone Creamery Enters South Africa Market*, VENTURES-AFRICA, Sept. 10, 2013, *available at* http://www.ventures-africa.com/2013/09/cold-stone-creamery-enters-south-africa-market/.

9 *Subway Chain Reveals MENA Growth Plans*, ARABIANBUSINESS.COM, Oct. 17, 2010, *available at* http://www.arabianbusiness.com/subway-chain-reveals-mena-growth-plans-356867.html.

food market.[10] International franchisors expanding across the continent are not limited to food franchises but rather cover a broad range of services and products, including tutoring, hotels, grocery chains, automotive products and services, and home maintenance and repairs.[11]

SMEs in Africa. African Development Bank research related to business failures has revealed that only 15% of franchised small and medium business enterprises ("SMEs") folded compared to an 80% failure rate among independent businesses.[12] This data point shows the significant impact that franchising could have on

---

10 Analeigh Vallie, *Burger King Eyes Expansion into SA*, BUSINESS DAY, SOUTH AFRICA, June 15, 2011, *available at* http://www.businessday.co.za/Articles/Content.aspx?id=145867.

11 In November 2013, Marriott International, Inc. announced that it signed a letter of intent with South African Protea Hospitality Holdings to acquire Protea Hotels' brands and its management business that operates or franchises approximately 116 hotels in South Africa and six other Sub-Saharan African countries. *Marriott Signs Letter of Intent to Acquire Protea Hotel Group's Hotel Operations and Brands*, Nov. 7, 2013, *available at* http://news.marriott.com/2013/11/marriott-signs-letter-of-intent-to-acquire-protea-hotel-groups-hotel-operations-and-brands.html. Tutor Doctor, a global tutoring franchise that provides home-based instruction to learners of all ages, recently announced the opening of its first franchise location in Tunisia. *Leading Tutoring Franchise to Debut in North Africa*, GLOBE NEWSWIRE, Nov. 14, 2013, *available at* http://globenewswire.com/news-release/2013/11/14/589990/10057655/en/Leading-Tutoring-Franchise-to-Debut-in-North-Africa.html. In 2011, Gap, Inc. announced its plans to open its franchised GAP stores in Egypt and Morocco. *Gap, Inc. Prepares to Open Its First Stores in Africa*, BLOOMBERG, June 29, 2011, *available at* http://www.bloomberg.com/apps/news?pid=conewsstory&tkr=GAP:GR&sid=a5iLj_fqYq3M. Pick n Pay, a large South Africa retailer, proposed plans in 2011 to expand its franchise operations elsewhere in Africa, particularly Mauritius and Mozambique. Samantha Enslin-Payne, *Pick n Pay Stretches Its African Footprint*, BUSINESS REPORT, June 24, 2011, *available at* http://www.iol.co.za/business/international/pick-n-pay-stretches-its-african-footprint-1.1088051.

12 In Kenya, research has revealed that nine out of ten bar and restaurant start-ups fail in their first nine months. Sarah Rundell, *More Chains for Africa*, AFRICA INVESTOR, Mar. 1, 2010, *available at* http://www.africainvestor.com/article.asp?id=6490.

the growth and stability of new business ventures on the continent.

Currently, SMEs account for more than 90% of private business in Africa. The franchising framework can be viewed as an effective tool to promote SME and private sector development, contribute to poverty reduction and wealth creation, and even promote quality health care.[13]

The potential opportunities under the franchising model are not only with international franchisors expanding into African markets but also domestic African SMEs adopting the franchise framework. Existing indigenous businesses in target countries have knowledge of the specific, local market demands. They have a proven product to be offered to consumers and a proven business format to offer to future franchisees.

In fact, indigenous franchising should prove more attractive to local consumers and be less sensitive to the need for product testing and adaptation in African markets, which may result in shorter gestation periods and lower failures rates for such franchises.[14]

---

[13] Health franchises are an attractive example of SMEs that have proven successful in various African communities. They help to encourage business development while also serving the dual goal of promoting quality health services and care. By collaborating with local medical clinics and converting them to franchisees, nonprofit organizations like LifeNet International aspire to increase patient count, quality of patient care, and build sustainable franchises. Center for Health Market Innovations, *Can Primary Care Franchising Work in East Africa? The LifeNet Model*. Apr. 1, 2011, *available at* http://healthmarketinnovations.org/blog/2011/apr/1/lifenet-international. In Ethiopia, the Biruh Tesfa (Ray of Hope) program has increased contraceptive use by 30% in the population of 10 million covered by its 92 clinics. In Zimbabwe, a franchise program called New Start, which tests and counsels for HIV, saw a great increase in visits from 1999 to 2003. *See, infra*, footnotes 211-215 and accompanying text.

[14] For example, Zain Nigeria, a mobile-telecommunications company (now known as Bharti Airtel Limited), had grown to more than 1,000 franchisees in rural Nigeria and the average franchised site produced a 160% return on original investment within the first year of launch. Jamie Anderson and

(Footnote continued on next page)

Legislative Reforms. The robust growth of franchising is likely to continue as legislative and economic reforms take hold on the African continent. For example, some African governments have enacted legislative reforms to amend laws that previously hindered the repatriation of royalties and franchise fees. In addition, some countries have also enacted franchise specific legislation. For example, South Africa enacted franchise legislation in 2008.[15] Tunisia drafted a legislative framework for franchising that took effect in 2010,[16] and Angola has had franchise laws in place since 2003.[17] Other countries on the continent are likely to follow their lead.[18]

Franchise Industry Associations. In some African countries, franchise associations provide industry oversight and also assist in the promotion of franchising. For example, well-established franchise associations such as the Egyptian Franchise Development Association[19] and the Franchise Association of

Ronan Moaligou, "*Slums and Warzones Create New Frontiers for the Industry*," Global Telecoms Business, Jan. 15, 2010, *available at* http://www.globaltelecomsbusiness.com/Article/2373676/Regions/25191/Slums-and-warzones-create-new-frontiers-for-the-industry.html.

15 *See* Taswell Papier, *Franchising in South Africa*, in FRANCHISING IN AFRICA 2014: LEGAL AND BUSINESS CONSIDERATIONS 330 (Kendal H. Tyre, Jr, Diana Vilmenay-Hammond and Courtney L. Lindsay II eds. LexNoir Foundation 2014).

16 *See* Yessine Ferah, *Franchising in Tunisia*, in FRANCHISING IN AFRICA 2014: LEGAL AND BUSINESS CONSIDERATIONS 358 (Kendal H. Tyre, Jr, Diana Vilmenay-Hammond and Courtney L. Lindsay II eds. LexNoir Foundation 2014).

17 *See* João Afonso Fialho, *Franchising in Angola*, in FRANCHISING IN AFRICA 2014: LEGAL AND BUSINESS CONSIDERATIONS 110 (Kendal H. Tyre, Jr, Diana Vilmenay-Hammond and Courtney L. Lindsay II eds. LexNoir Foundation 2014).

18 David J. Saunders, *Franchising Opportunities: Unlocking Africa's Potential*, AFRICA TRAVEL MAGAZINE, http://www.africa-ata.org/franchising.htm (last visited March 7, 2014).

19 *See also* the Egyptian Franchise Development Association website, www.efda.org.eg (last visited March 7, 2014).

South Africa[20] play an important role in promoting compliance with codes of ethics and industry standards, whether they relate to disclosure obligations by the franchisor or the resolution of disputes.[21] As is commonplace in other parts of the world, franchisors face losing association membership if they flout convention or commit abuses.

For several years, advocates for franchising on the African continent have lobbied for the creation of a Pan-African franchise association to serve as a resource center for the African franchise industry and for practitioners throughout the continent to foster an understanding of franchise "best practices."[22]

In May 2013, the creation of such an association became a reality. The Pan African Franchise Federation ("Federation") held its inaugural meeting in South Africa with delegations from Egypt, Ethiopia, Mauritius, Tanzania, and Nigeria. The Federation was originally formed as a result of a mandate issued by the World Franchise Council's (WFC) executive committee, which has sought to establish a franchise federation representing the franchise sector in Africa. Delegates believed that, because economic growth in developing countries is overtaking established economies, it was time that Africa formed an organization to assist with spearheading franchise growth throughout the continent.[23] The Federation will eventually join the European Franchise Federation and the Asia Pacific Franchise Confederation by applying to become a member of the

---

[20] *See also* the Franchise Association of South Africa website, www.fasa.co.za (last visited March 7, 2014).

[21] *See also* the Nigerian International Franchise Association website, www.nigerianfranchise.org (last visited March 7, 2014).

[22] African Development Bank, *Study on Franchising Opportunities in Africa*, 23 *(Background Paper for Franchise Africa Symposium, 2002), available at* http://www.franchise.org/files/AFDB%20Background%20Paper.pdf (last visited March 7, 2014).

[23] Kendal H. Tyre, Jr. and Courtney L. Lindsay II, Pan African Franchise Federation Holds Inaugural Meeting, NIXON PEABODY FRANCHISE LAW ALERT (June 2013).

WFC. The countries in the federation would then share the objectives of the WFC, including the desire to provide a leading and educational role in franchising on their home continent.

In the future, the Federation could potentially arbitrate disputes between franchisors and franchisees. This would be particularly important in those African countries where the judicial system is not particularly efficient. Chapter affiliates of the Federation could also, in effect, become self-regulatory bodies of the franchise sector in each country where it has a presence. Among other things, chapters could facilitate growth in the industry by organizing franchise shows and/or meetings between prospective master franchisees and international franchisors, managing the qualification process of interested franchisors, and organizing international trade missions and seminars on topics of interest.[24]

Challenges. Franchising in Africa is not without its challenges. A basic understanding of any franchise arrangement is that the intellectual property of the franchisor is licensed to franchisees for a limited time and under certain terms and conditions. To protect its intellectual property, the franchisor reserves sweeping rights in its franchise agreements with its franchisees. The "rule of law" is critical to maintaining and protecting property. Without the franchisor's ownership of its intellectual property, the franchisor would have no interest in teaching a potential competitor its proven trade secrets.

Concerns over the weak protection of intellectual property in Africa have been expressed by several brands, such as McDonald's.[25] McDonald's is in countries such as Egypt, Algeria, and South Africa, but Kenya, for example, still does not meet that particular franchisor's market entry criteria regarding

---

[24] An effective way to attract prospective franchising partners within a particular market is through the use of trade missions. These are sponsored by organizations such as the International Franchise Association. Randolph M. Wright and Scott D. Relf, *International Franchising: Expanding to Emerging Markets*, 84 MI BAR JNL. 18, 20 (2005).

[25] Rundell, *supra* note 12.

the protection of intellectual property.[26] Moreover, examples of recent court decisions underscore the fact that intellectual property expertise varies in Africa.[27]

Capital is another worry. Franchisors generally request franchisees commit over 50% of the total investment, but African banks are cautious lenders to SMEs and start-ups. However, reforms in the African banking industry are changing the lending landscaping. Local banks in Kenya now have franchise departments and are starting to look at franchising not as a business start-up, but as a support system for business enterprises that may merit a closer inspection.[28]

---

26 The franchisor has expressed its plans to enter the market in Zimbabwe. Roadwin Chirara, *Whet your appetite, McDonald's coming*, DAILY NEWS ZIMBABWE, Aug. 17, 2010.

27 In *Mega Power Centre CC t/a Talisman Plant and Tool Hire v. Talisman Franchise Operations (Pty) Ltd.*, a Namibian company, which was a franchisee of a South African company, provided large, "operator-intensive" tools and equipment to the Namibian building industry under the name "Talisman Tool Hire" for a number of years. When it discovered that a South African company intended to start a business with smaller, "non-operator-intensive" tools under the name "Talisman Hire," the Namibian company sued for "passing off." Passing off is a common law action. To maintain a suit for passing off, the plaintiff does not need to have a trade mark registration. Instead, the plaintiff must establish: (1) that it enjoys a reputation or goodwill in a name; (2) that the other party is, through the use of a similar name, misrepresenting that there is a connection with plaintiff's business; and (3) that plaintiff is likely to suffer damages. The Namibian judge, relying heavily on South African law, determined that no passing off had occurred despite the strength of common law decisions in favor of the plaintiff and the strength of the *Talisman* name. This case emphasizes the need for companies to register their marks in Africa. Had the plaintiff been able to rely on a registered trade mark instead of a common law claim for "passing off," the outcome would have likely been different. *See* Ilse Du Plessis, Edward Nathans Sonnenbergs, *South Africa: Namibian IP Case Highlights Pitfalls In Africa*, MONDAQ, July 29, 2013, *available at* http://www.mondaq.com/x/254536/Trademark/Namibian+IP+Case+Highlights+Pitfalls+In+Africa.

28 Rundell, *supra* note 12.

Supply chain issues present yet another challenge. For example, many sub-Saharan Africa countries are still in the early stages of supply chain development.[29] African franchisees are required to maintain adequate supplies of the products that fuel their businesses and those products must also meet the franchisor's particular quality standards. For example, KFC and other fast food brands require adequate supplies of chicken that meet their standards.[30] This may be difficult in certain African countries where the supply of chickens from local chicken farmers fail to meet the franchisor's criteria for not only food safety and security but also quality and quantity.[31] For example, South African KFC's sell almost 10% of the nation's commercially grown chickens.[32] In these instances, local franchisees are required to purchase their supply from outside the country from franchisor-approved suppliers.[33] To ensure adequate supply needs are met and to cut costs, some franchisors are working with their franchisees to secure local suppliers.[34]

29 Tielman Nieuwoudt, *Think Juba Not Jacksonville—supply chain trends in Africa*, How We Made It In Africa, Aug. 14, 2013, *available at* http://www.howwemadeitinafrica.com/think-juba-not-jacksonville-supply-chain-trends-in-africa/29094/.

30 Park, *supra* note 6.

31 *Id.*

32 *Id.*

33 Dinfin Mulupi, *KFC Expects More Global Fast-Food Chains to Enter the Kenyan Market*, How We Made It In Africa, July 24, 2012, *available at* http://www.howwemadeitinafrica.com/kfc-expects-more-global-fast-food-chains-to-enter-the-kenyan-market/18698/.

34 *Id.*

II. Legal and Contractual Overview

A. Standard Structures

When structuring the contractual arrangement for international franchise expansion, typical formats include single-unit franchise agreements, master franchise agreements, area development agreements, joint venture agreements, or area representative agreements. Often, international franchise agreements do not follow a standard form. In fact, they may be negotiated documents that take the form of a hybrid of these typical arrangements.

There are disadvantages and advantages for each form of international franchise agreement.

1. Unit Franchise Agreements

Franchise systems expanding into target countries with geographic proximity, or with similar languages, laws, customs, and cultural considerations will often offer new franchises to single-unit operators. They will simply amend the form of unit franchise agreement to conform to domestic standards in the target country. Under a single-unite franchise arrangement, the franchisee will acquire the right to open and operate only one unit for store. For example, a franchisee could be granted the right to open a single unit of Mr. Biggs in a single location in Nigeria.

Expansion through traditional single-unit agreements with different franchisees slows growth. It also results in increased cost to the franchisor in recruiting different prospective franchisees and providing operational support and training to each franchise arrangement. However, one or two single-unit agreements may be useful to test a concept in a new market, or to evaluate potential partners for area development or master franchise arrangements. In some instances, a single-unit franchisee may ask the franchisor to approve them for a second unit, then a third and so on, after proving they are capable operators. This is often called "sequential franchising."

2. Area Development Agreements

When the franchisee is well-financed, the parties may enter into an area development agreement. It is also common when the franchisee has corporate operational experience, and when expanding into target markets where language, laws, customs, and cultural considerations vary dramatically from those in the domestic market. Under this form of agreement, the franchisee—commonly known as the area developer—develops all franchise units in the target country by itself, or through affiliated corporations. For example, a franchisee could be granted the right to open 5 units of a KFC restaurant between 2014 and 2020. The development agreement governs the overall relationship. Typically, it specifies the territory, the time frame and the specific number of franchise units that the franchisee is authorized to open. A specified form of unit franchise agreement will be entered into with the area developer for each unit developed.

An area development arrangement enhances growth, eliminates the need to recruit perspective franchisees, and concentrates operational support to one franchisee, the area developer. However, the success of a franchise system using area development as an expansion strategy depends heavily on the expertise, business skill, and motivation of the area developers.

3. Master Franchise Agreements

Many franchisors expand internationally through master franchise arrangements. The master franchise agreement is entered into with the master franchisee, who is known as the sub-franchisor, and contemplates that the master franchisee will enter into subfranchise agreements with individual unit franchisees in the target market. The franchisor is typically not a party to the individual subfranchise agreements between the master franchisee and the subfranchisees. If the target country has applicable franchise registration or disclosure laws, the master franchise arrangement may result in two levels of registration and disclosure—one for the franchisor and master franchisee relationship and another for the master franchisee and subfranchisee relationship.

The master franchise arrangement typically results in rapid target market penetration and accelerated franchise system growth. It also attracts investors with the necessary financial resources and business experience. In less developed target markets, master franchise arrangements facilitate entry into the target market. Risk is allocated between the parties because much of the development and operational expansion risk is with the master franchisee. Under the master franchise arrangement, the strain on the franchisor's financial and management resources is less than what would be the case in direct unit franchising. If the master franchisee is successful, the return on invested capital to a franchisor is significant.

The disadvantage of a master franchise relationship to the franchisor is that the franchisor loses control of the sales process and operations in the target market. In addition, it may also need to comply with registration and disclosure laws in the target country. The franchisor shares fees from the subfranchisees with the master franchisee and so its profits are diluted. If the relationship fails and the master franchise agreement is terminated, the franchisor risks incurring the expense required to salvage the franchise system in the target market.

4. Area Representative Agreements

An area representative arrangement is another means to expand internationally. In this arrangement, the franchisor enters into an agreement with a local developer who is charged with expanding the franchise system in the target market, although the franchise agreements with individual franchisees are entered into directly between the franchisor and the franchisees.

The franchise agreements acknowledge the role of the area representative in servicing the franchisees. The area representative solicits and screens prospective franchisees and assumes post-sale operational responsibilities including recruitment, site selection assistance, training, advertising, inspections, operational assistance, and product and service sourcing. Typical fees payable to the area representative include a portion of the initial franchise fees, royalty fees, and perhaps other payments made by franchisees to the franchisor. Typically, the area representative receives 40 to 60 percent of the initial franchise fee and the ongoing royalties.

The advantage of an area representative structure is that the franchisor retains less contractual control over the franchise system but maintains a local presence in the market at a lower operational cost. Often, this means a more direct and efficient response to franchisees' needs.

There are some disadvantages of the area representative arrangement. The franchisor may be subject to vicarious liability claims based on the acts of the area representative. Moreover, it may be difficult to replace an area representative that does not adequately perform. Finally, profits are diluted to the franchisor since they must be shared with the area representative.

In some jurisdictions, the arrangement may result in complex franchise registration or disclosure compliance issues. Normally, there is no need for a separate registration and disclosure relating to the area representative arrangements. However, the area representative will often be registered as a broker where broker registration is required. Disclosure of the area representative arrangement in the franchisor's disclosure document, including the scope of the responsibilities of the area representative, is typically included.

5. Joint Ventures

International franchise arrangements may take the form of a joint venture agreement. Typically, a joint venture entity is established in the target market. The entity is often jointly owned by the franchisor and a local joint venture partner. The joint venture may take the form of a corporation, limited liability company, partnership, limited partnership, or another legal entity organized under the laws of the target country. The franchisor and the joint venture entity will often enter into a master franchise agreement. The joint venture entity will subsequently enter into subfranchise agreements with franchisees in the target market.

The franchisor and joint venture partner each contribute to the joint venture entity. The franchisor will typically contribute licensed rights to the use of trademarks and other intellectual property. It may also provide ongoing operational support. The domestic joint venture partner will often contribute investment capital, human resources, management, operational responsibilities, and certain services to franchisees.

A joint venture arrangement provides several advantages. Such arrangement:

- allows for rapid development and expansion of the franchise system in the target market,
- permits shared risk between the franchisor and the joint venture partner because costs are allocated between the parties,
- brings local market expertise and experience of the joint venture partner to enhance development,
- results in more control by the franchisor than a master franchise or area development arrangement because of the franchisor's equity ownership in the joint venture entity, and
- provides more potential for profit to the franchisor since it holds a direct ownership interest in the joint venture entity whose value may appreciate with the future success of the franchise system in the international market. In addition, the profit sharing in a joint venture arrangement may not be restricted to royalties, but could

include dividends or other forms of corporate reinvestment.

The disadvantage of a joint venture arrangement is that the agreements are often complex and subject to extensive negotiation.

A unique form of joint venture in the African context is "tandem franchising." Tandem franchising is a franchise model unique to South Africa and is an effective tool for the implementation of black economic empowerment (BEE) initiatives in that country.[35] The tandem franchise model is a joint venture arrangement between a franchisor, which acts as an appointed mentor, and a new franchisee. The new franchisee purchases a minority stake in the business, often as little as 10%, and manages the day-to-day business with substantial oversight and mentoring from the appointed mentor. This new franchisee, who may lack the business management experience to operate the business alone, operates the business in "tandem" with an experienced franchisor and mentor. Initially, the franchisor retains the majority stake in the business and shares in its profits while providing management support and mentoring to the franchisee at a substantial level. Gradually, the franchisee can use its share of the profits generated from the business to purchase additional shares and slowly take control over more of the business. Eventually, the franchisee can become the sole owner of the business, at which point, the franchisor mentor exits the arrangement and the tandem franchise converts into a standard franchise arrangement.

This type of program is typically negotiated to take place over a pre-determined period of time, ranging from 3-5 years. It has

[35] Black Economic Empowerment (BEE) is a program launched by the South African government to redress the inequalities of apartheid by giving certain previously disadvantaged groups of South African citizenship economic privileges previously not available to them. It includes measures such as employment preference, skills development, ownership, management, socioeconomic development and preferential procurement.

become an effective tool in ensuring empowerment initiatives and provides an entry into franchising for those individuals who may not possess the necessary skills, capital or collateral.

An example of successful tandem franchising is Pick 'n Pay, which is one of South Africa's most successful supermarket chains with over 200 stores. Through its "twinning" program, employees attend intensive training at the Pick 'n Pay Franchise Academy. Successful graduates are given the opportunity to become involved in a store on a tandem basis, while existing Pick 'n Pay franchisees are given the opportunity to open a second store in tandem with a recent graduate of the Franchise Academy.

There are several risks, however, of which franchisors should be aware. The franchisor would be required to make available a small stake in a new or existing business to a potentially inexperienced and unknown franchisee who is unable to contribute substantial finances. In addition, throughout the term of the tandem franchise arrangement, the franchisor would have to continually invest considerable resources to develop and train the franchisee into a self-sustaining and successful franchisee, with no guarantee of success. The typical attendant risks of the business would also affect the ultimate success of the franchised business.

6. Conclusion

A suitable international franchise arrangement for a particular franchise system in a specific target country, whether in Africa or elsewhere, must be determined on an individual basis. A franchisor's appetite for international growth, the ability to relinquish control, the desire for capital or debt reduction, and the willingness to share fees must be analyzed.

In addition, some thought must be given to certain cultural and business considerations including availability of product, supplies and sites, the receptiveness and adaptability of the franchise concept in the target market, and the sophistication of potential investors.

B. Typical Target Country Legal Issues

A franchisor expanding internationally must review and analyze the laws and regulations of the target country that impact the documents used for international expansion. Often, these laws and regulations dictate the modifications and changes to the franchise system that are necessary for its successful deployment in the target country.

1. Pre-Sale Disclosure

Many countries require disclosure of specific information to potential franchisees prior to the execution of an agreement or the payment of any money by the franchisee. The scope and types of information vary from country to country. The goal of most disclosure laws is to ensure that franchisors receive information necessary to make an informed decision. Compliance with some disclosure laws can be difficult due to the vague wording of the relevant legislation. In the case of newly enacted legislation, government regulators may not have had sufficient time to consider how the disclosure law should be interpreted and this may exacerbate the problem. Experienced local counsel should be retained if there are any questions regarding the interpretation of a country's disclosure requirements.

Many foreign laws specify that a certain number of days must pass between delivery of the disclosure document to the franchisee and the execution of an agreement or payment of money by the franchisee (e.g., Australia—14 calendar days; Brazil—10 calendar days; Indonesia—14 calendar days; Mexico —30 business days). Some countries (e.g., Romania) have no specified waiting period after the disclosure document is delivered.[36] Jurisdictions outside of Africa that require disclosure to potential franchisees include Australia,[37] Belgium,[38] Brazil,[39]

---

36 *See infra*, notes 37 through 56 and accompanying text.

37 *Trade Practices (Industry Codes—Franchising) Regulations 1998* under *Section 51AE* of the federal *Trade Practices Act 1974 (Cth)*.

Canada (Alberta, Ontario, Prince Edward Island, New Brunswick, and Manitoba),[40] China,[41] France,[42] Germany,[43] Indonesia,[44] Italy,[45] Japan,[46] Macau,[47] Malaysia,[48] Mexico,[49]

38 The *Law of 19 December 2005.*

39 *Brazilian Federal Law Number 8955/94* adopted on December 15, 1994, and effective as of February 14, 1995.

40 *Franchises Act, RSA 1980 cF-17* (Alberta); *Ontario Regulation 581/00, amendment to O. Reg. 199/05* (Ontario); *Franchises Act R.S.P.E.I. 1988, Cap. F14.1* (Prince Edward Island); *The Franchise Act, S.N.B. 2007, c. F-23.5, Mediation Regulation—Franchises Act, N.B. Reg. 2010-93* and *Disclosure Regulation—Franchises Act, N.B. Reg. 2010-92* (New Brunswick); *The Franchises Act, C.C.S.M. c. F156* and Man. Reg. 29/2012 (Manitoba).

41 *Measures for the Administration of Commercial Franchise*, effective as of February 2005; *Regulations on the Administration of Commercial Franchise*, effective as of May 1, 2007; *Administration of Commercial Franchise Operations Registration Procedures*, effective as of February 2012; and *Administration of Information Disclosure for Commercial Franchise Operations Procedures*, effective as of April 2012.

42 *Articles L330-3 and R-330-1*of the Commercial Code of France.

43 German pre-contractual disclosure requirements have been derived from German case law and from the German Franchise Association's code of ethics.

44 *Regulation of the Minister of Trade No. 53/M-DAG/PER/8/2012*, dated August 24, 2012.

45 *Law Number 129/04*, effective as of May 25, 2004.

46 *Medium-Small Business Retail Commerce Promotion Act* supplemented by the *Ministerial Order to Implement the Act*; *Guidelines on Franchising under the Antimonopoly Act.*

47 *Macau Commercial Code*, Book III, External Activity of an Enterprise Title VIII, Franchising Contract.

48 *Franchise Act 1998* as amended by the Franchise (Amendment) Act 2012.

49 Article 142 of the *Mexican Industrial Property Law* and the *Regulations of the Industrial Property Law.*

Romania,[50] South Korea,[51] Spain,[52] Sweden,[53] Taiwan,[54] United States,[55] and Vietnam.[56]

Most of the African countries surveyed do not require franchisors to provide pre-sale disclosure. Tunisia and South Africa are the exceptions. In July 2010, Tunisia enacted legislation dictating the minimum information that must be included in a disclosure document provided to the franchisee at least twenty days prior to signing the franchise agreement.[57] South African disclosure regulations are found in the country's 2008 Consumer Protection Act and came into effect on April 1, 2011. These regulations provide that the franchisor must provide the franchisee with a disclosure document at least fourteen days before signing the franchise agreement.[58]

---

50 *Government Ordinance number 52/1997*, as amended by *Law number 79/1998*.

51 *Act on Fairness in Franchise Transactions* as amended in February 2014.

52 Article 62 of *Spanish Act 7/1996 of January 15, 1996*, as amended by *Act 1/2010* and the *Royal Decree 201/2010 of February 26*.

53 *Act on Franchisor's Obligations to Provide Information* (*lagen 2006:484 om franchisegivares informationsskyldighet*), effective as of October 1, 2006.

54 *Rules on Disclosure of Information by Franchisors*, effective as of June 2, 1999 and further amended.

55 16 C.F.R. Part 436, *Disclosure Requirements and Prohibitions Concerning Franchising*, effective as of July 1, 2007, ("FTC Franchise Rule"). There are also 15 U.S. states that have adopted their own disclosure, registration, or notice laws.

56 *Commercial Law, effective June 14, 2005*; *Decree No. 35/2006/ND-CP*, dated March 31, 2006; *Circular No. 09/2006/TT-BTM*, dated May 25, 2006. Regulations on franchising are also found in the *Intellectual Property Law*, dated November 29, 2005, and the *Technology Transfer Law*, dated November 29, 2006.

57 *See* Ferah, *supra* note 16, at 358. See also Kendal Tyre, Diana Vilmenay and Yessine Ferah, *New Franchise Legislation in Tunisia*, NIXON PEABODY FRANCHISE LAW ALERT, (September 29, 2010).

58 *See* Papier, *supra* note 15, at 330.

2. Government Approvals, Registrations, Filing Requirements

An increasing number of countries have enacted regulations specifically affecting franchising.[59] Often, these laws include disclosure document requirements requiring the preparation and delivery of a disclosure document at a certain time before the execution of the definitive franchise documents. Other countries have enacted franchise laws requiring registrations, approvals, and/or filings with local government authorities before the offer or sale of a franchise. Other typical requirements could include, for example, competition authority approvals, trademark license filings, and central bank approvals. Compliance with these laws is important to ensure the enforceability of the franchise agreement. A few examples of these regulatory requirements are explored below:

a. Franchisor Registration

Before expanding to the target country, franchise counsel must determine whether the franchisor needs to register with any governmental authorities prior to offering or selling franchises in that jurisdiction. For example, a franchisor planning to sell franchises in Spain,[60] Malaysia,[61] Indonesia,[62] or Vietnam[63] must

[59] Some countries have issued self-regulatory or voluntary disclosure requirements through government agencies or franchise associations. The Franchise Association of South Africa's appeal to its franchisor-members to provide a disclosure document to prospective franchisees met with mixed results. In 1994, the FASA made the use of a disclosure document by franchisors a condition of membership. Today, the FASA's disclosure requirements are stronger than those required under franchise legislation contained in that country's *Consumer Protection Act, 2008*. *See* Papier, *supra* note 15, at 330. *See also* Mark Rose, *The Disclosure Documents — Your New Best Friend*, ENTREPRENEUR MAGAZINE ONLINE, South Africa, Nov. 16, 2011, *available at* http://www.entrepreneurmag.co.za/advice/franchising/researching-a-franchise/the-disclosure-document-%E2%80%93-your-new-best-friend/ (last visited March 7, 2014).

[60] Article 62 of *Spanish Act 7/1996 of January 15, 1996, on the Regulation of Retail Trading* as amended by *Act 1/2010* ("Article 62") is the statute regulating franchising in Spain and *Royal Decree 201/2010* (the "Royal

(Footnote continued on next page)

first complete a filing with the relevant governing authority. Some foreign registrations and filings must be updated annually and/or when an individual franchise is sold.[64] Compliance with registration requirements is critical. Franchisors may be prohibited from entering into or enforcing a franchise agreement before the approval of the franchisor's registration or filing. In some jurisdictions, the approval process may focus on one specific aspect of the franchise agreement. Currently, none of the surveyed African countries requires registrations or filings prior to offering or selling franchises in those jurisdictions.[65]

Decree") provides the rules and regulations that govern franchise activity in Spain. The Royal Decree imposes on all franchisor the obligation to register with the Registry of Franchisors before the execution of the franchise agreement. Registration forms are located at the Registry of Franchisors web site *available at* http://www.mcx.es (last visited March 7, 2014).

61 Section 6(1) of the *Franchise Act 1998* as amended by the Franchise (Amendment) Act 2012.

62 *Regulation of the Minister of Trade No. 53/M-DAG/PER/8/2012*, dated August 24, 2012.

63 *Commercial Law*, adopted by the National Assembly on June 14, 2005; *Decree No. 35/2006/ND-CP* dated March 31, 2006, and *Circular No. 09/ 2006/TT-BTM of the Ministry of Industry and Trade*, dated May 25, 2006.

64 *See Section 6(1) of the Franchise Act 1998* as amended by the Franchise (Amendment) Act 2012 (Malaysia) and *Regulation of the Minister of Trade No. 53/M-DAG/PER/8/2012*, dated August 24, 2012 (Indonesia); *Commercial Law*, adopted by the National Assembly on June 14, 2005; *Decree No. 35/2006/ND-CP* dated March 31, 2006, and *Circular No. 09/2006/TT-BTM of the Ministry of Industry and Trade*, dated May 25, 2006 (Vietnam).

65 Any reference in this book to "surveyed" African countries or jurisdictions refers to the countries reviewed in the latter portion of this work—namely, Angola, Botswana, Burundi, Cape Verde, Democratic Republic of Congo, Egypt, Ethiopia, Ghana, Kenya, Mozambique, Nigeria, Rwanda, South Africa, Tunisia, Zambia, and Zimbabwe.

b. Government Approvals

Many countries regulate the franchise relationship itself, as opposed to or in addition to regulating the offer and sale of the franchise opportunity. These countries require the franchisor to submit transactions for approval of their specific terms and conditions, including types and amounts of fees, choice of law provisions, termination rights, and non-competition provisions.

With the exception of Botswana,[66] Democratic Republic of Congo,[67] Ghana,[68] Kenya,[69] Rwanda,[70] and Zambia,[71] the African jurisdictions surveyed require central bank approval to remit payments abroad.[72]

---

66 *See* Bonzo Makgalemele, *Franchising in Botswana*, in FRANCHISING IN AFRICA 2014: LEGAL AND BUSINESS CONSIDERATIONS 161 (Kendal H. Tyre, Jr., Diana Vilmenay-Hammond, and Courtney L. Lindsay II, eds. LexNoir Foundation 2014).

67 *See* Emery Mukendi Wafwana et. al., *Franchising in Democratic Republic of Congo*, in FRANCHISING IN AFRICA 2014: LEGAL AND BUSINESS CONSIDERATIONS 203-04 (Kendal H. Tyre, Jr., Diana Vilmenay-Hammond, and Courtney L. Lindsay II, eds. LexNoir Foundation 2014).

68 *See* Divine K.D. Letsa and Elizabeth Ashun, *Franchising in Ghana*, in FRANCHISING IN AFRICA 2014: LEGAL AND BUSINESS CONSIDERATIONS 252 (Kendal H. Tyre, Jr., Diana Vilmenay-Hammond, and Courtney L. Lindsay II, eds. LexNoir Foundation 2014).

69 *See* John Syekei and Joseph Githaiga, *Franchising in Kenya*, in FRANCHISING IN AFRICA 2014: LEGAL AND BUSINESS CONSIDERATIONS 267 (Kendal H. Tyre, Jr., Diana Vilmenay-Hammond, and Courtney L. Lindsay II, eds. LexNoir Foundation 2014).

70 *See* Désiré Kamanzi, *Franchising in Rwanda*, in FRANCHISING IN AFRICA 2014: LEGAL AND BUSINESS CONSIDERATIONS 317 (Kendal H. Tyre, Jr., Diana Vilmenay-Hammond, and Courtney L. Lindsay II, eds. LexNoir Foundation 2014).

71 *See* Mabvuto Sakala, *Franchising in Zambia*, in FRANCHISING IN AFRICA 2014: LEGAL AND BUSINESS CONSIDERATIONS 383 (Kendal H. Tyre, Jr., Diana Vilmenay-Hammond, and Courtney L. Lindsay II, eds. LexNoir Foundation 2014).

72 *See infra* notes 95 through 104 and accompanying text regarding Currency Restrictions and Funds Repatriation at 26.

Under Tunisian law, for example, payments made by a Tunisian-based franchisee outside of the country are subject to the approval of the Bank of Tunisia.[73] A similar requirement is provided for under the laws of Angola,[74] Burundi,[75] Cape Verde,[76] Egypt,[77] Ethiopia,[78] Mozambique,[79] Nigeria,[80] South Africa,[81] and Zimbabwe.[82]

---

[73] *See* Ferah, *supra* note 16, at 367.

[74] *See* Fialho, *supra* note 17, at 112-13.

[75] *See* Gilbert Nyatanyi, *Franchising in Burundi*, in FRANCHISING IN AFRICA 2014: LEGAL AND BUSINESS CONSIDERATIONS 175 (Kendal H. Tyre, Jr., Diana Vilmenay-Hammond, and Courtney L. Lindsay II, eds. LexNoir Foundation 2014).

[76] *See* João Afonso Fialho, *Franchising in Cape Verde*, in FRANCHISING IN AFRICA 2014: LEGAL AND BUSINESS CONSIDERATIONS 187-88 (Kendal H. Tyre, Jr., Diana Vilmenay-Hammond, and Courtney L. Lindsay II, eds. LexNoir Foundation 2014).

[77] *See* Girgis Abd El-Shahid, *Franchising in Egypt*, in FRANCHISING IN AFRICA 2014: LEGAL AND BUSINESS CONSIDERATIONS 215-16 (Kendal H. Tyre, Jr., Diana Vilmenay-Hammond, and Courtney L. Lindsay II, eds. LexNoir Foundation 2014).

[78] *See* Yohannes Assefa and Biset Beyene Molla, *Franchising in Ethiopia*, in FRANCHISING IN AFRICA 2014: LEGAL AND BUSINESS CONSIDERATIONS 229-31 (Kendal H. Tyre, Jr., Diana Vilmenay-Hammond, and Courtney L. Lindsay II, eds. LexNoir Foundation 2014).

[79] *See* Diogo Xavier da Cunha, *Franchising in Mozambique*, in FRANCHISING IN AFRICA 2014: LEGAL AND BUSINESS CONSIDERATIONS 280-81 (Kendal H. Tyre, Jr., Diana Vilmenay-Hammond, and Courtney L. Lindsay II, eds. LexNoir Foundation 2014).

[80] *See* Theo Emuwa and Tiwalola Okeyinka, *Franchising in Nigeria*, in FRANCHISING IN AFRICA 2014: LEGAL AND BUSINESS CONSIDERATIONS 301-02 (Kendal H. Tyre, Jr., Diana Vilmenay-Hammond, and Courtney L. Lindsay II, eds. LexNoir Foundation 2014).

[81] *See* Papier, *supra* note 15, at 334.

[82] *See* Nellie R.F. Tiyago-Jinjika, *Franchising in Zimbabwe*, in FRANCHISING IN AFRICA 2014: LEGAL AND BUSINESS CONSIDERATIONS 398 (Kendal H. Tyre, Jr., Diana Vilmenay-Hammond, and Courtney L. Lindsay II, eds. LexNoir Foundation 2014).

In South Africa, the South African Department of Trade and Industry ("DTI") and the South African Reserve Bank ("SARB") must approve the payments to the franchisor. DTI and SARB have established their own guidelines that dictate the nature and amount of royalty payments deemed acceptable. For consumer goods and/or know-how, the acceptable royalty percentage is between 0% and 4%. Intermediate and final capital goods and/or know-how have an acceptable royalty percentage range of 0% to 6%. Registration of a franchise agreement may be declined by the SARB or the DTI if the royalty fee payable by the franchisee to the franchisor would exceed the stipulated maximum percentage.[83]

In Ethiopia and Nigeria, certain aspects of the franchise agreement may fall under the purview of each country's technology transfer regulations, and any agreement subject to these regulations must be submitted to each country's respective regulatory authority for approval and registration.[84]

Ethiopia's 2012 *Investment Reenactment Proclamation 769/2012* mandates that technology transfer agreements be submitted to the Ethiopia Investment Agency for approval and registration. It defines "transfer of technology" to mean "the transfer of systemic knowledge for the manufacture of a product, for the application of improvement of a process, or for the rendering of a service, including management and marketing technologies."[85] The definition does not include the mere sale or lease of goods.[86] Franchise agreements may fall under the purview of the law if a franchise agreement includes, for example, a marketing technology, proprietary business processes, and/or specified machines that could be used for the production of goods or for

83 *See* Papier, *supra* note 15, at 332-34.

84 *See* Assefa and Molla, *supra* note 78, at 227-28 and Emuwa and Okeyinka, *supra* note 80, at 295-96.

85 *Id.* Article 2 (10).

86 *Id.*

rendition of a service. In these instances, the franchise agreement may require registration.

Nigeria's approval process is particularly burdensome. The National Office for Technology Acquisition and Promotion ("NOTAP") is the agency charged with registration of all foreign technology agreements in Nigeria. NOTAP imposes a number of conditions on the agreement of the parties that must be fulfilled before NOTAP will approve registration. These include limits of 5% of the net sale value or profit before tax on royalty payments as well as limitations of ten years on the term of each agreement.[87]

c. Trademark License Filings

Trademark offices in some countries require the filing of the franchise agreement or a short form license agreement that shows that the trademarks used in the franchise system have been licensed to the local franchisee for use in the target country. Generally, the documents must be translated into the local language before their submission. Trademark authorities in countries requiring the filing of franchise agreements or the short form license agreements include Brazil,[88] Columbia,[89] Ecuador,[90] Guatemala,[91] Peru,[92] and Panama.[93]

---

87 *See* Emuwa and Okeyinka, *supra* note 80, at 296-98.

88 *Brazilian Law No. 9279* of May 14, 1996.

89 *Trademark Law* contained in the *Andean Pact Decision 486* concerning industrial property, effective December 1, 2000.

90 *Industrial Property Law* in force since May 1998 and the *Andean Pact Decision 486* concerning industrial property.

91 *Intellectual Property Law of November 1, 2000.*

92 *Industrial Property Act*, in force since January 1, 1994, and the *Andean Pact Decision* concerning industrial property, in force since December 1, 2000.

93 *Intellectual Property Law*, in force since November 10, 1996, and the *Executive Decree No. 7* of February 17, 1998.

Although some trademark offices provide only a ministerial review of the terms and conditions of the licensing arrangement, failure to file with these authorities can have serious repercussions. In Mexico, for example, which is typical of many countries, the filing is not technically required but is highly recommended because the failure to file can result in an inability to pursue claims against third-party infringing parties.[94] In Russia, approval of a trademark license agreement by the trademark office must occur prior to the granting of a valid trademark license. A failure to register will invalidate the trademark license portions of the franchise agreement.[95]

In those African countries surveyed, most require (or the authors recommend) the filing of a registered user agreement or a short trademark license agreement with the trademark authorities. In many cases, such a filing would enable parties to pursue claims against third-party infringers. The one clear exception to this is Egypt. It was recommended that parties not register the trademark license in Egypt because of the difficulty in deregistering a license, especially in the event of a dispute between the parties. It is unclear whether the trademark office will acknowledge and respect a decision to terminate or not renew a license agreement. The lack of registration with the trademark authorities in Egypt does not affect the enforceability of any agreement between the parties.[96]

3. Currency Restrictions and Funds Repatriation

Some target countries require that any commercial transactions within their borders be conducted in the domestic currency of the country. Other countries restrict the amount of domestic currency that can be converted into foreign currency, restrict the

---

94 *Industrial Property Law* (as last amended April 2012).

95 *Part IV of the Russian Civil Code,* which came into effect on January 1, 2008.

96 *See* El-Shahid, *supra* note 77, at 217.

amount of foreign currency that can be withdrawn from the country, or prohibit funds to be expatriated at all.

If appropriate funds cannot be withdrawn from the target country, it may be necessary to leave all profits earned in the target country for further expansion opportunities or as an offset against expenses incurred in the country. As an alternative, the franchisor may acquire products available in the target country with domestic currency, and thereafter sell such products in the free market to obtain freely tradable currency.

Of those African countries surveyed, with the exception of Zambia, there are no specific restrictions concerning the exchange, repatriation, or remittance of payments under the franchise agreement in immediately available U.S. Dollars.[97]

The laws differ in some of the other African jurisdictions. For example, the Bank of Mozambique (the "BoM") serves as a foreign exchange control authority. The BoM must authorize the repatriation or payment of funds outside of Mozambique. Any currency transfers between resident and non-resident entities will be subject to different requirements depending on the nature of the underlying transactions.[98] Similarly, in South Africa, any payments by a franchisee resident in the country will be subject to the South African Reserve Bank's exchange control requirements. A South African franchisee is not permitted to make payments under a franchise agreement to an offshore franchisor without the SARB's prior approval.[99] Likewise, regulatory bodies must authorize transfers of payments in countries like Angola,[100] Cape Verde,[101] Ethiopia,[102] Nigeria,[103]

---

[97] *See* Sakala, *supra* note 71 at 383-84.

[98] *See* da Cunha, *supra* note 79, at 280.

[99] *See* Papier, *supra* note 15, at 334.

[100] *See* Fialho, *supra* note 17, at 112-13.

[101] *See* Fialho, *supra* note 76, at 187-88.

[102] *See* Assefa and Molla, *supra* note 78, at 229-231.

Tunisia,[104] and Zimbabwe[105] before certain payments under the franchise agreement may be made.[106]

4. Anti-trust, Competition, and Trade Practice Laws

Most developed countries have anti-trust, competition, or trade practice laws that are applicable to franchise operations. For example, laws impacting suggested pricing, misleading advertising, price discrimination, co-operative advertising allowances, telemarketing, tying, exclusive dealing, and market restriction must be analyzed and incorporated as necessary into the franchisor's documents and into the franchise system.

Anti-trust or competition laws typically address two types of activity: collusion among parties that limits consumers' choices in selecting products or services, and abuse of franchisor's superior bargaining position to the detriment of the other party to an agreement.

Most franchisors use in-term and post-term covenants not to compete to protect their systems. Typically, non-compete covenants are enforceable if they include reasonable limitations as to the time, geographic area, and the scope of activity restricted. Some countries, however, have additional restrictions on non-compete provisions. For example, in certain circumstances, European Union countries may restrict in-term covenants not to compete to five years (and post-term covenants to one year).[107]

[103] *See* Emuwa and Okeyinka, *supra* note 80, at 301-02.

[104] *See* Ferah, *supra* note 16, at 367.

[105] *See* Tiyago-Jinjika, *supra* note 82, at 398.

[106] *See supra* notes 66 through 85 and accompanying text regarding Government Approvals at 22-25.

[107] Frank Zaid and Kendal Tyre, International Franchising Basic Track Workshop: *A World Tour of The Basics of International Franchising*,

(Footnote continued on next page)

In those African countries surveyed, with a few exceptions, covenants not-to-compete are generally enforceable, so long as the restraint is reasonable, limited in scope and geography, and necessary to protect the interests of the individual or entity who seeks to enforce the restraint.

South African courts will retain discretion to enforce a non-competition restraint and will consider the merits of the enforceability of each restraint on a case-by-case basis after assessing the restraint. In balancing the various considerations, a South African court will consider the following questions:

- Does the franchisor have an interest deserving of protection upon termination of the franchise agreement?
- If so, is such interest being prejudiced by the franchisee?
- If so, how does the franchisor's interest weigh against the franchisee's interest in not being rendered economically unproductive for a period of time?
- Is there some broader aspect of public policy, unrelated to the personal interests of the individuals concerned that demands that the restraint should or should not be enforced?

A restraint will not be enforced in South Africa if it is unreasonable or contrary to the public interest.[108]

Non-competition provisions are generally enforceable in Nigeria but the Nigerian regulatory agency, NOTAP, has specific conditions for such provisions that must be observed. Specifically, the agreement cannot:

(Paper Presented at the International Franchise Association's 38th Annual Legal Symposium, May 2005) at 7.

[108] *See* Papier, *supra* note 15, at 347-50.

- require the franchisee to acquire equipment, tools, parts, or raw materials exclusively from the franchisor or any other person or given source;

- prohibit or restrict the exportation of the franchisee's products or services;

- compel or oblige the franchisee to sell the products manufactured by it exclusively to the franchisor or any designated person or source;

- prevent the franchisee from using complementary technologies;

- compel the franchisee to use personnel designated by the franchisor either on a permanent basis or for any unconscionable period; or

- require the franchisee to appoint the franchisor as its exclusive sales agent.[109]

Angola provides that a post-term non-compete is only enforceable if both parties agree to the provision and it (i) does not exceed two years and (ii) is limited to the territory areas and clients covered by the franchise agreement.[110]

5. Agency Laws

The relationship between franchisor and franchisee is not typically considered an agency relationship in most countries. In certain countries, however, franchisees are deemed agents of the franchisor and are subject to commercial agent or sales representative laws. These laws protect sales agents who market and distribute the products or services of a principal. They often entitle the franchisee to reasonable compensation or

[109] *See* Emuwa and Okeyinka, *supra* note 80, at 306-07.

[110] *See* Fialho, *supra* note 17, at 122.

indemnification, which is triggered upon a termination of the relationship without "good cause." Compensation in some instances may be triggered regardless of the reason upon any termination or expiration of the franchise agreement. Other agency laws in some countries define "good cause" narrowly such that a franchisee will almost certainly be entitled to compensation upon any expiration or termination of the agreement.

In several Middle Eastern countries, the amount of compensation that may be owed to the franchisee under an agency law varies from country to country. However, it is often left to the discretion of local courts. They typically consider the circumstances as a whole. This would include the franchisee's actual investment and a reasonable prediction of future profits. A standard award would be the equivalent of one year's total profits (averaged over four to five years) of the franchisee. Compensation for the goodwill of the business and any unused inventory could also be awarded.[111] The amount of compensation may be higher if the parties have a long-term relationship and the franchisee shows extensive investment in the franchise.

If agency laws are deemed applicable in certain target countries, local courts may assume jurisdictions notwithstanding a contrary jurisdiction and/or venue clauses in the parties' agreement. Moreover, there are even special agency law courts that are made up of agents who hear the cases.[112]

One method for avoiding registration is to ensure that the franchisee itself is at least partially owned by foreign nationals of the target country, and thus ineligible to serve as a commercial agent. Alternatively, franchisors include features in the agreement that would make the overall relationship more difficult to register, refrain from execution formalities required

---

[111] Zaid and Tyre, *supra* note 105, at 8.

[112] Joyce Mazero and J. Perry Maisonneuve, *Franchising in the Middle East and North Africa*, (Paper Presented at the American Bar Association 32nd Annual Forum on Franchising, October 14–16, 2009) at 10.

in the registration process, and seek protection against the exposure arising out of registration under the commercial agencies law.

Of those African countries surveyed, Angola's franchise legislation is guided by the country's laws of agency. As a result, there is a risk that upon termination of a franchise agreement, Angolan courts could look to agency case law precedents and award an indemnity similar to awards that are typically made in Middle Eastern countries. Such an indemnity would be calculated on a case-by-case basis not exceeding the annual average of profit generated by the franchisee during the last five years (or the average of the period in which the contract was in force, if it was not in force for five years).[113]

6. Arbitration

Many international franchisors turn to arbitration as a means of dispute resolution due to the uncertainty and lack of development of judicial systems in a number of foreign countries. A franchisor expanding internationally should review the local laws of the target country with respect to the ability to enforce arbitral decisions. International treaties or target country laws relating to the enforcement of an international arbitration award must also be analyzed. Over 145 countries have adopted the *Convention on the Recognition and Enforcement of Foreign Arbitral Awards* (the "New York Convention"). Under the New York Convention, arbitration awards are recognized and enforced with little interference from foreign courts in the signatory countries. Of those African countries surveyed, Botswana,[114] the Democratic Republic of the Congo,[115] Egypt,[116] Ghana,[117] Mozambique,[118] Nigeria,[119] Rwanda,[120] South

---

[113] *See* Fialho, *supra* note 17, at 119.

[114] *See* Makgalemele, *supra* note 66, at 167.

[115] *See* Wafwana et al., supra note 67, at 207-08.

[116] *See* El-Shahid, *supra* note 77, at 219.

[117] *See* Letsa and Ashun, *supra* note 68, at 257.

Africa,[121] Tunisia,[122] and Zambia[123] are signatories to the New York Convention.

Arbitration is popular because of the perception that it will be conducted in a neutral setting, and because the parties can tailor the procedural rules to be used in their arbitration. Some of the disadvantages of arbitration include the potential high costs, the potential for unpredictable results stemming from the arbitrators not being bound by legal precedent, and the concern that arbitration awards are not generally appealable.

7. Execution Formalities

Each country has its own execution formalities, including witness requirements, spousal acknowledgements, notarization requirements, legalization requirements, or payment of stamp duties. Franchise agreements may also need to be authenticated before they are deemed enforceable by the courts of a particular jurisdiction. In some countries, the execution procedures differ depending on the location of the party when it executes the agreement. Others require that any documents required for government approval must be translated into the local language and that the translated form of the agreement must be signed. If possible, franchisors should specify in their franchise agreements that regardless of whether the agreement is translated into another language, the English language version of the document must be executed by the parties and will govern any dispute between the parties.

118 *See* da Cunha, *supra* note 79, at 287.

119 *See* Emuwa and Okeyinka, *supra* note 80, at 306.

120 *See* Kamanzi, *supra* note 70 at 322.

121 *See* Papier, *supra* note 15, at 343.

122 *See* Ferah, *supra* note 16, at 373.

123 *See* Sakala, *supra* note 71 at 389.

Of the African countries surveyed, there were no execution formalities noted, with the exception of Zambia. In Zambia, franchise agreements must be authenticated according to the provisions of Zambia's *Authentication of Documents Act* to be enforceable.[124] Documents executed in the United Kingdom are sufficiently authenticated if they are executed before a notary public and signed and duly sealed by such notary public. As for the execution of documents from any other jurisdiction outside Zambia, other than the United Kingdom, the signature and seal of the notary public must be certified by the consular office in Zambia of that foreign jurisdiction.

In addition, most of the African jurisdictions surveyed had no requirement that a franchise agreement be translated into the local language to be enforceable. English is generally acceptable. However, where an agreement is required to be filed or registered with a government authority or enforced by a local court, local laws often require that the agreement must be translated into the local language. This is true of Angola,[125] Cape Verde,[126] the Democratic Republic of the Congo,[127] Ethiopia,[128] Mozambique,[129] and Tunisia.[130]

C. Drafting International Franchise Agreements — Typical Legal Terms

There is no such document as a "standard" franchise agreement, but rather a checklist of "standard" issues that must be considered before drafting a franchise agreement. Drafting an

---

124 *Id.* at 391

125 *See* Fialho, *supra* note 17, at 124.

126 *See* Fialho, *supra* note 76, at 196.

127 *See* Wafwana et al., *supra* note 67, at 210.

128 *See* Assefa and Molla, *supra* note 78, at 239.

129 *See* da Cunha, *supra* note 79, at 289.

130 *See* Ferah, *supra* note 16, at 374.

agreement before an issues list has been canvassed will only prove to be problematic.

Preparing a "standard" form of international franchise agreement complicates the issue further. The typical drafting issues must be considered in addition to legal, socio-economic, cultural, linguistic, and commercial factors of two or more countries. A number of these issues are explained below[131]:

1. Territorial Rights and Limitations

The franchisor must define the scope of the franchise system for which exclusivity is being granted. Most franchisees will seek a franchise agreement that provides them the exclusive geographical right, license, and privilege to use the franchise system in a local segment of the market or the entire jurisdiction. Exclusivity issues are not, however, limited to geographical considerations.

It is not uncommon for a franchisor to grant third parties exclusive or reserved rights to sell the franchisor's products or services within the exclusive territory. If this is the case, these rights must be specifically carved out in any documents being drafted or under consideration.

Notwithstanding the exclusive rights granted to a franchisee, most international franchisors reserve to themselves certain rights, such as the right to acquire a competitor or be acquired by a competitor, to sell the same or similar products or services associated with the franchise system or the right to sell such products or services through other channels of trade, including the Internet, or to specific customers, and national or international accounts. These reserved rights often place the franchisor in competition with the franchisee or its subfranchisees, so the franchisor may be required to disclose

---

[131] Portions of this section C were adapted from Zaid and Tyre, International Franchising Basic Track Workshop: *A World Tour of The Basics of International Franchising*, *supra* note 105.

those reservations depending on the laws of the relevant jurisdictions.

Because an international franchisor imparts know-how, trade secrets, and confidential information relating to the operation of the franchised business, the franchisee should covenant to deal exclusively with the franchisor and the franchise system, and not to compete (at least during the term of the franchise agreement). Any such covenants require a number of drafting considerations, including the geographical scope of the restriction, to whom the covenant will apply, and exceptions for potential existing businesses of the franchisee.

Exclusivity in terms of the territorial restrictions applicable to the franchisee should be clearly defined. A map or description of the boundaries as they exist at the time of executing the franchise agreement could be included in the agreement.

Finally, if international franchisees wish to expand the franchise system beyond the boundaries of the target country to adjoining countries, rights of first refusal or options to develop additional countries may be provided for in an international franchise agreement. These rights are often granted when the adjoining countries have similar cultural, language, and/or commercial characteristics. These rights may also require that certain quotas or target sales figures be reached before the rights may be exercised or may have time restrictions on the exercise of the options following which the options will be forfeited.

2. Fees

The initial fee for international franchise rights is typically calculated in one of two ways. It is either a fixed fee or a fee based on quota or performance. International franchisors may frequently underestimate the costs involved in expanding their franchise systems internationally, particularly in less developed or emerging target countries, accordingly some franchisors control their cost by requiring the reimbursement of their expenses in developing products and services for the franchise system for target markets. Examples of reimbursed costs may include:

- expenses incurred in connection with governmental reviews, registrations, and approvals; and

- expenses incurred by the franchisor for training the franchisee and its staff, communications expenses, translation and other development costs for the operations manual and other materials, and legal and other professional costs incurred related to the development of the franchise system documents.

As for "development" fees incurred by the franchisor for the opening of individual franchisee locations, the agreement may provide for payment to the franchisor for fees for a specific number of initial or additional outlets. Fees may be incurred on a fixed-amount basis, a per unit basis, or in accordance with some formula basis. Agreements typically express continuing fees as a royalty percentage of gross sales or revenues of the franchisee. Continuing fees may also be expressed on a fixed-fee basis for each unit developed. Fees may be expressed on a constant or variable percentage. Alternatively, the agreement may provide for minimum periodic fees, usually on a quarterly or annual basis.

Definitions of gross or net sales typically provide for certain exclusions, including refunds, discounts, taxes, and other similar nonprofit items to the franchisee. In some instances, the fees will be subject to an inflation factor or adjustment based on a cost of living or other index. This type of adjustment is especially important in jurisdictions with historically high inflation records.

The agreement must describe the mechanics for payment, including the frequency of payment, any interest on late payments, and the methods of payment. For example, the agreement could provide for payment to a designated bank account of a franchisor. If withholding taxes are exigible on fees paid to the international franchisor from the target country, the agreement may be written to break up specific components of the fees into certain services that may not be subject to withholding tax. These components may include technical assistance services, training, rights to know-how, trademark license fees, site selection, inspection, and consultation fees.

a. Currency

The franchise agreement may provide for a particular conversion method to the franchisor's home country currency that results in a specific payment in that currency on a particular date. A franchise agreement should allow the franchisor to select a different currency, designate the source from which the exchange rate quotations are to be obtained, and specify the conversion date on which the franchisee must purchase the required currency. Typically, the currency conversion date is the date on which periodic payments are due under the agreement. For reimbursements and other irregular payments, the currency conversion date should be the date the franchisor incurs the expense or the date it issues an invoice. For late payments, the conversion date should be, at the franchisor's option, either the date payment was due or the date of actual payment. If currency conversion is not possible because of governmental regulations or other factors, alternatives for the franchisor should be stipulated, including the possibility of payment in tangible or intangible property. If currency conversion continues, the agreement may provide for a suspension or termination of the franchise agreement after a specified period.

If subfranchising is involved, the franchisor may require payment by subfranchisees directly to the franchisor to avoid the risk of non-payment by the franchisee.

b. Withholding Taxes

Withholding taxes will normally be charged on royalty, interest, and similar payments from a franchisee to a franchisor residing outside of the target country. The franchisee will generally be required to calculate, withhold, and remit such taxes to the target country tax authorities. The franchisee will also be required to provide the franchisor tax receipts for the payments made so that the franchisor can claim foreign tax credits in its home country.

Some international franchisors require a gross up of all fees including a component for any taxes withheld in the target country. The "tax gross-up" method shifts the burden of target country withholding taxes to the franchisee. The franchisee pays both the withholding tax and the royalties (or other applicable fees) at the full contract rate agreed to by the parties. If the franchisor reimburses the franchisee for its withholding tax payments to the extent that the franchisor receives foreign tax credits for withholding taxes paid by the franchisee, the franchisor can mitigate the negative financial impact on the franchisee. This mitigation method is complicated by the complexities of calculating allowable foreign tax credits. It may not work where the target country government objects to any provision that benefits the franchisor at the franchisee's expense.

The "unbundling" method is another technique for avoiding foreign withholding tax issues. "Passive" income, such as royalties, is taxed in some target countries at higher rates than "active" income earned for the provision of services. Such services would include field supervision, training, and business counseling. The "unbundling" method separates the fees assessed for trademark and business system usage—the passive income—and the fees that compensate the franchisor for training, consultation, and other benefits or services provided by franchisor—the active income. Each set of unbundled fees are subsequently taxed at the applicable rate. This may result in tax savings for the franchisor.

The applicable taxes vary widely by country in those African countries surveyed. For example, in Tunisia, payments due under a franchise agreement are subject to a value added tax ("VAT") of 18% and withholding tax of 15% depending on whether the franchisor is resident in the country.[132] The VAT tax in Ethiopia

[132] *See* Ferah, *supra* note 16, at 367-68.

is 15% and the withholding tax is 5% of royalty fees.[133] In Nigeria, the applicable withholding tax rate for royalty payments made under a franchise agreement is 10% of the payment. Nigeria has a *Companies Income Tax Act*, which states that deductions made from a payment may not be regarded as an additional cost of the contract but as tax due on the payment. Therefore, a gross-up clause in Nigeria would be unenforceable if it provided that the person making the payment was obligated to pay withholding tax or any other deductions in addition to the contract price. However, a gross-up clause drafted to provide that the recipient would receive the amount it would have received prior to any deduction would be acceptable.[134]

Gross-up provisions are common and enforceable under all of the African countries surveyed. As in most countries across the globe, including those African nations surveyed here, the applicable taxes can be reduced if the entity receiving the payment is incorporated in a country with which the taxing jurisdiction has a double taxation agreement.

3. Development of Territory

International franchise agreements often specify development rights and obligations of the franchisee defined in terms of a specific number of outlets that are required to be owned and operated by the franchisee or by sub-franchisees. These rights will often be defined in a development schedule. The schedule will typically specify a minimum number of outlets to be opened and operated within a certain period.

The international franchise agreement will specify the aggregate number of outlets that must be opened and in operation at the end of each development period. The relevant provision must also cover any closed or terminated outlets and the ability of the

---

[133] *See* Assefa and Molla, *supra* note 78, at 231-32.

[134] *See* Emuwa and Okeyinka, *supra* note 80, at 303.

franchisee to carry forward outlets developed beyond the schedule requirements.

Some drafters of international franchise agreements extend development obligations in certain countries to political subdivisions or geographic territories rather than expressing them on a broader target country or other geographic basis.

In most agreements, the franchisee is required to own and operate at least one and perhaps more franchise outlets. The agreement may provide that the franchisee must open and operate a certain number of outlets itself or own and operate outlets for a certain period before being allowed to subfranchise. The franchisee may also be required to own and operate a specified number of outlets during the term of the agreement to be allowed to continue subfranchising.

For outlets to be developed by subfranchisees, the franchisor may require certain information provided to it before approving such outlets or subfranchisees. The franchisor may stipulate site selection criteria and franchisee selection criteria rather than approving each outlet and subfranchisee individually. As an alternative, the franchisor may require the right to approve each site either during an initial period or during the entire term of the franchise agreement.

As for development obligations, the franchisor must establish clear growth targets with the franchisee. Often, development targets in international franchise agreements are not met.[135] To

[135] Arturs Kalnins, *Biting Off More Than They Can Chew: Unfulfilled Development Commitments in International Master Franchising Ventures*, 5.12 *CHR REPORTS* 1, 8 (2005). Specifically, research revealed that in a sample of 142 ventures of 53 U.S.-based franchisors in 37 countries: (1) only 55 (39 percent) of the ventures survived to the end of the development term which was typically five years; (2) the median number of units that were intended to be open was 34; (3) of the 55 ventures that survived to the end of the development term, the median number of units opened was 3; and (4) only six (11 percent) of the ventures satisfied their development obligations.

counter this, international franchisors should consider growth incentives and providing rewards for good performance. For example, if a franchisee opens more than "x" complying units in a particular city or region within "y" period, it may be granted the right of first refusal over additional territory.

If the franchisee fails to comply with its development obligations, a number of alternatives may be triggered. The most severe would be the termination of the franchise agreement. Alternatively, the franchisee's development rights may be terminated. Under this scenario, the franchisee would continue to service existing subfranchisees. The franchisee may also trigger the right to continue limited development on a right of first refusal basis, or its exclusivity may be terminated. This would allow the franchisee to continue developing but in competition with the franchisor or some other newly appointed franchisee.

Surrendering of a portion of the territory for which exclusive rights were granted could be another consequence of failing to comply with the development schedule. This would permit the franchisor to further develop the territory or to enter into a franchise or other agreement with a new franchisee or developer.

Yet another alternative when drafting development obligations is to require the parties to renegotiate a reduced development schedule. This may be a viable option particularly when the franchisee may be able to demonstrate that the original development schedule was unrealistic because of economic or market changes.

4. Term and Post-Term Rights and Obligations

The term of an international franchise agreement is typically expressed for a certain number of years and extension or renewal rights are usually included. Conditions of renewal will be similar to those provided for in the franchisor's home country unit franchise agreement.

Post-term rights and obligations of the parties must be provided for in the agreement, if the document expires or terminates. The franchisee may be allowed to continue as a subfranchisor on a non-exclusive basis and to operate its existing owned or operated outlets. However, further development rights for additional units will normally terminate. Alternatively, if the franchisee is precluded from continued operation of the franchise system, de-identification obligations of the franchisee and its subfranchisees must be stipulated. In some instances, the franchisor may include a right to purchase the franchisee's and the subfranchisees' outlets on expiration.

Upon expiration or termination of the international franchise agreement, typical post-term covenants include return of the franchisor's proprietary materials, including operations manuals, agreements, advertising and promotional materials, products and supplies, and trademarked products on a pre-determined formula or third-party determination basis.

As indicated above, the post-term non-compete covenant of the franchisee requires an understanding and application of applicable laws in the target country, as well as the definition of prohibited activities, the geographical scope of application, and the time period for the covenant. A drafter will also need to determine the persons to whom the covenant applies, such as the franchisee, principals of the franchisee, family members, and designated shareholders.

5. System Adaptation and Modification

Often franchisors must modify their franchise systems so that they will be accepted in the target country. The franchisor's trademarks are one of the essential elements of the franchise system that may be subject to modification. The franchisor must determine whether its trademarks can be used in the target country or whether they must be modified. The franchisor must also ensure that it complies with all appropriate legal requirements to maintain continuing ownership of its principal trademarks and any modified or translated versions.

Other typical franchise system modifications in the target country include site and franchisee selection procedures, specifications for system facility, equipment, fixtures, furnishings, decor, signage, and location standards. In addition, approved products and services are often modified to local customs, tastes, laws and regulations, and cultural and religious standards. Training procedures and facilities, as well as advertising and marketing programs, may also be impacted.

Some international franchisors maintain approval rights over each and every such change and modification, but this approach is often impractical. The franchisor approves certain critical matters relating to the franchise system and retains a right to approve, at its option, less critical changes in the system. The franchisee will typically be required to modify or change the operations manual to comply with local standards, but in any event the franchise agreement should specifically state that all modified versions of the operations manual will be owned by the franchisor including specifically all copyrights in and to the modified versions.

The form of subfranchise agreement used by the franchisee for subfranchisees is often attached as an exhibit to the international franchise agreement and requires approval by the franchisor. An international franchisor will often require approval of any modifications, or may allow for some non-material changes to comply with local requirements. If the franchisee develops the form of subfranchise agreement, the franchisor should prescribe for certain mandatory provisions and for an absolute right to approve the form of subfranchise agreement. Finally, there should be a separate form of subfranchise agreement for each such unit owned and operated by the franchisee or its affiliate.

6. Governmental Approvals

In a number of jurisdictions, governmental authorities must approve the proposed franchise agreement prior to the parties entering into the agreement or enforcing its terms and conditions. Often these governmental approvals will be a condition precedent to the effectiveness of the franchise agreement in the jurisdiction. The franchise agreement should stipulate which party is responsible for obtaining such approvals. Other pre-conditions in the franchise agreement that may be stipulated include foreign investment notifications or approvals, completion of trademark registrations and obtaining visas or work permits for certain specified personnel.

7. Proprietary Marks

One of the earliest considerations that an international franchisor should undertake in respect of international franchising is the protection of its trademark around the world. The franchisor must determine the availability of its trademarks in the target country. If the trademarks have not been registered, applications should be applied for as soon as possible after the relevant searches are undertaken to identify the existence of the same or confusingly similar trademarks. Once the registration process is underway, the franchisor's principal trademarks should be registered for additional classes of products and services, if possible, to allow for future expansion. If modified, translated, substitute, or additional trademarks are necessary, the franchisor should protect and register those trademarks as well.

Subject to the trademark laws of the target country, the franchise agreement should impose upon the franchisee and all subfranchisees proper provisions for use of the franchisor's trademarks. Often these provisions are similar to those that would typically be provided for in the home country unit franchise agreement. The agreement must further stipulate:

- compliance with any registered user or licensing registrations in the target country;
- marking and public notification of ownership; and

- appropriate legal proceedings to protect the trademarks against infringing uses; this may include provisions relating to who initiates those procedures, the selection of counsel, the payment of expenses, and the control of proceedings.

The franchise agreement should also provide that translated versions of its trademarks, and new trademarks in the future, regardless of whether they are introduced by the franchisee, subfranchisees, or otherwise, will be owned by the franchisor. It will also provide for the right of the franchisor to substitute new, different, or modified trademarks for use in the target country, with a provision concerning the financial or other obligations of the franchisor if it exercises such right.[136]

8. Franchisor's Obligations

The franchisor will often provide certain services to and fulfill certain obligations to international franchisees on a periodic and continuing basis. For example, a franchisor will typically conduct an initial training session for the franchisee. Topics typically covered during such training include site selection, operating systems, systems standards, and marketing. If the international franchise agreement provides for subfranchising, training may also include the recruitment and training of subfranchisees, the servicing of subfranchisees, and the sourcing of equipment and products for subfranchisees.

Following the initial training, the franchisor may mandate periodic additional training related to the introduction of new products and services, the modifications to existing facilities and/or system standards. Subsequent training sessions may take the form of conferences, seminars, or workshops. Attendees may include representatives of the franchisor and/or the relevant suppliers.

---

[136] *See supra* notes 86 through 94 and accompanying text regarding Trademark License Filings at 25-26.

The international franchise agreement must specify where the training session will be conducted, the costs of who will cover the costs related to such training and what, if any, support franchises may provide with respect to obtaining any travel visa to attend such training sessions.

If the training will be conducted in a particular language, such as English, the franchisor should specify this in the franchise agreement and, if appropriate, stipulate that training program attendees must be fluent in the designated language and/or provide that the franchisee will be responsible for the expense of any interpreter required for the program attendees.

The franchise agreement should mandate that the franchisee and its designated personnel satisfactorily complete all initial training programs. If the franchisee and its personnel fail to satisfactorily complete the initial training, the consequences should be set forth in the agreement. For example, the franchisee could be required to attend additional training at the franchisee's expense or replace any personnel that did not successfully complete training or, at the discretion of the franchisor, terminate the agreement.

The franchise agreement may also specify certain ongoing assistance to be provided by the franchisor, such as:

- periodic inspections of outlets to ensure they comply with the system standards;

- support consultations with the franchisee with respect to operating problems and changes in system standards; and

- additional services and assistance requested by the franchisee that may incur a charge at designated per diem or other rates.

9. Franchisee's Reporting and Payment Obligations

An international franchisor will typically require certain reports submitted to it relating to the performance of the franchised units in the target country. The reports will cover units of the franchisee and, if applicable, any subfranchisee. The franchise agreement must therefore prescribe the type and frequency of reports required, including operational reports outlining the number of outlets opened or under development, the identification of subfranchisees, the locations of all outlets, the revenues from each outlet and other operating statistics submitted to the franchisor.

Financial statements will generally also be submitted to the franchisor. The financial reporting requirement in some target countries may differ from generally accepted accounting principles in the franchisor's home country. Consequently, conversion of financial statements and reports may be required.

The agreement may specify that reporting obligations may be satisfied by electronic means, including e-mail, and this may require special computer hardware and/or software as required by the franchisor.

Special payment terms may be required in certain target countries, especially where there are temporary or permanent restrictions on payment. For example, a franchisor may require payments to a designated bank or other financial institution or intermediary located in the target country. The franchisor could also require payment in the form of tangible property or drawdown payments against deposits lodged in the franchisor's home country.

Finally, a franchisor will typically require the right to: (i) inspect rights of the franchisee's and subfranchisees' outlets, (ii) audit statements submitted by the franchisee, and (iii) review the books and records of the franchisee and outlets operated by the franchisee and subfranchisees.

The franchisee may also be required to furnish franchisor copies of inspection reports performed by the franchisee and related to outlets operated by the franchisee and subfranchisees. The parties will typically negotiate whether the inspection and audit rights of the franchisor must be subject to prior notice.

10. Other Franchisee Obligations

A typical international franchise agreement will contain additional obligations pertaining to the franchisee. This may include site selection, acquisition, and development, training, system standard compliance, insurance policies and maintenance, target country law compliance, advertising and promotion, supplier arrangements and, if applicable, selection of subfranchisees and training and assistance to subfranchisees.

11. Supply and Suppliers

Prior to entering into an international franchise agreement, the franchisor must investigate anti-trust and competition laws of the target country, particularly as they relate to supplier matters. Often, the parties will negotiate the franchisor's right to designate approved suppliers or sources of products and services. Often the supplier or a source of products or services will include the franchisor or the franchisor's affiliates. If the franchisor receives rebates, advertising allowances, concessions, or other payments from designated suppliers, subject to target country anti-trust of competition laws, the franchisor should disclose such payments in the franchise agreement.

The franchisor will typically provide standards and specifications for approval of suppliers to the franchisee. The franchisor may stipulate a right to limit the number of suppliers, to inspect and monitor the supplier's premises and facilities, to receive samples of the supplier or source of products to ensure such samples comply with the franchisor's standards for testing purposes, and to change or disapprove an approved supplier or source of supply upon notice to the franchisee.

If the franchisor will share with the franchisee and/or its subfranchisee any rebates or other payments from suppliers, the franchise agreements should disclose these payments.

For goods or supplies sold to or provided by approved suppliers to the franchisee for use in connection with the franchise in the target country, the franchise agreement should restrict, subject to the target country's anti-trust or competition laws, resales outside the target country, to prevent grey marketing or unauthorized parallel importation in other foreign countries, where another franchisee has already been appointed or may be appointed in the future.

12. Advertising and Marketing Fund

Franchisors may administer a national advertising fund in their home countries as part of their franchise system. Franchisees in these domestic systems often contribute a percentage of gross sales to the fund. Similarly, an international franchise agreement typically establishes and administers an advertising and marketing fund for the target country to which franchisees must contribute. In forming an advertising and marketing fund in the target country, the franchisor must consider what the franchisee will contribute and the benefits to be obtained. The franchisee should have access to any advertising promotions and marketing materials, and to use such materials in the target country, subject to any necessary translations and modifications based on the customs, culture, and local laws of the target country. The franchisee's contribution to the fund may be a percentage of aggregate revenues from the franchise system in the target country, or an individual percentage of royalties or fixed fees paid by the franchise units of a franchisee or subfranchisee.

The right of the franchisor to approve marketing programs in the target country must also be addressed in the franchise agreement. The agreement should provide the criteria for granting approval, the time limits for granting such approval, and the method by which approval must be obtained by the franchisee. Alternatively, the franchisor could require the franchisee to consult with the franchisor before initiating a marketing program of a material nature, if the franchisor does not retain rights to approve such programs.

13. Transfer and Assignment

The personal qualifications of controlling shareholders of its international franchisees are of vital importance to international franchisors. As a result, a franchisor will generally restrict the ability of an international franchisee from transferring its ownership interests, the franchise agreement, or all or substantially all of the franchisee's assets without the franchisor's prior approval. Also, it may strengthen the enforceability of a transfer restriction if the international franchise agreement contains an acknowledgment by the franchisee that the restrictions are reasonable and necessary for the proper management of the system.

In some instances, franchisors require franchisees to place transfer restrictions in their organizational documents to prohibit transfers to innocent third parties by putting them on notice of the restrictions. This technique is permissible in most jurisdictions. However, some target countries, such as Taiwan, for example, will not allow transfer restrictions in a company's articles.[137] The practice is also not customary in Australia.[138] Several countries permit the placement of transfer restrictions in organizational documents subject to certain restrictions. Panama permits certain transfer restrictions in an entity's charter documents except that an absolute prohibition of share transfers will be void, and Costa Rica requires shareholder approval and several other conditions before transfer restrictions can be added to a company's articles.[139]

---

[137] Zaid and Tyre, *supra* note 105, at 26.

[138] *Id.* Australia has, however, codified that right to impose reasonable transfer restrictions. *See Australia's Franchising Code of Conduct*, Clause 20.

[139] Joyce Mazero, *Impact of Other Local Laws*, in FUNDAMENTALS OF INTERNATIONAL FRANCHISING, 240-41, ABA Forum of Franchising

(Footnote continued on next page)

The franchise agreement should provide whether change in control of the franchisee is prohibited or subject to the approval of the franchisor.

A drafter of the franchise agreement may limit the right of the franchisee to transfer the franchise agreement, or to transfer a controlling interest in the franchisee, subject to the franchisor's right of first refusal. Typically, these transfers are subject to the franchisor's right of first refusal, unless the transfer involves a non-controlling interest below a specified ownership level, transfers among existing shareholders or owners, or a public offering of securities in the franchisee entity.

The franchisor may often restrict a public sale of equity interests in the franchisee entity or permit a public offering only after with the franchisor's prior approval. If the franchisor allows a public offering, it typically will require the original owners to retain a minimum threshold of ownership of the franchisee entity and require prior approval of the prospectus or any other registration document filed with a regulatory authority. The franchisor will want to confirm that references to the franchise agreement, the franchisor, and the franchise system are accurate. The franchisor will also usually require indemnities.

In those African countries surveyed, the authors were asked to advise whether there are any restrictions on a franchisor's ability to restrict transfers by a master franchise including any interest in or assets of the master franchisee. Transfers are generally permissible so long as the other party gives prior consent. For example, a restriction on transfer would be valid in Mozambique so long as the terms of the contract are not contrary to Mozambican law.[140] For another example, language in the Ethiopian Commercial Code suggests that transfers may not be

(Richard M. Asbill & Steven M. Goldman eds, 2001). *See also* Zaid and Tyre, *supra* note 105, at 26.

[140] *See* da Cunha, *supra* note 79, at 282-85.

made without the written consent of the franchisor.[141] Other countries differ, however. Egypt has no definite restrictions.[142] South Africa permits agreements to provide for certain restrictions on transfer favoring the franchisor if, for example, the master franchisee intends to dispose of the franchised business. It also allows for step-in rights in favor of the franchisor where there are concerns relating to the prudent management of the franchise entity and franchisee.[143]

14. Liquidated Damages

Most target countries enforce liquidated damage provisions. As a result, franchisors often include them in international franchise agreements, because damages may be difficult to prove in foreign courts and other proceedings. They also deter the franchisee from engaging in activities that could cause irreparable harm to the franchisor, such as violations of transfer restrictions, non-competition, confidentiality, and trademark or other intellectual property protections. Foreign courts review liquidated damage amounts to ensure that the amount of damages stipulated is commensurate with the damages of the franchisor. As a result, the franchise agreement should only provide for that amount of liquidated damages based on a reasonable expectation of the damages that may occur. Foreign courts view excessive liquidated damage amounts as a penalty and reduce such amounts to an amount that approximates the actual damages resulting from the breach. Moreover, in certain target countries, the inclusion of liquidated damage amounts in an international franchise agreement may not be beneficial to the franchisor. In the Dominican Republic, for example, the courts may use the amounts specified as liquidated damages as a cap on damages, even if actual damages exceed such amount.[144]

---

141 *See* Assefa and Molla, *supra* note 78, at 235.

142 *See* El-Shahid, *supra* note 77, at 217.

143 *See* Papier, *supra* note 15, at 339-40.

144 Mazero, *supra* note 137, at 280-81.

15. Indemnification

Indemnification provisions allocate losses and expenses between the parties. In drafting these provisions, the parties should address (i) who is indemnified; (ii) who initiates, controls, and pays for an indemnitee's legal counsel; (iii) who has authority to settle disputes; (iv) whether the parties must mitigate damages; and (v) whether the indemnification provision survives termination of the agreement.

In international franchise agreements, the franchisees are usually required to indemnify franchisors for any losses or expenses involving (i) any lawsuit, dispute resolution proceeding, settlement, or investigation; (ii) a breach of the agreement; and (iii) any acts and omissions in the construction or operation of the franchisee's unit(s). Moreover, in some instances, franchisors indemnify franchisees for third-party actions related to the franchisee's authorized use of the franchisor's trademarks.

Most target countries will enforce indemnification provisions provided that parties are not indemnified for their own gross negligence or intentional acts. Italy and other countries, however, will generally require mitigation of damages.[145] Moreover, in other jurisdictions, drafters should be aware that overly broad indemnification provisions are vulnerable to challenge. In these target countries, indemnification is often restricted to what was reasonably foreseeable at the time of execution of the franchise agreement.

16. Default and Termination

An international franchise agreement stipulates a variety of items constituting default of the agreement. Cure periods may be negotiated for certain events, but others will provide for the right of the franchisor to terminate the franchise agreement.

---

145 *Id.* at 266.

Standard defaults include a breach of representations or warranties by the franchisee. Other defaults may include franchisee's failure to comply with the development schedule; failure to meet target quotas or development obligations; and breach of any bankruptcy or insolvency provisions of the agreement.

In addition, there may be certain events, which if not met, result in termination. These events include failure to obtain any required government approvals, failure to register trademarks, and compliance with exchange controls that prevent payment of fees to the franchisor for some period of time.

Depending on the negotiation of the parties, cure periods will provide the franchisee a reasonable period of time to cure those defaults that can be cured.

Many target countries have general agency laws requiring that the franchisor have "good cause" to terminate or fail to renew a franchise agreement, provide the franchisee prior notice of a termination or non-renewal, and give the franchisee an opportunity to cure a breach. Some countries regulating the termination of franchise agreements include Australia, Italy, Malaysia, Romania, and Russia.[146] In most target countries "good cause" for termination includes franchisee's failure to comply with material provisions of the agreement, including a failure to make payments under the agreement, and a felony, abandonment, fraud, bankruptcy, or insolvency of the franchisee.

In those African countries surveyed, the authors were asked to comment on any laws relating to termination of contractual agreements such as agency laws, any required indemnity provisions, and notice or "good cause" requirements. Egyptian law permits the parties to provide for indemnification of non-

---

[146] *See* European Franchise Federation website, http://www.eff-franchise.com/spip.php?rubrique21 (last visited March 7, 2014). *See also* Zaid and Tyre, *supra* note 105, at 29.

defaulting parties and liquidated damages.[147] Under Tunisian law, if Tunisian authorities believe that the termination of a franchise agreement is the result of anticompetitive conduct, it may prevent termination of the agreement.[148] South African law provides that parties are free to stipulate to the terms governing termination. However, certain termination provisions may be governed by the *New Companies Act* (in the case of termination by insolvency) and the *Consumer Protection Act*.[149]

17. Dispute Resolution

Because parties to the franchise agreement typically want to avoid judicial proceedings, it is common for alternative dispute resolution methods and requirements to be specified in the agreement.

The first step in attempting to resolve any dispute in many international franchise agreements is the requirement that the senior executives of the parties meet in an attempt to resolve any disputed issues prior to the commencement of any further dispute resolution proceedings. The agreement should require the parties to meet in good faith to resolve the dispute. It should also specify who are the required participants, the location of any meeting, the minimum period of time for the meeting, and who incurs the costs of such meeting.

If the senior executive officers of the parties are unable to resolve the dispute, non-binding third-party mediation is typically the next step. The agreement should provide for who the mediator will be or how the mediator will be selected, the place of mediation, the procedures for mediation, and who incurs the costs of the mediation.

---

[147] *See* El-Shahid, *supra* note 77, at 218.

[148] *See* Ferah, *supra* note 16, at 371.

[149] *See* Papier, *supra* note 15, at 340-41.

If mediation cannot resolve a dispute, the agreement may provide for formal arbitration. However, certain dispute items may fall out the purview of arbitration so that the parties may seek immediate relief. These items include equitable remedies, remedies with respect to use or misuse of the franchisor's trademarks, and remedies with respect to non-payment.

All details concerning the arbitration should be provided in the international franchise agreements, including whether the arbitration will be held in the home country, the target country, or in a neutral location. Arbitration rules should also be specified. Typical rules include the rules of the American Arbitration Association (*Commercial Arbitration or International Arbitration Rules*), the International Chamber of Commerce, the United Nations Conference on International Trade Law (UNCITRL), and the London Court of International Arbitration.

The agreement should specify the number of arbitrators, how they will be selected, the language of the arbitral records, the jurisdiction for enforcement of the arbitral award, the governing law, and who has responsibility for expenses and fees of the arbitration as well as responsibility for payment of each party's own fees and expenses.

If any disputes are to be resolved by judicial determination, provisions must be included in the franchise agreement specifying a number of items. Each of the franchisor and the franchisee will typically want the governing law of the franchise agreement to be the law of its home country. Regardless of the choice of law, in many cases, parties to the franchise agreement will seek remedies before target country courts even if only to enforce arbitral or judicial awards or decisions granted in the home country.

The laws of the target country will also control intellectual property issues (e.g., trademark infringement claims), currency restrictions imposed by the target country, withholding taxes, disclosure requirements, and competition restrictions.

In providing for choice of forum, the franchisor may want to designate the forum for dispute resolution within the home country, while the franchisee may want to designate the forum within the target country. To resolve the issue, the agreement could provide that the courts of the domicile of the party that does not commence legal proceedings will serve as the choice of forum. Another alternative is to confer concurrent jurisdiction on the courts of the domicile of each party.

Because the judicial systems in some target countries do not recognize equitable remedies, the parties may need to specifically provide for preliminary relief in the form of interlocutory injunctions, temporary restraining orders, orders of specific performance, and other similar types of relief in the agreement.

It will also be necessary to specify who is responsible for fees and costs, although in some judicial systems it is within the discretion of the court to order costs. Nevertheless often the losing party pays all fees, expenses, and costs of the other party.

Other dispute-related issues to cover in an international franchise agreement include a period of time for asserting claims, severability of agreement provisions, waiver of jury trial, and waiver of exemplary or punitive damages.

In those African countries surveyed, the country authors were asked to confirm whether the choice of law of a foreign jurisdiction would likely be upheld under the law of his or her country. They were also asked to confirm whether a court in his or her country would honor an election of international arbitration dispute resolution. Most of the answers were consistent. It is preferred that the franchise agreement be governed by and interpreted under the laws of the African target country; however, in a number of cases the courts will generally hold the parties to the laws of another jurisdiction so long as the parties have agreed to it and the choice of law does not conflict with domestic public policy. In short, courts in the countries surveyed would likely honor an election of international arbitration dispute resolution and enforce arbitral judgments.

Moreover, Botswana,[150] Egypt,[151] Ghana,[152] Kenya,[153] Mozambique,[154] Nigeria,[155] Rwanda,[156] South Africa,[157] Tunisia,[158] and Zambia[159] are signatories to the New York Convention so an arbitral award under international rules will likely be enforced in these jurisdictions.

18. Consequences of Termination

The consequences of terminating an international franchise agreement can be complicated, especially if subfranchisees are involved. As a preliminary matter, it must be determined whether the agreement will provide that the franchisee has any continuing rights to operate the franchisee's own outlets and those of subfranchisees post-termination. If a franchisee will be prohibited from continuing operation, the agreement must, upon termination, automatically reassign subfranchise agreements to the franchisor. It may also provide for a right to purchase existing outlets on a pre-determined formula basis. The franchisor will need to review the laws affecting the preparation of conditional assignments in the target country to draft the appropriate assignment provisions in both the franchise agreement and the individual unit subfranchise agreements.

If the franchisee is to be barred from further involvement in the franchise system, appropriate covenants should be included in

---

[150] *See* Makgalemele, *supra* note 66, at 167-68.

[151] *See* El-Shahid, *supra* note 77, at 219.

[152] *See* Letsa and Ashun, *supra* note 68, at 257.

[153] *See* Syekei, *supra* note 69, at 272.

[154] *See* da Cunha, *supra* note 79, at 287.

[155] *See* Emuwa and Okeyinka, *supra* note 80, at 306.

[156] *See* Kamanzi, *supra* note 70, at 322.

[157] *See* Papier, *supra* note 15, at 342-43.

[158] *See* Ferah, *supra* note 16, at 372-73.

[159] *See* Sakala, *supra* note 71, at 389.

the agreement relating to non-competition, non-solicitation, non-use of trade secrets and confidential information, and cessation of all use of trademarks and proprietary products.

The agreement may also provide for conditional rights of assignment of all leases and subleases entered into by the franchisee. As a precautionary measure, the franchisor should review the enforceability of such provisions under the target country laws as well as any formal requirements for drafting the appropriate assignment language.

Finally, the franchise agreement should provide the franchisor with an option to require a defaulting franchisee to sell the agreement and related rights and assign any subfranchise agreements to a qualified third-party purchaser designated by the franchisor. This allows the franchisor to locate a new franchisee and to assign to the new franchisee the system rights.

19. General Agreement Provisions

An international franchise agreement should include the general contract provisions that would typically be included in a contract, such as provisions relating to the entire agreement, the binding effect of the agreement, counterparts, governing language, effective headings, notices, and independent contractors.

Appropriate disclaimers should also be included and adapted for the laws of the target country. Relevant disclaimers may provide that:

- the franchise system is proprietary,
- the franchisee had an opportunity to obtain independent advice and counsel,
- the franchisee assumed the risks of entering into the international franchise agreement,

- the franchised business has adequate capitalization and working capital,

- the franchisee has provided adequate representations and warranties relating to financial statements submitted by to franchisor, as well as to the identity of and ownership interests of shareholders and principals of the franchisee entity, and

- the franchisee has acknowledged that it does not and will not operate any competitive business.

D. Conclusions

Africa is a rapidly changing continent, and franchising is increasingly seen as a viable means to expand businesses, spur the development of SMEs, and increase foreign investment in the target countries of the African continent. Given these factors, counsel and business executives in the franchise industry should understand the impact and consequences of various franchise structures, the law of the target countries in which the franchise will operate, and the options in drafting key contractual provisions of the international franchise agreement. Throughout the expansion process, it is critical that the franchisor obtain experienced legal, accounting, banking, and other professional advice in the target country and that an appropriate selection be made of the franchisee in the target country to launch a successful franchise venture in the African continent.

Financing the African Franchise Venture

Benjamin Gyepi-Garbrah, Jr. and
Manbegrot Shimellis
SATIG LLC

Washington, D.C.

I. Capitalization and Costs

Franchising startup costs often vary significantly depending on the type of franchise, the franchisor, and the terms of the particular agreement. Well-established brand-name outlets can cost hundreds of thousands of dollars. Franchising costs can be divided into two categories: initial fees and ongoing fees (including royalty payments and advertising fees). In addition, franchisees may also face other administrative and legal expenses. An entrepreneur's ability to amass adequate free cash or cash equivalents to meet the total financing requirements to start up a franchised business is often referred to as the capacity for capitalization.[160]

It is imperative for prospective franchisees to understand all of the attendant costs and the financing alternatives. Surveys in Africa indicate that general commercial lending standards require entrepreneurs to invest 33% to 50% of the total franchise investment (i.e., a debt : equity ratio of 2:1 to 1:1), including an operating line of credit for working capital purposes, in free cash or cash equivalents.[161] About 75% to 90% of franchisees in

[160] African Development Bank, *supra* note 22, at 18.

[161] *Id.*

Africa that initially inquire into a franchise lack the necessary unencumbered investment capital to secure financing.[162]

A. Initial Franchise Fees

Franchise fees are the initial upfront fees that franchisees pay the franchisor. This fee, which may or may not be refundable, is effectively the price of buying into the franchise system, and may range from a few hundred dollars to several hundreds of thousands of dollars for larger well-established franchises.[163.] It includes the right to use the franchise brand, trademark, trade secrets, training, operating procedures, and manuals.[164] Franchise fees are usually due when the franchise agreement is executed, but installment plans are also a feasible alternative.[165]

The following table gives a sense of the average franchise fees by sector in two African countries—South Africa and Egypt.

Average Franchise Fees[166]

Sector	South Africa	Egypt
Automotive, building & home services	US$3,150	N/A
Business, education & training	US$22,344	US$3,300
Fast-food, restaurant	US$9,773	US$14,992
Retail	US$11,471	US$1,300
Average	**US$12,358**	**US$12,807**

162 *Id.*

163 Dennis L. Foster, *Encyclopedia of Franchises and Franchising* 98, FACTS ON FILE, INC. 1989.

164 Mark. P Friedlander, Jr. & Gene Gurney, *Handbook of Successful Franchising 3rd Edition*, 13-14, LIBERTY HALL PRESS 1990.

165 Foster, *supra* note 161, at 290.

166 Wouter Deelder & Robin A. Miller, *Franchising in Frontier Markets: What's Working, What's Not, and Why?* (Report by Dalberg Global Development Advisors, 2009).

B. Ongoing Fees

Ongoing fees include franchise royalties, contributions to the franchisor's national or regional advertising fund, charges for special services or assistance, payments to franchise associations, costs of auditing the franchisees business, mandatory minimum advertising expenditures, and contract renewal fees. Franchisees might also encounter transfer fees, if they sell or assign their franchise.[167]

Franchise royalty fees are typically calculated as a set percentage of the franchisee's gross sales receipts.[168] Some franchisors even demand a minimum royalty fee independent of the franchisee's actual performance.[169]

Advertising fees are separate payments by the franchisee for the franchisor's promotional services. Most franchisors maintain a cooperative advertising fund pool into which franchisees contribute a percentage of their outlet's gross revenue. This pool of advertising fees funds major advertising campaigns to benefit all franchisees.[170] While the most common advertising fee is a royalty on the gross revenues of the franchisee's outlet, fixed fees are also an alternative.[171] Advertising fees can be a contentious issue, and research suggests that the best arrangement is to give the franchisor ultimate authority over budgeting for and spending on advertising, while requiring the franchisor to consult with the franchisees in developing the advertising plan for the franchise system.[172]

---

167 Foster, *supra* note 161, at 99.

168 *Id.* at 98.

169 Andrew J. Sherman, *The Franchising Handbook* 300, Andrew J. Sherman ed., AMACOM BOOKS 1993.

170 Foster, *supra* note 161, at 34.

171 *Id.* at 110.

172 Sherman, *supra* note 167, at 179.

C. Other Expenses

New franchises can take several years to reach profitability. In the meantime, franchisees will need working capital, a pool of money to cover their overhead expenses such as training, audit, legal, public offering review, lease negotiation, insurance requirements, and consulting fees charged by the franchisor or its affiliates.[173] To assist them in calculating how much capital they will need to meet these overhead expenses, franchisees should obtain an estimate of the working capital requirements from the franchisor.

II. Financing Sources

Given their relatively high startup costs, many franchises are launched with financial assistance from external parties such as banks, savings and loans, investment firms, leasing companies, financial partners, or venture capitalists. Funding obtained from these sources is mobilized for four general purposes:

- seed capital,
- startup capital,
- working capital, and
- expansion capital.[174]

Franchisees seeking financing to open a new franchise outlet are usually seeking startup capital for the initial upfront investment.[175] Franchisees operating "mezzanine level"[176] and "mature"[177] franchise systems are generally seeking working and

---

[173] *Id.* at 290.

[174] Foster, *supra* note 161, at 83.

[175] *Id.* at 84.

[176] A "mezzanine level" of growth is often described as a franchise system between 20 and 60 franchisees and 5 to 10 years of franchising.

[177] A "mature" franchise system is often described as a franchise system with 60 or more franchisees and 10 years or more in franchising. Mature level franchisors are usually run by professional managers.

expansion capital to sustain their current operations and grow into secondary and tertiary markets.

As the chart below demonstrates, there are four broad categories of funding:[178]

Debt Instruments	**Equity Financing**	**Asset Based Financing**	**Other Alternatives**
Trade credit • Open account trade credit • Notes payable trade credit • Consignment trade credit Bankers acceptances Letters of credit • Export letters of credit • Import letters of credit • Standby letters of credit • Revolving letters of credit • Irrevocable letters of credit • Transferrable letters of credit Transaction loans Floor planning Commercial paper Revolving credit Term loans Banks • Debentures • Subordinated debentures • Insurance bonds • Mortgage bonds • Zero coupon bonds Mortgages	Common Stock Preferred Stock • Cumulative • Non-cumulative • Callable	Accounts receivable financing Accounts receivable factoring Inventory financing	Warrants Convertible bonds Leasing Sale leaseback Employee stock ownership plan (ESOP)

[178] Sherman, *supra* note 167, at 386.

Financing the African Franchise Venture

A. Conventional Lenders

Conventional lenders, such as banks, savings and loans, and credit unions, are the most commonly utilized capital source for franchises.[179] They offer market interest rates, subject to the borrower's credit worthiness, and often demand collateral in the form of a personal property pledge from the borrower, such as a mortgage on a home or title to business assets.[180] Conventional lenders in Africa are often characterized by high interest rate spreads and margins due to a lack of competition, diseconomies of scale, high risk, and the absence of a well-established credit rating system.[181] Data collected in 2007 indicates that the average annualized commercial bank prime lending rates[182] across Africa ranged from a high of 578.96% in Zimbabwe to 6% in Libya.[183] In addition to high initial rates, unexpected upward interest rate adjustments can leave borrowers stuck with unaffordable payments. Interest rate risk, coupled with onerous collateral requirements and lengthy terms of up to 30 years can be burdensome.[184]

Among conventional lenders, commercial banks are typically the first source of debt financing. Bankers are generally more lenient on businesses with franchise brand names and a lengthy history of consistent cash flows. Approved franchisees and favored brands may borrow at a debt/equity ratio of 2:1, instead of the

---

179 *Id.*

180 *Id.*

181 *Nigeria: AfDB Decry High Interest Rates By African Banks*, ALLAFRICA.COM, (2011), http://allafrica.com/stories/201109170187.html (last visited March 7, 2014).

182 The "prime rate" is the interest rate that lenders charge their most credit-worthy customers.

183 Central Intelligence Agency, *The World Factbook, Country Comparison: Commercial Bank Prime Lending Rates*, https://www.cia.gov/library/publications/the-world-factbook/rankorder/2208rank.html (last visited March 7, 2014).

184 Sherman, *supra* note 167, at 386.

standard 1:1 rate.[185] Franchises with few outlets and locations are not as attractive, partly because they might not perform well across different regions and economic environments. Lenders usually approach each application on a case by case basis, taking into account the franchisee's personal status and circumstances, and poor risk candidates will not be granted a loan merely because they are allied with a brand name franchise system. Because franchisees are often required to disclose whatever information the bank needs to assess the application, in some instances they protect sensitive information through a confidentiality agreement with the investigating bank.[186]

Bankers take into consideration the following factors in determining whether to grant credit to a borrower:[187]

- character: track record and history of repayment;
- cash flow: capacity to meet payment obligations, sufficiency of projected cash flows to meet obligations, and offer investment returns;
- capital: net worth of the business, liquidity, debt/equity ratio; and
- collateral: tangible assets such as homes, machinery, equipment.

Bankers will also consider:[188]

- the franchise system: size, performance, brand value, capital requirements, cash flows, franchisor support;
- established unit: (if the franchisee is buying an existing unit), unit history, condition, demographics of the area; and
- operator: history of existing operations, management structure, track record, viability, reputation, industry, available training, ethics.

---

185 *Id.*

186 *Id.* at 68-69.

187 Nicole Coppo, *Your Blueprint to Franchising Success* 26, SUCCEED, 2006

188 *Id.*

Financing the African Franchise Venture

Notable banks catering to franchises in Africa include ABSA Bank ("ABSA"), First National Bank ("FNB"), Sanlam Bank, Nedbank, and Standard Bank. The sophistication of services that banks offer to franchisees varies from country to country, and is generally correlated to the sophistication of the franchising sector in that country. Currently, South African banks such as ABSA and FNB maintain divisions that cater specifically to the franchising sector.

In order to facilitate bank loans to franchisees, some African governments have undertaken initiatives designed to incentivize banks. For example, South Africa's Khula Credit Guarantee scheme ("Khula Guarantees") provides various guarantee solutions to registered commercial banks and financial institutions in the private sector. Under the guarantee, Khula Enterprise Finance Limited, a part of the South African Department of Trade and Industry, guarantees 80% of a qualifying loan, up to ZAR1,000,000 (approximately US$120,700). Khula Guarantees can only be utilized when a borrower meets a bank's basic lending criteria, but fails to secure a bank loan due to insufficient collateral security.[189] Similarly, the Government of *Nigeria's Small-Medium Industry Equity Investment Scheme* ("SMIEIS") requires every Nigerian bank to set aside 10% of its pre-tax profit to fund small and medium-sized businesses investment proposals, including franchises, through equity participation.[190]

Bank lending to franchises is growing, partly driven by the franchising sector's apparent immunity to the recent global downturn. As Thabiso Ramasike, Head of Franchising at South Africa's Standard Bank noted:

---

[189] *Individual Guarantee Scheme* (2003), KHULA ENTERPRISE FINANCE LTD., *available at* http://www.westerncape.gov.za/Text/2003/khula_credit_guarantee.pdf.

[190] Basil Anthony Ngwu Onugu, *Small and Medium Enterprises in Nigeria: Problems and Prospects* (2005).

> With franchising showing more resilience than other business sectors of the economy, the likelihood of a franchise business being approved funding is much higher than normal non-franchised business. This is particularly evident in the fast food, retail, fuel retail, telecommunication, and automotive sectors. There is greater support, sharing of best practice, and predictability, especially in the well-run franchised brands.[191]

B. Franchisor Funding

Many franchisors offer direct or indirect financing, sometimes up to 100% of the initial fee. Franchisors can assist franchisees through equipment leasing and real estate acquisition programs, and credit lines for supply and opening inventory purchases. Franchisors can assist franchisees by: identifying suitable financing sources, fostering relations with lenders, assisting in loan package presentations, establishing vendor programs, designing internal leasing programs, providing loan guarantees, and remarketing agreements.[192] They can also retain third parties, such as finance and leasing firms or product distributors, to fund up to 100% of the initial investment.

South Africa's Jenny Wireless is a notable example of a low-cost African franchisor that lends significant support to its franchisees. The company assists its franchisees in establishing wireless networks, and its support services are available in all African countries. In addition to its low start-up costs, Jenny Internet handles all billing and support services, leaving the franchisees free to handle the technical work instead of being

---

[191] Jacqueline Martinez, *Franchising in Africa Continues to Innovate and Show Growth*, BIZASSIST.CO.ZA, Nov. 15, 2011, *available at* http://www.bizassist.co.za/news.asp?Cat=Sme&Ref=2921 (last visited March 7, 2014).

[192] Sherman, *supra* note 167, at 382.

mired in administrative minutiae.[193] Similarly, Kenya's Kula Korner restaurant chain undertakes the provision of equipment and the construction of its restaurants, which it offers to franchisees as a complete package.[194]

C. Venture Capitalists

Venture capitalists or "angel investors" invest in risky startups, when banks are unable or unwilling to do so. In exchange for control of what, in their estimation, will flourish into a profitable business, venture capitalists are willing to accept the higher risk associated with startups. Venture capitalists expect an ownership stake in the franchise in exchange for funding.

Venture capital is a viable source of equity financing for rapidly expanding franchisors unable to meet the collateral and debt repayment terms of traditional debt lenders.[195] Soft costs such as personnel and marketing, for which debt financing is challenging to obtain, are particularly amenable to venture capital financing. Venture capital financing requires a management team capable of negotiating the transaction and addressing various issues, including dilution, control, investment returns, and risk mitigation. The structure of the transaction will hinge on the type of the forms of securities to be used: preferred stock, convertible debentures, debt securities without warrants, or common stock.[196]

In comparison, some private equity shops eschew franchise investments, which they regard as startups with unjustifiably

---

[193] *How We Made it in Africa*, http://www.howwemadeitinafrica.com/case-study-connecting-rural-africa-to-the-internet/15624/ (last visited March 7, 2014)

[194] *How We Made it in Africa*, http://www.howwemadeitinafrica.com/interview-how-i-started-kenyas-own-version-of-mcdonalds/7356 (last visited March 7, 2014).

[195] Sherman, *supra* note 167, at 375.

[196] *Id.*

high risks. A number of firms, such as Kenya's Centum Investment, have sizable investments in franchises, and view franchising as a viable means of diversifying their portfolios. Notable examples of venture capital and private equity firms that invest in franchises in Africa include GroFin Capital (Mauritius), Social Venture Capital (SOVEC) (Netherlands), and Greenfields Venture Capital (South Africa)

With the growth of private equity and venture capital in Africa, a number of professional organizations, such as the South African Venture Capital Association, have emerged to facilitate the dialogue between investors and entrepreneurs. These organizations serve as a forum, bringing together investors and capital seekers.

D. International Development Funds

In addition to private sector sources, franchisees also have the option of reaching out to international development organizations for startup up capital.

The International Finance Corporation ("<u>IFC</u>") offers a range of financing solutions for businesses, including loans, syndicated loans, equity financing, quasi equity finance, equity and debt funds, structured finance, intermediary services, risk management products, local currency financing, sub national finance, and trade finance.[197] However, securing IFC financing can be a lengthy and complicated process, and may entail relatively tight restrictions and covenants.

The IFC's Private Equity Group has been engaged in private equity funds in emerging markets for over 25 years, and in 2000, it established a dedicated team to invest in private equity funds. The IFC presently maintains a US$3 billion portfolio, committed to over 180 funds, and remains a key player in the emerging

---

[197] *International Finance Corporation*, http://www.ifc.org/wps/wcm/connect/CORP_EXT_Content/IFC_External_Corporate_Site/What+We+Do/Investment+Services (last visited March 7, 2014).

market funds space, where it has backed approximately 10% of the funds.[198]

The African Development Bank's (AfDB) Fund for African Private Sector Assistance (FAPA) is another source of grant funding for technical assistance and capacity building for both public and private sector clients. A key component of FAPA's agenda is to stimulate SME growth and job creation by advancing franchising in Africa. As of November 2009, FAPA grant approvals for African franchises totaled nearly US$2 million.[199] AfDB also lends financial support to the franchise sectors of its member countries through other means. For example, in 2009, AfDB extended a US$40 million loan facility to the Government of Egypt to finance the Franchising Sector Support Program ("FSSP") in Egypt, which is expected to create 375 franchise outlets.[200]

The Overseas Private Investment Corporation ("OPIC") is the development finance institution of the United States government. OPIC provides long-term financing solutions to U.S. franchisors interested in expanding into international emerging and frontier markets. Additionally, OPIC finances the business entities involved in international franchise relationships. OPIC's loan amounts range from US$100,000 to US$4 million, and terms range from 3 to 8 years, with an interest-only grace period of up to six months.[201] OPIC financing requires significant U.S.

---

198 *International Finance Corporation*, http://www.ifc.org/funds (last visited March 7, 2014).

199 African Development Bank, http://www.afdb.org/en/topics-and-sectors/initiatives-partnerships/enhanced-private-sector-assistance-for-africa-epsa-initiative/ (last visited March 7, 2014); *see also* Kendal Tyre, *Franchising Sector in Egypt Receives Financial Boost*, NIXON PEABODY FRANCHISE LAW ALERT (June 29, 2009).

200 African Development Bank, http://www.afdb.org/en/news-and-events/article/afdb-supports-the-franchising-sector-in-egypt-4702 (last visited March 7, 2014).

201 Overseas Private Investment Corporation, http://www.opic.gov/financing/loan-structures/franchise-loan (last visited March 7, 2014).

involvement in the franchising transaction. This requirement can be met through a minimum 25% ownership by a U.S. small business as the franchisee or by significant involvement in the project by a U.S. franchisor, including:

- small business concepts and systems constructed or originally developed by a U.S. franchisor and employed by the franchisee;
- a long-term franchise agreement among the U.S. franchisor, the local in-country master franchisor, and the franchisee;
- local use of the U.S. franchisor's trademark or brand name; and
- a U.S. franchisor with a long-term financial interest through the acceptance of franchise fees.

In addition to the U.S. content requirement, franchise projects must also satisfy OPIC's *General Requirements*, such as environmental and social sustainability, respect for human rights, absence of negative impact on the U.S. economy, and positive development effects on the host country.[202]

In 2011, OPIC initiated a new facility for franchises in Africa. The facility, which will likely function as a working capital facility through local banks, is intended to assist local entrepreneurs, as well as U.S. companies. OPIC has indicated that its standard underwriting criteria will apply to the new franchise funding facility. As of the end of 2011, the new initiative was still in its preliminary phase as a concept paper.

In addition to international development organizations, domestic development institutions can also serve as a source of franchise funding. For example, the Development Bank of Namibia provides wholesale and individual finance facilities to

---

202 *Id.*

franchisees that meet certain citizenship, financial, and business criteria.[203]

Similarly, the Government of Botswana established the Citizen Entrepreneurial Development Agency (CEDA) in 2001 to surmount financial challenges faced by SMEs, including franchises, through structured finance solutions and credit guarantee schemes.

In the same vein, South Africa's Industrial Development Corporation (IDC) endeavors to facilitate the entry of entrepreneurs into the franchising industry by directly funding individual franchise operations with a minimum requirement of ZAR1 million (approximately US$120,900). Additionally, the IDC maintains a wholesale facility implemented in 1999 that has primarily been used to fund franchise businesses.

E. Finance Companies and Leasing Firms

Finance companies, leasing firms, and property management businesses that provide fractional funding for the franchisee's investment are another source of franchise financing.[204] Examples include General Electric Capital Corporation, which provides financing for inventory, equipment, and fixtures. While there are few financing companies catering specifically to franchises in Africa, that number is rising. South Africa's Franchise Finance is an example of a specialist franchisee loan origination organization set up to address the specific needs of the franchising sector. Established and administrated by

---

203 Development Bank of Namibia, http://www.dbn.com.na/index.php?option=com_content&view=article&id=64:franchise-finance&catid=35:private-sector-finance&Itemid=26 (last visited March 7, 2014).

204 Sherman, *supra* note 167, at 68-69.

franchising professionals, Franchise Finance assists franchises in obtaining funding by serving as a loan originating agency.[205]

Leasing companies may purchase equipment or real estate to lease back to the franchisee. Property management firms may invest in the real estate that the franchisee requires, via conventional or leaseback programs.

F. Franchisee Equipment Leasing Programs

Because equipment leasing is 100% financing, it conserves and frees up vital working capital, creates more operating time, and increases profitability.[206] Nevertheless, equipment leasing can be complicated: financing programs change without notice, available funds suddenly fail, and lease marketing is often misleading. There is no one-size-fits-all approach to leasing, and every franchisor must develop its own program.[207]

Potential lessors can be grouped into five broad categories: individuals, independent leasing companies (finance leasing companies, service leasing companies), lease brokers, captive leasing companies, and banks.

There are two basic categories of equipment leases: financial leases and operating leases. Financial leases are longer term leases under which the sum of lease payments due is roughly equal to the equipment's purchase cost. Financial leasing is part of the franchisee's financial, instead of its operating, policy. All other equipment leases are generally grouped into the operating lease class. Operating leases are typically shorter term and part of the company's operating policy. Within both categories of

---

[205] http://www.franchisefinance.co.za/WhoIsFF.htm (last visited March 7, 2014).

[206] Sherman, *supra* note 167, at 391.

[207] *Id.*

leases, there are a few variations: leveraged, non-leveraged, and service leases.[208]

The following table provides a brief sketch of the variations.[209]

Lease Type	Term	Typical Transaction	Description/Notes
Finance lease	Substantial portion of asset's economic life	Underwritten and direct lessor	Payout-type lease
Net Finance lease	Substantial portion of asset's economic life	Underwritten and direct lessor	Payout type lease; lessee has all ownership rights and duties
Leveraged lease	Typically for substantial portion of asset's economic life	Underwritten	Usually net finance lease
Nonleveraged lease	From a few hours to substantial portion of asset's economic life	Direct lessor	Any lease where no third-party debt involved
Operating lease	Hours to years	Direct lessor	Usually nonpayout

1. Advantages of Equipment Leasing

Leasing can reduce the risk of equipment obsolescence if the lessor's investment return is based upon a sale or re-lease of the equipment at the end of the term. It is an effective solution to obsolescence if the equipment is needed for a limited time frame only. Leasing also helps to preserve existing funds or bank lines for other uses. Service leases enable franchisees to obtain technical or administrative services from the lessor, thereby saving time and resources. Leases also enable franchisees to get around internal capital budget restrictions, because the lease rental payments can be accounted for as an operating expense,

208 *Id.*

209 *Id.* at 402.

even though they are long-term financing, similar to capital expenditures. Because lessors actually own the equipment, and are more willing to handle used equipment, they have less stringent financial requirements than traditional lenders.[210]

2. Disadvantages of Equipment Leasing

Equipment lessees forego the possibility of realizing a gain, should the equipment appreciate in value during the term of the lease. Equipment value appreciation is a common occurrence, resulting from inflation or buyer demand.[211] Because the lessee's right to use the equipment terminates when the lease ends, the lessee might run into problems if a replacement is not available and if the lessor refuses to renew the lease.[212] Equipment financing programs should be molded to the franchisee's customer profile and managerial and financial capabilities. Lessees who depend on third-party franchise funding should not rely on only one financing relationship. Bank affiliated and non-bank leasing companies may cut off funding without warning and without considering customer commitments. Contractual lease obligations can be ineffective in a sluggish and unpredictable court environment and are often filled with loopholes that allow the lessor to walk away.

Franchisors might consider establishing their own financing company or establishing at least three funding relationships. Franchisors should also control the lease application and documentation process to ensure that problems are remedied swiftly. Developing a uniform set of lease documents generally acceptable to all funding sources avoids having to redesign the application for every situation.

---

210 *Id.*

211 *Id.* at 408.

212 *Id.* at 409.

G. Other Financing Alternative

Soft loans, also known as "off balance sheet financing" are loans with below-market interest rates, sometimes as low as zero-interest. Soft loans can be sourced from family and friends, and they typically lack specified repayment terms and can be recalled at any time. Franchisees can mitigate the risk of a soft loan being recalled at an inconvenient time by specifying terms and conditions in a written contract.

Strategic alliances with third parties that can provide funding for the franchise venture offer another funding alternative. However, strategic partners typically demand a degree of control over the franchise management, in addition to the shares of profits they will receive. Therefore, franchisees should select partners with whom they share complementary business skills and common strategic objectives. The terms and conditions of the strategic partnership should be clearly delineated in a partnership agreement.

III. Micro-franchising

Micro-franchising is a business model and development tool that applies tested concepts and methods of conventional franchising to small and medium enterprises in the developing world. Micro-franchising usually targets the delivery of development-related services such as water, sanitation, health care, energy, and transportation.

Successful micro-franchising requires several key elements: uniform branding, systems, and training; careful location screening; and rigorous quality controls enforced through regular inspections. In addition to their minimal initial costs, micro-franchises provide franchisees with a significant portion of the required start-up capital, and encourage owners to raise the equity through family and friends. The price of services charged includes the franchise fee. Using this system instead of calculating franchise fees as a percentage of gross receipts removes the owners' incentive to under-report sales or deviate from franchise-wide price schedules. The ability to purchase quality inventory wholesale and inexpensively distribute to outlets enables micro-franchisees to maintain competitive prices, while paying franchise fees and interest, and earn a profit.[213]

Micro-franchise competitive advantages include the ability to source low-cost, high-quality inventory; centralized management of political and regulatory issues; and a critical mass of branches that can share best practices and leverage economies of scale. Further, franchisees enjoy training, marketing support, technical counsel, and a reputable, trusted brand name.[214]

Micro-franchise models are gaining popularity in African markets because they enable local entrepreneurs to own and operate sustainable, lucrative businesses. Micro-franchising discourages corruption because noncompliance with the franchisor can result in the franchisee losing its franchise. The risk of losing their investment and business is more powerful than any short-term gains from dishonesty. By aligning the incentives of clients, government regulators, and franchisees, micro-franchises can deliver high quality service to underserved communities, while maintaining a profitable return on investment, particularly in complicated and unprofitable endeavors such as health care distribution.[215]

IV. Micro-franchise Financing

Because they do not always produce financial returns at the scale that traditional investors demand, funding micro-franchises can often be a challenge. Micro-franchise founders and managers often lack business experience and the financial history that banks require to extend loans. Before they can begin generating significant revenues, micro-franchises require a substantial

213 *About the HealthStore Foundation*: http://www.cfwshops.org/how_you_can_help.html (lasted visited March 7, 2014).

214 *Id.*

215 *Id.*

amount of time to develop and test their business models and recruit franchisees. This longer time frame for profitability implies a longer loan repayment time horizon. Because most micro-franchisees have a limited range of funding options, the micro-franchisor will often have to provide financial support to their franchisees.[216]

Micro-franchises face additional unique costs, including expenses related to travel, translation, investigating international legal issues, and establishing a supply chain and distribution system. Like traditional franchises, micro-franchises incur different costs at different stages of their maturity, and rely on some sources of funding more than others during the various stages of their development.[217]

[216] Nicolas Sireau, *Microfranchising: How Social Entrepreneurs Are Building a New Road to Development* 69, GREENLEAF PUBLISHING LIMITED, (2011).

[217] *Id.* at 72.

Franchising Costs: Traditional Franchising and Micro-Franchising[218]

	Traditional Franchising	Micro-franchising
Franchise fees	• Buy-in fees are often a profit source for franchisor • Covers cost of training, support, site selection	• Minimal cost, minimal barrier • Covers costs, ensures franchisee is invested in venture • May be waived on philosophical grounds
Build out costs	• Pays for furniture, fixtures, signage, equipment • Usually must satisfy branding, image standards	• Pays for furniture, fixtures, signage, equipment • Micro-franchisor might finance or subsidize it • Must often meet branding, image standards
Inventory costs	• Initial stock often paid for in advance	• Initial stock often available on consignment
Supply fees	• For purchasing other items for business operation (computers, machinery)	• For purchasing other essential items for business operations, but very limited • Computers and machinery often financed by micro-franchisor
Working capital	• For day-to-day operations	• For day-to-day operations • Likely to be matched closely to business' actual cash flows
Legal fees	• Ensures compliance with local and national laws • Contract regulates and enforces overall business relationship	• Ensures compliance with local laws • Contract defines business relationships, but enforcement via formal legal system is uncommon
Travel & training	• Usually borne by franchisee	• Usually borne by micro-franchisor

218 *Id.* at 71.

A. Self-financing

Often referred to as "boot strap financing," self financing includes loans from friends or family. This method of financing is very common and successful throughout Africa. For example, the Fan Milk franchise in Ghana sells ice cream and dairy goods via individual franchisees that pay about US$55 to join the franchise network. The majority of Fan Milk franchisees self fund the bulk of their franchise costs.[219]

B. Revenue Sharing or Consignment System

Also known as "pay as you go" or "pay from profits," this financing model enables micro-franchisees to continue paying small sums to the micro-franchisor until the original costs, fees, and applicable interest charges are fully repaid. This method is particularly useful when the micro-franchisee receives a product instead of cash and when the micro-franchisee introduces new products as it lowers the risk for the micro-franchisees and incentivizes them to add offerings with which they may be less familiar.[220]

For example, VisionSpring (formerly Scojo) uses the method to provide women micro-franchisees with a startup inventory of diagnostic kits and eyeglasses. Instead of having to pay for the material upfront, the micro-franchisees use their sales revenue to repay the cost of inventory. While this model was successful in recruiting low-income women, VisionSpring discontinued its use due to the complicatedness of recovering the cost of managing and consigning the inventory, and the high turnover rate in sales associates. VisionSpring's experience suggests that this financing option is effective where managers can cost-effectively manage recovery costs.[221]

---

[219] *Id.*

[220] *Id.*

[221] *Id.* at 74.

C. Grants

Grants can provide a crucial supply of funds in the early stages of micro-franchise development. While corporations and individuals often provide grants of one kind or another, government and nongovernment development agencies and foundations are the most common sources of grant funding. Grants usually entail major screening processes, disbursement conditions, and follow up requirements to guard against fraud and ensure that the funds will be deployed according to the grantor's agenda.[222]

D. Program-Related investments

Program-related investments (PRI) are investments by organizations that further the organizations' goals, and enable them to maximize the use of their philanthropic dollars. The investments are usually in the form of equity or loans carrying below-market rates. The investing organizations make these investments with the expectation of returns from repayments or a return on equity, and they rely on a broad range of options, including loans, loan guarantees, linked deposits, and equity investments. The investments usually go toward funding capital projects, providing bridge loans, or offering liquidity to loan funds. Presently, there is a growing trend of making equity investments in charitable organizations or commercial ventures for charitable purposes.[223]

Charitable organizations typically extend PRIs as supplementary financing vehicles to ventures with which they have preexisting and established relationships. Should the grantee need additional funding, the grantor might recommend a PRI in place of a grant. PRIs enable the grantee to access capital at favorable rates, while yielding a return on investment that enables the grantor to recycle its funds for other charitable purposes. PRIs can serve as

---

222 *Id.*

223 *Id.* at 75.

a transitional step in fostering long-term sustainability and improving the grantees' cash flows.[224]

E. Micro-loans

Micro-loans are very small loans to finance startup or expansion, and can range in size from a few hundred to several thousand dollars.[225] Micro-loans are usually extended by micro-finance institutions, and generally carry an interest rate that is below in-country market rates. Because they require frequent partial repayment (usually weekly or monthly), micro-loans carry effective interest rates ranging from 20% to 50%.[226] Micro-loan funding for micro-franchising is still in its early stage because the payment terms are often not synched to the cash flow cycles and needs of most micro-franchisees. In response, many micro-franchise institutions have created new micro-loan solutions.[227]

Village Phone, a micro-franchise opportunity tied to a micro-loan organization was started in Bangladesh under the oversight of Grameen Bank, and has since been replicated in Uganda, Rwanda, the Philippines, Cambodia, Haiti, and Indonesia. The initiative offers dependable, inexpensive, and commercially sustainable telecommunications to the world's rural poor. Local entrepreneurs, relying on micro-loans, can purchase a Village Phone kit that includes a cellular phone, an external antenna, a discounted service plan, and an operations manual. The entrepreneurs then rent the use of the phone on a per-call basis, thereby providing an affordable telecommunications service in their community, while generating sufficient income to repay their loan and lift their income level. After repaying the loan, the franchisees keep the Village Phone kit for future use.[228]

---

224 *Id.*

225 *Id.*

226 *Id.*

227 *Id.*

228 *Id.* at 76.

F. Loans

Commercial banks prefer to extend short-term demand loans, seasonal lines of credit, or single-purpose loans for machinery or equipment, and are often hesitant to offer long-term loans to SME's or social-purpose firms, particularly if the loan is unsecured. Therefore, micro-franchises will often seek micro-loans, grants, and PRI funds before resorting to commercial bank loans. Nonetheless, loans can be a viable funding option for micro-franchisors that have demonstrated healthy growth rate.[229]

G. Equity

Equity investments are the buying and holding of shares of stock by investors. An equity investment often requires the assistance of investment bankers and attorneys to navigate the regulatory environment and to find potential investors, making the cost of this option in proportion to the relative size of most micro-franchisors prohibitively expensive.[230] Therefore, micro-franchisors seeking equity financing should first consider private equity, venture capital, angel investors that tailor their investment criteria and approach to the needs of micro-franchisors.

H. Venture Capital

Venture capitalists provide capital, contacts and relationships, and management support, in exchange for a significant percentage of ownership or a position in the company or its board. Venture capitalists are typically intimately involved in the companies they invest in, and often use their networks to connect the company with potential partners and additional resources. Generally, venture capitalists look for small firms with the potential to return ten times the original investment within a five year investment horizon. Most venture capitalists intend to

---

[229] *Id.*

[230] *Id.* at 77.

collect their investment during an IPO, sale to a larger firm, or with follow on sales of company shares. Venture capitalists presently play a minimal role in the micro-franchising arena, and any role they do play is usually limited to supporting and funding the micro-franchisor rather than the micro-franchisee.[231]

I. Angel Investors

Angel investors, a sub-category of venture capitalists, invest their own funds rather than the pooled funds of other investors. Because angel funds provide smaller amounts than venture capital but higher amounts than seed loans or grants, they fill the funding gap between seed funding and venture capital. Thus, they can be a tremendous resource for micro-franchisors seeking second round financing. Angel investors also tend to invest for reasons beyond simply monetary returns, bridging pure venture capital and social investors. While most angel investors seek repayment, they also offer generous terms and flexible schedules.[232]

J. Social Investors and Impact Investing

Social or impact investors seek to achieve both financial return and social impact while still relying on the same methods as venture capitalists. They utilize a double, sometimes triple bottom-line approach to their investment capital and they usually assign real value to the social and environmental return in their investment decisions. They are often willing to forego higher economic returns for potential social or environmental impacts. In addition to traditional valuations, social investors focus on the social outcomes of the micro-franchise, such as quantity of medicines distributed, number of children educated, or lives saved. Most social investors mobilize both debt and equity funding, and source their funds from philanthropic and commercial sources. Social investors tend to be more flexible on

---

[231] *Id.*

[232] *Id.*

repayment terms depending on their evaluation of what is most suitable for the social purpose recipient. They are willing to accept longer time frames for their investment returns, and they often serve as consultants or marketers and can play critical roles in addressing management challenges, fostering partnerships, and in sharing what they learn with a broader audience. Notable social venture organizations include Acumen Fund and Bamboo Finance.[233]

K. Micro-equity Conversion

Micro-equity conversion, also known as the sliding scale of ownership or the "build, own, operate, and transfer" (BOOT) model, refers to the paced transfer of ownership of the micro-franchise to an operator selected and tutored by the micro-franchisor.[234] Conversion involves significant training and mentoring, with the ultimate aim of transferring 100% of the ownership to the operator. This method can take up to a year, or longer. The operator sometimes earns a salary and may also share in profits once the micro-franchisor recoups its start-up costs. The model assumes that the operator uses funds from the salary and profit sharing to purchase ownership, gradually becoming more invested in the business.[235]

"Build, own, operate, and transfer" or BOOT, describes the process from the point of view of the micro-franchisor. NGOs that sponsor the creation of a micro-franchise, but want to withdraw from fulltime sponsorship and management often rely on the micro-equity or BOOT models to withdraw from sponsorship without shuttering the business or harming its stakeholders.[236]

---

233 *Id.* at 78.

234 *Id.*

235 *Id.* at 79.

236 *Id.*

L. In-kind and Management Support

In-kind support from a funder can have significant financial value. Support can come in the form of providing products or raw materials to a micro-franchisee at no cost or at a discount. This kind of support from board members and investors is common and appropriate for micro-franchisees and micro-franchisors to request and pursue.[237]

For example, global management consulting, technology services, and outsourcing company Accenture has a program that enables gifted mid-career managers to gain hands-on experience with social-purpose organizations in developing countries. Under the program, Accenture covers the managers' in-country costs, including salary, housing, and health insurance, while the managers complete their in-country training and practice.[238]

M. Micro-franchise Funding Life-cycle

Each micro-franchise funding source entails varying degrees of difficulty, complexity, and shared risk. Although each option can be pursued at any stage, some funding options are more likely to be utilized at start-up, while others are more suitable for the growth or maturity phase of an enterprise.

Startup	Growth	Maturity
Personal savings	Internal Cash Flow	Internal cash flow
Loans from friends	Bank loans	Secondary infusions
Micro-loans	Micro-loans	Loan guarantees
Consumer Credit	Asset-based loans/leases	

Source: Sireau, 82

[237] *Id.*

[238] *Id.* at 80.

V. Micro-franchising Case Studies

A. HealthStore Foundation

Created in 1997 in Kenya to improve access to high quality essential drugs and basic health care and prevention services in the developing world, The HealthStore Foundation (HSF) oversees 85 Child and Family Wellness (CFW) shops and clinics to address and target the most common illnesses across Africa.[239] Most CFW shops hit profitability and provide living incomes to health workers and nurses approximately six months after startup. Until 2009, profitability at the franchisor or country level was not a priority, and income from the franchisee recouped a mere 5% of the costs, with the remainder covered with funds raised through grants and private donations.[240] In 2008, the HSF network required US$850,000 in core support from HSF, whose overall revenues comprised initial franchise fees from franchisees and mark-ups on products sold to franchisees. That same year, HSF served over half a million people for an all-inclusive cost to donors of US$2.42 per visit.[241]

Previously, franchisees invested US$300 of their own money, matched by a US$1,200, 3-year, 1% interest rate loan from HSF to cover initial inventory, as well as US$3,500 in donor support. HSF is funded by various institutions such as U.S.AID, Acumen Fund, ExxonMobil Foundation, and individual donors.[242] The total list of funding sources includes franchise fees, grants, donations, product margins, and below market loans.[243]

---

[239] *About the HealthStore Foundation*, *supra* note 211.

[240] Sireau, *supra* note 214, at 82.

[241] *Id.*

[242] *About the HealthStore Foundation*: http://www.cfwshops.org/donors.html (last visited March 7, 2014).

[243] *Id.*

B. Fan Milk

The Fan Milk Limited Company sells ice cream, juices, and dairy products in Ghana through retailers and a network of 8,000 bicycle-vendor micro-franchisees. On average, vendors buy daily inventory worth US$33 and earn a daily profit of US$5.50. Vendors make a fixed profit and receive monthly commissions on sales. Their initial startup cost of US$14 goes toward covering equipment purchases. The Fan Milk micro-franchisor provides free bicycle repair, training on product handling, and awards to top salespersons. Vendors are required to save 10% of their profits, to be deposited in a bank account and returned to them when they leave the network. The average vendor stays with the company for eight years, and most intend to start their own business or further their education after they leave the network.[244]

Fan Milk Limited earns about US$10 million in profits annually, and its sources of funds include operating funds, self-financing, and equity.[245]

C. Coast Coconut Farms

Started in 2006 by the Pope Foundation, Coast Coconut Farms, as recently as 2012, offered East Africa farmers access to capital, equipment, and training to create organic coconut oil from wild coconuts.[246] To cover their initial equipment purchase costs, Coast Coconut micro-franchisees obtain a 6-month, US$350 micro-loan from Yehu Micro-finance Trust, a micro-finance institution in coastal Kenya that serves rural economically disadvantaged entrepreneurs. Coast Coconut Farms' sources of

---

[244] Sireau, *supra* note 214, at 87-88.

[245] *Id.*

[246] The website for Coast Coconut Farms appears not to be available as of March 7, 2014.

funds include self-financing, micro-loans, social investors, program-related investments, grants, and in-kind support.[247]

D. Sanergy[248]

Sanergy, Inc.[249] tackles sanitation issues in the urban slums of Kenya. With an estimated eight million Kenyans living in these densely populated and informal settlements, the lack of physical space, infrastructure, and resources has created a sanitation crisis when it comes to the disposal of human waste. Residents are forced to rely on unsanitary options such as "flying toilets"—a local Kenyan euphemism referring to defecating into plastic bags that are then tossed onto the streets. There is also the problematic use of pit latrines that release untreated human waste into the environment. Approximately, four million tons or 90% of fecal sludge from Kenya's slums are discharged into waterways and fields every year.

Sanergy takes a systems-based approach to solve the sanitation crisis by designing and manufacturing portable toilets. Developed by Sanergy engineers, Sanergy's "Fresh Life Toilets" are pre-fabricated at local workshops, have a small footprint that enables installation close to homes and are cost-effective. They also include hand-washing features.

Sanergy connects with local residents who purchase and operate its hygienic sanitation facilities. These operators become franchise partners. Sanergy provides the operators with its Fresh Life Toilets, training, access to financing, ongoing operational and marketing support, and a daily waste collection service. In

---

[247] Sireau, *supra* note 214, at 87-88.

[248] The following text is an excerpt from *Entrepreneurs and franchisors tackle issues of the developing world while turning a profit*. Kendal H. Tyre, Keri A. McWilliams and Courtney L. Lindsay II, NIXON PEABODY FRANCHISE LAW ALERT (November 2013).

[249] *About Sanergy*, *available at* http://saner.gy/about-us (last visited March 7, 2014).

turn, the operators generate local demand and ensure that the facilities are kept clean. The company then collects the waste-filled cartridges from the toilets and replaces them with clean empty cartridges on a daily basis. The human waste is removed from the community by wheelbarrow, handcarts, and/or truck. Next, Sanergy converts the waste at a centralized facility into useful by-products such as organic fertilizer. The fertilizer is transported to agricultural regions where it is used for farming. Fertilizer is a valuable commodity in East Africa and is scarce relative to its need. Sanergy also re-uses the urine and captures the biogas released by the waste.

Micro-franchising is rapidly becoming a popular option for tackling development issues because it is a relatively simple model that applies a tested system to a new problem. Despite its similarities to traditional franchising, micro-franchising has unique characteristics that parties must address when seeking and securing funding.

Inclusive Business in Africa

John Luiz, Jonathan Goldberg and Lauri E. Elliott

Conceptualee, Inc.

Charlotte, North Carolina

The principles of good management apply universally and, in this respect, doing business in Africa is much like doing business elsewhere—with some nuances. However, having said that, it is evident that the business environment (including the social, economic, legal, and political dimensions) is highly complex in Africa because of the continent's unique history, diversity, geography, political, and institutional landscape.

The result is that one cannot do business here without recognizing that this legacy has shaped the business environment in ways that cannot be ignored. And, along with the legacy, future trends call for new forms of business that will be profitable but also consider people and the planet.

I. Realities of Doing Business in Africa

A multinational corporation entering South Africa with the aim of using it as a platform to do business in Africa needs to understand that it will have to confront the country's apartheid legacy and the country's attempt to overcome that legacy. The South African government has adopted a complex system in these efforts that affect various components of the business environment. A case in point is Broad-Based Black Economic Empowerment (BBBEE) legislation, which requires black ownership so as to redistribute assets to those who were previously disadvantaged under apartheid. This legislation has been contentious, and certainly experience elsewhere on the continent has not been without controversy or corruption.

However, it is clear that political and social stability in South Africa is contingent upon rectifying these injustices.

From an international business perspective, this raises the apparent costs of doing business on the continent and may elicit the question of why businesses should have to pay for crimes of the past. However, what is often overlooked is that it does have unexpected payoffs. Local empowerment companies bring with them local knowledge and contacts, which may be of benefit and allow more effective access to the local market. The South African case is not unique, and various African countries have adopted analogous indigenization programs with similar objectives and specifications.

Also, any company doing business on the continent must take into consideration the complexity of leading in such a diverse context. Managers in Africa need to contend with challenges that may be foreign to outsiders.

There is a sense of social responsibility that goes hand in hand with leadership in Africa. It is impossible to be only profit-driven and be sustainable on this continent with its culture, its challenges, and its history. A manager needs to deal with the scourge of poverty, unemployment, and HIV/AIDS not only because it is the right thing to do but because it makes good business sense in a region where firms are expected to be embedded in the community in which they operate.

Leaders in industrialized countries may deal with diversity at a superficial level at home (e.g., gender, race), but in Africa they are forced to confront diversity in its most stark manifestation where it has often erupted into real conflict. Operating in these surroundings requires a sensitive, and often brave, response from companies. This, in turn, affects the human resources environment in Africa and allows one to understand why the region has developed such complex labor relations systems and why trade unions have taken on their particular roles.

And in terms of strategy, it is necessary to be creative and innovative, as well as understand the peculiarities of this market.

For example, there is a strategic challenge facing entrants into Africa about whether their existing products are even saleable or scalable on the continent. A lack of purchasing power, or a lack of infrastructure, in developing countries suggests that "down-scaled" or even different product portfolios might be required to harvest this potential. Thus, a business needs to ensure that its products are affordable, available, accessible, and attractive in the market it is entering.

And if not, an important strategic question arises, "Should a new product that suits the purchasing power of the African market concerned be developed?" And, if it is, will its costs of development be covered by cash flows emerging from the market involved? Also, will the contextual conditions and the operating infrastructure permit scaling of the opportunity?"

However, it is important to understand that starting operations in Africa within the next five years can be a strategic advantage moving forward. If you look to Africa for short-term gains only, you will likely not find success. Just as with emerging regions like Brazil or China, the long-term outlook is strong and more sustainable.

Some good news is that the business atmosphere in Africa has improved dramatically over the past decade and is likely to continue doing so. For example, NEPAD seeks to provide business with a predictable environment in which the rules of the game are understood and more familiar. This will make adaptation easier.

But there are still threats to the process. NEPAD has not received uncontested support both by the general populace, who question its pandering to Western ideas, and by renegade regimes clinging to power.

Bad neighbors also still exist in Africa and contagion from these neighbors remains a threat and, indeed, there is ample literature on the negative externalities that go with bad neighbors, as in the case of the current situation in the Ivory Coast and the spillover of people into Liberia.

And, the consolidation of the political and economic liberalization since the late 1980s has yet to be completed. Therefore, the threat of reversal remains real, but declining.

However, the potentially higher risk in Africa is matched by significantly higher returns and this has seen a recent scramble for quality assets in Africa as companies recognize the potential of these large, untapped markets. Incomes are rising in Africa and soon the large population will translate into significant consumer markets.

II. Empowering Your Bottom Line by Empowering Others

While South Africa's BBBEE codes have been cause for contention, the revised codes of 2007 introduced a framework that is surprisingly insightful at its foundation. It is actually a framework that would be broadly beneficial to business looking at how to shape successful businesses in Africa, no matter the country.

One of the key problems with the original set of BEE codes is that it focused on achieving equity through ownership schemes primarily. In this context, some blacks became wealthy in South Africa while many others remained behind. And, firms who entered arrangements often did not find mutual value in the arrangement other than they had fulfilled requirements of doing business with the South African government.

There are seven strategies, or categories, within the BBBEE codes, which are social development, procurement, skills development, employment, enterprise development, management, and ownership. If you create a holistic framework, using most, if not all, of the strategies you can build your company's internal capacity and consumer base.

The starting point for being able to empower your bottom line by empowering others is the mindset of the leadership of the enterprise. Without a sustainable commitment to the new approach and cascading it through an enterprise, the initiative is bound not to produce significant results. If the leadership team is not committed to this approach, cannot have a change of mindset, and understand that business cannot carry on into the future on the same basis as before, the results of BBBEE will not be achieved.

BBBEE should rather become part of the strategic imperative of enterprises as the only way to survive and prosper in South Africa. In order to be sustainable it must become truly broad-based and not only benefit a small minority.

On the African continent, many countries have not had a participative empowerment approach and although they have been independent for longer than South Africa, they are still grappling with this problem. The consequential result is draconian legislation, for instance, introduced in Zimbabwe which states that businesses over the next five years must have 51% black Zimbabwean shareholding.

Political interference has taken shape in many of these economies as a direct result of not bringing a sufficient number of the population into the main stream of the economy.

The proposed approach is founded on the principle of a broad-based approach as opposed to a narrow one. This is put out in the BBBEE Codes of Good Practice[250] and the approach is for enterprises to score up to 100 points for BBBEE across the seven distinct categories.

The question is how do enterprises get into this more sustainable broad-based approach of transformation? It can be deduced that the approach is far broader than the past practices and should, if correctly implemented, have a far greater impact on transformation. The key to unlock this desired result is, however, implementation.

---

250 Detailed information can be found at the Department of Trade and Industry of South Africa at http://www.dti.gov.za/bee/beecodes.htm.

As a result of the generally poor scores in the element of management and employment equity that make up 30% of the scorecard, pressure is placed on enterprises to score well in the other categories.[251] This correctly modeled could create the opportunity in getting a shift away from the emotional charged issue of ownership requirements. For example, Microsoft has successfully developed a BBBEE strategy, approved by the South African government, which is not based on ownership schemes.

The key to BBBEE strategy for most enterprises must lie in the 15 points allocated for skills development. Most South African enterprises currently are facing a major skills shortage in key areas of their enterprises. This will likely be the case for foreign firms as well, and be a typical scenario across Africa.

It is therefore a business imperative to invest heavily in skills development for a sustainable future. This approach calls for a new strategic intent, through skills development, and for an enterprise to buy into implementation of BBBEE based not only on the "right" thing to do but the "best" thing to do for the sustainability of the company. The underlying assumption is that if a business rationale for implementation of an initiative could be found, it has far greater chances of succeeding than a legislative penalization approach.[252]

Moving forward BBBEE schemes can be incorporated into competitive and sustainable strategies, instead of solely legislative requirements, for businesses. While there are costs associated with BBBEE, these costs can be seen as investments for sustainable business practices in South Africa and even applied to other markets in Africa and emerging regions.

---

[251] Goldberg, J., & Balshaw, T. (2008). *Broad-Based Black Economic Empowerment: Final Codes and Scorecard*, Cape Town, South Africa: Human & Roussau Publishers.

[252] *Id.*

A Case Study of BBBEE in South Africa

A motor manufacturer, such as DaimlerChrysler South Africa, could be taken as an example. They will not be fined or penalized directly for not implementing the Act through legislation. They do, however, do business with the government insofar as the sale of vehicles and trucks are concerned. They further rely heavily on government incentives for their exports programs. It is in this area when the government deals with them, where they apply the legislation to impose direct pressure on DaimlerChrysler South Africa to comply with BBBEE. Further down the supply chain, a family-owned consultancy firm wanting to do business with DaimlerChrysler South Africa would have to get a good BBBEE score to enable Daimler Chrysler South Africa to get a good score under procurement.

A motor manufacturer is limited in the area of procurement in that major procurement comes from international enterprises that are not in a position to comply with the codes from an ownership perspective. Private imports are excluded from the measurement. This will translate into even more pressure being imposed on those suppliers in order to comply with the legislation and Codes of Good Practice.[253]

The above knock-on effect is illustrated by the consultancy firm now having to get its empowerment credentials up to speed. It would also be forced to look at its own procurement. Here, it could be assumed that one of the major expense items is travel. The consultancy will now put pressure on its travel agent to become BBBEE compliant.

The family-owned travel agent, whose quest, in time, is to have a good broad-based black economic empowerment rating, looks at its suppliers and so on. The cascade effect of BBBEE will be experienced throughout most enterprises' supply chains—any

[253] Goldberg, J., & Balshaw, T. (2005). *Cracking Broad-Based Black Economic Empowerment*. Cape Town, South Africa: Human & Rousseau Publishers.

business that ignores it will be ill-advised and this would lead to a loss of business. This is deemed a much better way to monitor implementation than through government monitoring and constant political pressure.

As a result of this knock-on effect, all these enterprises have to focus on the elements of the scorecard. The elements that bring the sustainable benefits to your future customers and employees are procurement (as in the above example), skills development (the only way to ensure the right employees to do the job), enterprise development (creating more black entrepreneurs to participate in the main stream of the economy) and socio-economic development (help by the enterprise linked into aspects of the business like in the General Motors example above). The elements of employment equity and management control are therefore a natural progression underpinned by a strong skills development initiative. Ownership then becomes not a necessity, but a personal enterprise's choice of whether the enterprise needs to go down that route strategically.

III. The Broader Application of Inclusive Business

From a business perspective, I totally agree with others that handing part of your company over to a group just because of its ethnicity, or disadvantaged status, is not a value proposition. I would refuse and take my business elsewhere. (I [Lauri] am African American so I can say this more directly perhaps than others).

However, if I can create value for my firm while addressing transformation or empowerment requirements, I am all for it. In fact, I systematically look for ways to do so.

One of today's mantras is "Doing Well by Doing Good." This is really the context in which business operates today globally, not just in Africa. We need to be concerned with the triple bottom line—people, profit, and planet. We need to create sustainable societies and economies from which all can benefit. Hence, the term "inclusive" has become a key message for today and the future.

There are innumerable ways to precisely define inclusive, depending on the context. Suffice it to say that when we think of business, or inclusive business, we are speaking of firms trying to engage with low-income consumers and communities for the purpose of sustainable development. Sustainable development typically covers social, economic, or environmental issues.

The concept of inclusive business has not dominated the business environment as of yet, but its profile has significantly risen in the last five years. Multinationals like Cadbury, Coca-Cola, and Unilever have implemented inclusive business models. Whatever the motive for implementing inclusive business models, there is no denying that by developing inclusive business models these companies will ultimately be benefiting their bottom lines, building strong foundations in emerging markets.

The concept of inclusive business models is about to go mainstream, if it hasn't already. The last several decades of exuberate growth, but increasing economic inequity, has put social, political, and economic pressure on governments around the world. This pressure, if not released well, will create negative consequences. Business is part of the solution as recognized by the call for inclusive growth from global business leaders at the 2011 World Economic Forum. So, the key question is no longer if or when to do it but how you should do it.

This is where we return to using the principles behind South Africa's BBBEE code as a framework for inclusive business. As discussed, doing business in Africa requires dealing with its legacy and future trends, which means that firms need to find innovative ways to deal with poverty, unemployment, and social issues in the communities in which they operate.

Like strategic philanthropy, I believe that inclusive business models should bring value to the business enterprise. The approach I use most often I call, "Creating Your Own

Consumers." In essence, by helping people build sustainable lives both socially and economically, you are developing your consumer base.

Let's explore one scenario. Besides poverty, unemployment, and social issues, companies often have difficulty finding skilled workers in local markets. Let's say a technology firm, ECHOSOUND, which will be providing products and services to retail customers, wants to enter a local African market. How can the company use the seven strategies to its benefit?

First, knowing that an increasing number of skilled workers will be needed to serve the local market in the medium term, ECHOSOUND decides to sponsor a math, science, and technology program for a secondary school serving low-income students. This would be applying the social development strategy aligned with business objectives.

As the students finish successfully and go on to university, ECHOSOUND provides scholarships and internships for students during university. This is applying the skills development strategy.

Once the students complete college, ECHOSOUND hires them, which applies the employment strategy. The additional bonus is that through internships and summer work programs the students not only learned about basic workforce skills and made some money, but also became familiar with ECHOSOUND's company culture and operations. Having designed innumerable entry worker programs and consulted with companies with low-performing, entry-level workers, I know the transition from school to work is costly to a company when it takes a well-paid, skilled worker two to three years to reach adequate performance.

As these former students work for ECHOSOUND for three to five years, they then become assets to the company and potential managers. With this virtuous cycle, ECHOSOUND is developing both the local community and itself. The people ECHOSOUND has brought up through the ranks and possibly made managers, perform well and understand the business.

If some of ECHOSOUND's talented personnel decide to go out on their own (the company should expect this), ECHOSOUND can create enterprise development programs to help these entrepreneurs, if the business ideas fall within the business ecosystem of the company. And, as these entrepreneurial enterprises develop, ECHOSOUND can procure goods and services from them. Therefore, ECHOSOUND implements both the enterprise development and procurement strategies.

The company can also work on an ownership strategy by offering employees shares in the company, and/or elevating senior management to owners in the company. Some companies may choose to follow an employee-owned company model like Southwest Airlines in the United States.

In South Africa, a great example is Axiz, one of the leading technology distributors in South Africa. Axiz was started in the late 1980s by Anthony Fitzhenry and Simon Hodgson. Under Fitzhenry's leadership, Axiz transformed to an employee-owned company in 2003. In addition, they have developed several inclusive business models also working with communities like a tree planting venture.

In this scenario, the methods used by ECHOSOUND are typical programs companies do anyways in the West to some degree. So, the ideas are not totally foreign. However, if implemented aligned with South Africa's BBBEE codes, or other empowerment or transformation requirements in other African countries, companies set great foundations with government and society in African countries with the potential to reap rewards as well.

There are innumerable sources and examples of inclusive business models,[254] so one model does not have to fit all. The key is to know your business strategy, then find or create an approach that fits your business imperative.

---

[254] For further resources on inclusive business, visit http://www.afribiz.net/insightareas/inclusive-business.

Transformation, empowerment, and inclusive business are no longer costs of doing business, but investments made to grow a sustainable business. And as these approaches become widespread, they will help directly and indirectly address the broader, larger issues of poverty, unemployment, disenfranchisement, and other social dynamics at play.

IV. Conclusion

The realities Africa faces today are similar to most developing regions, and alarmingly on the increase in the West. There is no easy answer in the complex environment of today's world. Solutions need to be holistic and systematic, focusing on the causes not the effects.

Inclusive business is certainly not a new idea, but its evolution, still in progress, to a mainstream concept is different. In some respects, some businesses have found the cost of doing business that is not inclusive is higher than the cost of doing business that is inclusive. What is clear is that many firms with long-term strategies for emerging markets are shifting priorities and approaches.

In Africa, many governments have some level of transformation requirements, such as minimum indigenous ownership requirements. However, a holistic approach that benefits both the people and business on a large, systematic scale is not evident. The effect is that governments will try to institute more regulations to make sure their people benefit. This, in the end, is not necessarily the best scenario for the people or the business. However, inclusive business models will help both governments and businesses meet their imperatives while benefiting people.

Franchising in Angola

João Afonso Fialho

Miranda Correia Amendoeira & Associados

Lisbon, Portugal

Angola

I. Introduction

A. Historical Background of Country

Since 2002, after 27 years of civil war, Angolans are rebuilding their country. Fighting between the Popular Movement for the Liberation of Angola (MPLA), led by José Eduardo dos Santos, and the National Union for the Total Independence of Angola (UNITA), led by Jonas Savimbi, followed Angola's independence from Portugal in 1975. Peace seemed imminent in 1992 when Angola held national elections, but the conflict picked up again by 1996. Up to 1.5 million lives may have been lost—and 4 million people displaced—in a quarter century of fighting. Savimbi's death in 2002 ended UNITA's insurgency and strengthened the MPLA's hold on power. President dos Santos held legislative elections in September 2008, pushed through a new constitution in 2010 and had elections held in 2012 that resulted in his installation.

B. Economy of the Country

Angola's high growth rate in recent years was driven by its oil sector and high international oil prices. Oil production and its supporting activities contribute about 85% of GDP. Increased oil production supported growth averaging more than 15% per year from 2004 to 2007 but the global recession and lower prices led to a contraction in GDP in 2009. A postwar reconstruction boom and resettlement of displaced persons has led to high rates of growth in construction and agriculture as well. Much of the country's infrastructure is still damaged or undeveloped from the 27-year-long civil war. Remnants of the conflict (e.g., widespread land mines) still mar the countryside even though an apparently durable peace was established after the death of rebel leader Jonas Savimbi in February 2002. Subsistence agriculture provides the main livelihood for most of the people, but half of the country's food must still be imported. Since 2005, the government has used billions of dollars in credit lines from China, Brazil, Portugal, Germany, Spain, and the European Union to rebuild Angola's public infrastructure. The global recession that started in 2008 temporarily stalled economic growth. Lower prices for oil and diamonds during the global recession slowed GDP growth to 2.4% in 2009 and to 3.4% in 2010. Many construction projects stopped because Luanda accrued US$9 billion in arrears to foreign construction companies when government revenue fell in 2008 and 2009. Angola abandoned its currency peg in 2009, and in November 2009 signed on to an IMF Stand-By Arrangement loan of US$1.4 billion to rebuild international reserves. Consumer inflation declined from 325% in 2000 to 10% in 2012. Higher oil prices have helped Angola turn a budget deficit of 8.6% of GDP in 2009 into a surplus of 12% of GDP in 2012.

C. Franchise Legal Overview

Franchise-specific regulations have been in force in Angola since 2003. *Law 18/03, of August 13, 2003, on Distribution, Agency, Franchising and Concession Agreements* ("Franchise Law") governs franchise transactions in Angola, as well as distribution, agency, and commercial concession agreements.[255]

II. Regulatory Requirements

A. Pre-Sale Disclosure

Please describe any pre-sale franchise disclosure or similar requirements that may apply to franchise transactions.

No pre-sale franchise disclosure or similar requirements apply to franchise transactions under the laws of Angola.

[255] Editor's note: see Appendix at the end of this chapter for the original Portuguese text and an English translation of the Franchise Law.

B. Governmental Approvals, Registrations, Filing Requirements

Please describe any necessary government approvals, registrations, or filing requirements that may apply to franchise transactions.

Angolan law does not provide that the effectiveness of a franchise transaction is dependent on any formalities beyond the execution of a written contract, such as government approvals, registration or filing requirements.

Notwithstanding the foregoing, an Angolan franchisor or franchisee will be subject to the normal registration procedures and filing requirements for performing business activities in Angola, such as, inter alia, commercial companies' registration, commercial exploration permits, and import/export licenses. See also Section III (Currency) and Section V (Trademarks) of this chapter relating to bank approval for cross border payments and notice requirements under the Angolan Industrial Property Law.

The *New Angolan Private Investment Law*, approved by *Law No. 20/11*, of May 20, 2011, sets out a list of foreign investment transactions that are subject to the prior approval of the Angolan government through the Angolan Private Investment Agency (*Agência Nacional de Investimento Privado*) ("ANIP"). Franchise agreements are not included in that list. Therefore, franchise agreements where the franchisor is a foreign company and the franchisee is a local company will not be subject to these approvals. However, the franchisee may be subject to the *New Angolan Private Investment Law* if its shareholders are foreign entities that have established a legal presence in the country through the incorporation of a local company or the acquisition of shares in an Angolan company. Under the *New Angolan Private Investment Law*, a foreign entity with an investment project approved by ANIP may repatriate its funds and profits. The minimum investment amount required by the *New Angolan Private Investment Law* for the approval of an investment project is US$ 1,000,000.

C. Limits of Fees and Typical Term of Franchise Agreement

Please describe any limits upon the nature and extent of fees and the term of a typical franchise agreement.

In accordance with the Franchise Law, the parties to a franchise agreement may freely determine the applicable franchise fees, and may include: (a) the payment of a fee to enter the franchise agreement; (b) payment of a royalty—periodical fee, fixed, or variable—which can be calculated on the basis of the turnover, gross revenues, or quantity of goods supplied; and (c) payment of an advertising fee.

The term (i.e., time frame) of a franchise agreement may be freely established by the parties. However, if the parties fail to agree on the term of the franchise agreement, it is considered to have an indefinite term. Contracts with a fixed term, which continue to be executed by the parties notwithstanding the expiration of their respective deadlines, are also deemed to have become agreements with an indefinite term.

III. Currency

If all payments under a franchise agreement must be made in immediately available U.S. Dollars, please advise as to any restrictions, reporting requirements, or regulations concerning the exchange, repatriation, or remittance of U.S. Dollars.

As a rule, Angolan companies cannot open and operate offshore bank accounts. Angolan companies can only open and operate bank accounts with local banks unless a special authorization is obtained from the Angolan Central Bank ("BNA"), which seldom grants them. Moreover, foreign exchange operations between resident and non-resident entities may be subject to Angolan authorities' prior approval and licensing.

Pursuant to *Decree 21/98*, of July 24, 1998, and the recently enacted BNA Order 13/13 of August 6, 2013, cross border payments under contracts (such as franchise agreements) are subject to prior approval and licensing from BNA where the relevant payments and/or contract value is greater than US$1,000.000 or US$3,000,000 per year, depending on whether the foreign exchange resident entity with whom the relevant contract is entered into is an oil service provider (duly registered with or having entered into a contract program with the Ministry of Petroleum) or not.

In order to obtain BNA's approval, the interested party must submit a request to the local bank attaching all documentation that evidences and explains the relevant transaction. To that end, a Portuguese translation of the franchise agreement shall be required. The commercial bank will then liaise with the BNA to obtain the necessary license. BNA will then issue the foreign exchange license authorizing the bank to carry out the relevant operation.

IV. Taxes, Tariffs, and Duties

Please do not provide any in-depth comments on tax structuring. However, please provide your general comments on the typical amount of withholding tax that would apply and whether a "gross-up" provision contained in a franchise agreement would be enforceable in your country.

A. Tax General Overview

A major tax reform is currently underway in Angola. Some Angolan taxes have already been revised such as the Investment Income Tax (applicable to interest, dividends and royalties), the Stamp Duty (an indirect tax applicable to documents, like receipts confirming payments in connection with the sale of goods and services, and certain transactions, including leases, financing arrangements, imports, etc.) and the Consumption Tax (an indirect tax on certain services and operations). Additionally, the publication of new statutes was expected for 2013, especially in relation to Industrial Tax and Industrial Tax withholding, transfer pricing (reportedly aligned with OECD Guidelines), invoicing requirements, and Personal Income Tax, etc.

B. Withholding Tax

From an Angolan tax standpoint, payments made under a franchise agreement may trigger industrial tax withholding, as well as investment income tax withholding, depending on the nature of the payments made by the franchisee to the franchisor (i.e., initial fee, provision of services, or royalty fees). Since Angola has no international double taxation treaties in force, there is no available mechanism to reduce or eliminate the assessment of withholding tax in Angola and, thus, international tax relief for non-resident investors can only be obtained in their home jurisdiction.

C. Gross-up Provision

Tax gross-up clauses are valid and contractually binding pursuant to Angolan Tax Law and should preclude any economic loss in the event that any tax is due to the Angolan Tax Authorities on any payments made under a franchise agreement. Notwithstanding, such clauses, from a tax standpoint (although they can be enforced between the parties), are not binding for the tax authorities since it is not legally possible to assign the responsibility for payment of any taxes in Angola.

D. Industrial Tax[256]

The provision of services from the franchisor to the franchisee (e.g., technical assistance, management services, advertising, publicity, training, etc.) made by or accounted for as a cost by

[256] Under the tax regime reform, the Industrial Tax rate is expected to drop to 30%; the current rate is 35%. The Industrial Tax withholding rate is expected to increase to 6.5%; the current standard rate is 5.25%, with a reduced rate of 3.5%.

Angolan based entities[257] is subject to 5.25% industrial tax withholding pursuant *to Law No. 7/97*, of October 10, 1997 ("*Lei sobre a Tributação das Empreitadas*") on managerial, technical services, and other services, as well as services related to construction work.

According to the position consistently held by the Ministry of Finance, industrial tax withholding is still due regardless of the Angolan tax status of the service provider, or the place where the services are rendered. In other words, it is applicable to local and foreign service providers and to services rendered in Angola or abroad provided the same are accounted for as a cost by an Angolan-based entity. Given the above, industrial tax withholding is due either on payments made to resident (payment on account of the final industrial tax due in Angola) or non-resident suppliers, deemed as their final tax liability in Angola.

Given the broad scope of *Law No. 7/97*, payment of fees as a consideration for the rendering of services will be subject in Angola to 5.25% industrial tax withholding.

E. Investment Income Tax

The term "royalties," as defined in the *Investment Income Tax Code* approved by *Legislative Presidential Decree 5/11*, of December 30, 2011 ("*Código do Imposto sobre a Aplicação de Capitais*"), means any type of remuneration, irrespective of its nature, either for the concession of the right to use a copyright over literary, artistic, or scientific work, including cinematographic movies as well as movies and tapes broadcasted through radio or television, patents, designs, models, plans, and secret formulas or processes, as well as for the use or the right to use industrial, commercial or scientific equipment, or information concerning acquired industrial, commercial, or scientific experience.

[257] Angolan-based entity means a company resident for tax purposes in Angola or a non-resident entity with a permanent establishment therein.

Therefore, royalty fees paid under a franchise agreement will be subject to 10% investment income tax withholding provided that the royalties are paid by an Angolan resident franchisee or by a non-resident franchisee with a permanent establishment in Angola.

V. Trademarks

Please advise us as to whether there are any special requirements for granting a valid trademark license, including the use of a registered user agreement or a short trademark license agreement and any required filing of such an agreement with the trademark authorities.

Intellectual property in Angola is regulated by the *Industrial Property Law* ("IP Law"), *Law 3/92*, of February 28, 1992. Article 65 of the IP Law establishes a notification requirement with the Angolan Trademark Office ("*Instituto Angolano da Propriedade Industrial*") for agreements pertaining to the creation, transmission, and termination of licensing of any sort of intellectual property rights regulated under the IP Law, including patents, designs, trademarks, etc. This notification requirement is only necessary to create legal effects between the licensee and third parties.

Paragraph 2 of Article 65 sets out that the notification may be carried out by any persons "interested" in the agreement.

VI. Restrictions on Transfer

Please advise as to whether there are any restrictions on (1) a franchisor to restrict transfers by a master franchisee, any interest in a master franchisee, or the assets of the master franchisee or (2) the ability of a master franchisee to control and/or restrict transfers of a subfranchisee's rights under a master franchise agreement, interest in the subfranchisee, or the assets of the subfranchisee.

Angola

The Angolan legislation does not set forth any specific restrictions on the franchisor's ability to restrict the (i) transfers by a master franchisee, (ii) any interest in a master franchisee, or (iii) the assets of the master franchisee. Nor do any restrictions exist relating to the master franchisee's ability to control and/or restrict (i) transfers of a subfranchisee's rights under a master franchise agreement, (ii) any interest in the subfranchisee, or (iii) the assets of the subfranchisee.

Considering the private nature of the franchise agreement and the underlying principle of private autonomy, the parties may, within the scope of their contractual freedom, introduce such clauses as they see fit, provided they are not unlawful or against public order.

The general principle of contractual freedom is enshrined in the *Angolan Civil Code*, and other provisions of Angolan legislation further support this principle, e.g.:

- the *Angolan Civil Code* rules on the assignment of the parties' contractual position provide that neither party may assign its contractual position without the previous consent of the other party;

- the Franchise Law provision on "subcontracting" provide that the franchisee will not be able to enter into any subfranchisee agreement without the franchisor's express consent;

- the *Angolan Commercial Companies' Law* and practice grant shareholders several control mechanisms, allowing the shareholders to, inter alia, restrict the transfers of participating interests; and

- the *Angolan Civil Code* allows for the transfer of assets subject to the verification of conditions.

VII. Termination

Please advise us as to any laws relating to termination in your country, such as agency laws, required indemnity provisions, notice or "good cause" requirements, or other laws affecting termination of a franchise agreement. Please describe.

As noted in Section II.C., the Franchise Law provides that the provisions governing termination of agency agreements apply to the termination of franchise agreements.

The causes for termination included in the Franchise Law are (i) the parties' mutual agreement, (ii) expiration of the contract, (iii) unilateral termination, and (iv) termination following breach of contract.

In case of unilateral termination, the Franchise Law establishes the following prior notice requirements: (i) one month's notice, if the agreement lasted less than one year; (ii) two months' notice, if the agreement lasted between one and two years; and (iii) three months' notice if the agreement lasted longer than two years. Failure to comply with these notice requirements obliges the defaulting party to pay compensation assessed on the basis of the agent's (or franchisee's) average monthly payback of the previous year.

In case of termination due to a breach of the franchise agreement, the non-defaulting party is entitled to compensation and such compensation should be determined based on equitable grounds.

However, the most relevant issue with regard to compensation is the possibility of having to pay a compensation based on "client goodwill," which may be required in addition to the foregoing types of compensation. This compensation is due if three requirements set forth in the Franchise Law occur:

- the activity of the franchisee entailed new clients or an increase of the franchisor's existing client basis, to an extent which would not occur without the activity of the franchisee;
- the other party will benefit significantly from the activity performed by the franchisee, after termination of the contract; and
- the franchisee stops receiving any consideration for deals negotiated or completed after the termination of the contract with any of the clients entailed by its activity.

Notwithstanding the foregoing, the franchisee may be indemnified for "client goodwill," which is a concept set out in Portuguese law for termination of agency agreements. This is a result of the uncertainties generated by Portuguese court decisions, which in an informal manner set the precedents for Angola, because many Angolan judges have completed their legal studies in Portugal. Portuguese courts apply the "agency" principles and termination regime to all types of franchise agreements.

This indemnity would be calculated on a case-by-case basis, but may never exceed an amount equivalent to an annual indemnity, based on the annual average of profit generated by the franchisee during the last five years (or the average of the period in which the contract was in force, if it was not in force for five years).

It is clear that, applying these rules to franchise agreements would not constitute a linear operation and would not result in providing adequate compensation to the party that would have helped the other to promote its business. In fact, in an agency agreement the agent receives a small percentage of the total amount received by the principal, whereas in a franchise agreement, the franchisor is the party receiving a small percentage. Accordingly, determining the exact extent to which the agency termination compensation clauses should apply to the termination of franchise agreements proves to be very difficult, if not impossible. Unfortunately, there is no court decision that helps to clarify this issue, as most Angolan court rulings are not published.

VIII. Governing Law, Jurisdiction, and Dispute Resolution

A. Choice of Law of Foreign Jurisdiction

Please confirm whether the choice of law of a foreign jurisdiction would likely to be upheld under the law of the country, except for certain matters such as trademarks, bankruptcy, and competition matters, which we assume would be governed by the law in your country.

The Franchise Law expressly sets forth that parties may freely choose the law governing their agreements provided that the choice of law corresponds to a serious interest of the parties or has a relevant connection with any element of the contract. A foreign law is deemed to have a connection with the underlying contract if it is the law of: (i) the domicile of the parties (or of one of them), (ii) the place where the agreement is performed, or (iii) the place where the contract was signed.

In case the parties fail to choose the applicable law, the Angolan conflict of law principles and provisions shall apply. In accordance with such principles, the law of a foreign jurisdiction will not be applicable if it is deemed contrary (i) to the public policy principles of Angolan law (which will always apply, even if the governing law chosen by the parties is not Angolan law), and/or (ii) to any mandatory provision of an Angolan statute. This means that a foreign law can be chosen by the parties to govern a franchise agreement; however, Portuguese courts (which very often set the precedents for Angola) have considered that the laws governing compensation based on "client goodwill" correspond to a serious interest of the parties and are mandatory irrespective of the law governing the franchise agreement. Again, it must be noted that there are no Angolan court precedents in this regard.

Finally, it is worth mentioning that it is not rare for Angolan parties to refuse or at least to resist signing documents not governed by their "home law."

B. International Arbitration Dispute Resolution

Please confirm that a court in your country would honor an election of international arbitration dispute resolution, and therefore refuse to hear any disputes arising under a franchise agreement.

Arbitration is generally accepted in Angola and governed by the *Angolan Arbitration Law* (*Law No. 16/03*, of July 25, 2003). Under the *Angolan Arbitration Law*, the parties to a contract may submit their disputes either to: (i) ad-hoc arbitration (i.e., arbitration organized without the support of an arbitral institution), for example, under the *UNCITRAL Arbitration Rules*; or (ii) institutional arbitration under the arbitration rules of an international arbitration institution such as the ICC Arbitration Court, except for disputes that fall under state courts' exclusive jurisdiction and disputes that relate to inalienable or non-negotiable rights, which are not arbitrable.

In principle, the seat of the arbitration as per the *Angolan Arbitration Law* may either be in Angola or abroad. However, this general rule may be subject to limitations depending on the type of dispute in question. There are certain disputes that cannot be submitted to arbitration located outside Angola or cannot be submitted to arbitration at all.

The Angolan Franchise Law expressly recognizes the parties' right to submit their disputes to arbitration, provided that the arbitration clause expressly defines (i) the substantive applicable law, (ii) nature/type of disputes that may be submitted to arbitration, and (iii) the designated arbitral institution and the seat of the arbitration.

It should be further emphasized that, Angola has not ratified the *Convention on the Recognition and Enforcement of Foreign Arbitral Awards* (the "New York Convention"). Therefore, an arbitral award rendered outside Angola has to be reviewed and confirmed by an Angolan court (see Angolan procedural law).

In principle, the scrutiny of local courts should not be on the merits of the case submitted to arbitration, except where the foreign arbitral award violates Angolan public policy. In this latter scenario, the court may refuse to confirm, recognize, and enforce the foreign arbitral award should the contents of the relevant award be deemed to offend public policy. If one of the parties is successful in obtaining the recognition of the foreign arbitral award, then the recognized award is enforceable in Angola in the same way that a judgment/award originally rendered in the country is enforced.

IX. Non-Competition Provisions

If the franchise agreement prohibits the master franchisee from engaging in certain competitive activities during the term of the agreement, and for a 12-month period after the termination or expiration of the agreement, please comment on the enforceability of non-competition covenants in your country.

The Franchise Law sets forth that a franchisee cannot carry out any activities that compete with the franchisor's activity provided that the parties have entered into a non-competition agreement. Under the Franchise Law, non-competition agreements are enforceable provided that: (i) both parties agree on it, (ii) the duration of the non-competition agreement does not exceed two years, and (iii) the non-competition clause is limited to the territory/area and clients covered by the franchise agreement.

X. Language Requirements

Does the law in your country require that a franchise agreement be translated into the local language in order to be enforceable between the parties?

The *Angolan Commercial Code* sets out the general principle that commercial contracts are valid in any language. The only exception to this rule is related to sales contracts and services agreements—as well as other trade documents—to be entered into with end consumers in the Angolan market. In this type of contract, the use of Portuguese language is mandatory.

The *Angolan Commercial Code* further determines that in case of a dispute on the interpretation of any commercial agreement drafted and executed in two different languages, e.g., Portuguese and English, then the Portuguese version shall prevail. This is a mandatory rule and cannot be subject to any agreement to the contrary between the parties.

Additionally, we note that if the agreement is to be filed with any public authority or in court in a foreign language, then a certified Portuguese translation will be required.

XI. Other Significant Matters

Please advise as to whether there are any significant matters not addressed above of which a franchisor should be aware in connection with its entering into a franchise agreement in your country.

The Franchise Law sets forth that the franchisor is responsible and liable for the quality of products supplied and services provided, notwithstanding the responsibility and/or liability imposed on the franchisee. The wording of the law is not clear and there is no case law that could aid in construing the real scope and extent of this rule. However, the phrasing of this legal provision leaves it open to the interpretation that, should the franchisee fully comply with all of the requirements set forth in the franchisors' instructions and manuals, then the latter will be held liable for any damages caused to consumers.

Appendix — Angola Law on Distribution, Agency, Franchise and Dealership Contracts (in English)

ASSEMBLEIA NACIONAL
[National Assembly]

Law No 18/03
of 12 August

Distribution, agency and franchise contracts have become increasingly important in the field of domestic and international trade as a means to develop new markets, increase product and service awareness and reduce costs. Although less used, companies have also found dealership agreements to be important tools in seeking new lower cost markets.

Despite the lack of specific legislation on such contracts, entrepreneurs in Angola have also used some of these contractual mechanisms to some extent, particularly in relation to agency and commission.

Although franchise contracts have not as yet been generally accepted at national level, the country's short-term development could benefit from their use.

It has accordingly become necessary to incorporate these types of contracts into our legal system as a way of increasing guarantees for the contracting parties and ensuring the safety of trade.

Therefore, pursuant to Article 88(b) of the Constitutional Law, the National Assembly hereby approves the following:

Law on Distribution, Agency, Franchise and Dealership Contracts

Angola

CHAPTER I
Agency Contracts

SECTION I
General Provisions

ARTICLE 1
(Notion)

1. An Agency Contract is an agreement whereby a natural or legal person undertakes to promote contracts on behalf of another party on an autonomous and stable basis in return for payment.
2. Agency contracts may grant agents a certain area or a particular group of customers.

ARTICLE 2
(Agency with representation)

The agent may enter into contracts on behalf of another party only if the latter has conferred the necessary powers upon them in writing.

ARTICLE 3
(Form of contract)

Agency contracts shall be in written form.

ARTICLE 4
(Claims and urgent measures)

1. Irrespective of whether the powers of representation provided for in Article 2 hereof exist or not, claims or other declarations relating to business entered into through the agent may be brought against that agent.
2. The agent shall have standing to call for the urgent measures deemed essential to safeguard the principal's rights.

ARTICLE 5
(Recovery of amounts receivable)

1. The agent may recover amounts receivable only when expressly authorised to do so in writing by the other party.
2. An agent upon whom powers of representation have been conferred shall be deemed to be authorised to recover amounts receivable arising out of the contracts entered into thereby.
3. Should the agent recover amounts receivable without the necessary authorisation, Article 770 of the Civil Code shall apply thereto, without prejudice to the scheme laid

down in Article 25 of this Law.

ARTICLE 6
(Exclusivity)

Unless otherwise agreed in writing, the agent shall not pursue activities which compete with the activities of the principal, while the latter shall not use other agents for the applicable branch of activity within the same area or the same group of customers.

ARTICLE 7
(Sub-agency)

1. Unless otherwise agreed in writing, the use of sub-agents shall be permitted.
2. The rules of this law shall apply, mutatis mutandis, to the sub-agency relationship.

ARTICLE 8
(Good faith)

In fulfilling their contractual obligations, the agent and principal shall act in good faith to ensure completion of the contract.

SECTION II
Obligations and Rights of the Parties

ARTICLE 9
(Obligations of the agent)

The obligations of the agent are in particular:

a) to comply with the instructions of the other party which do not undermine their autonomy;
b) to provide the information requested thereof or which is necessary for sound management, particularly that relating to customer solvency and seriousness;
c) to inform the other party of the market situation and prospects;
d) to be accountable in the terms agreed or whenever so justified.

ARTICLE 10
(Obligation of secrecy)

1. The agent, even after termination of the contract, shall be prohibited from using or revealing to third parties the secrets of the other party which are entrusted thereto or which they become aware of in pursuing their activity,

except in the event of breach of contract to the extent permitted by the rules of professional ethics.

2. Infringement of the provisions of the preceding number shall render the agent civilly liable in general terms, particularly those of Article 798 *et seq.* of the Civil Code.

ARTICLE 11
(Non-competition obligation)

1. The parties may agree in the contract that the agent shall not pursue activities which compete with the activities of the other party after termination of the contract.

2. The non-competition obligation may be agreed only for a period not exceeding two years and shall be confined to the area or group of customers entrusted to the agent.

ARTICLE 12
(Assurance of compliance)

1. The agent may, by written agreement, provide assurance that third-party obligations will be met, provided they relate to a contract negotiated or concluded thereby.

2. Such assurance shall be valid only when the contract is specified or the persons guaranteed are individually identified.

ARTICLE 13
(Temporary impossibility)

An agent who is temporarily prevented from fulfilling a contract, totally or in part, shall immediately notify the other contracting party accordingly in writing.

ARTICLE 14
(Rights of the agent)

The rights of the agent are in particular:

a) to obtain from the other party all the information and means necessary for pursuing their activity in the light of the circumstances;
b) to be informed immediately of the acceptance or refusal of contracts negotiated and contracts which may have been concluded without the necessary powers;
c) to receive a list of the contracts concluded

and commission owing at the frequency laid down in the contract by no later than the final day of the month following the quarter in which the right to commission is acquired;

d) to ask to be provided with all the information, particularly an extract from the other party's books of accounts, required to verify the amount of commission owing;
e) to receive payment of the remuneration in the terms agreed;
f) to receive special commission, which may accumulate, relating to the costs of recovering amounts receivable and the *Del Credere* Agreement;
g) to receive compensation for the obligation not to compete after termination of the contract.

ARTICLE 15
(Right to notification)

In the event of a reduction in the other party's capacity, the agent shall be entitled to immediate notification that the other party is only in a position to conclude a number of contracts substantially below the number agreed or to be expected, according to the circumstances.

ARTICLE 16
(Remuneration)

Unless agreed by the parties, the agent's remuneration shall be calculated according to practice or, failing that, according to equity.

ARTICLE 17
(Right to commission)

1. The agent shall be entitled to receive commission for contracts promoted thereby and for contracts concluded with customers attracted thereby, provided they are concluded prior to termination of the agency relationship.

2. Should they have an exclusive right to a geographic area or group of customers, the agent shall also be entitled to receive commission for acts concluded during the contract

with customers in that area or group of customers.

3. The agent shall only be entitled to receive commission for contracts concluded after termination of the agency relationship if it is demonstrated that they were negotiated thereby or, if he prepared them, that their conclusion is due principally to the activity pursued by him, provided in both cases that they are concluded within a reasonable time subsequent to termination of the agency contract.

ARTICLE 18
(Successive agents)

The agent shall not be entitled to the commission provided for in Article 17(1) during the contract if such commission is owed, by virtue of Article 17(3), to the agent who preceded him, without prejudice to the commission being shared equally between both, when circumstances justifying such action exist.

ARTICLE 19
(Acquisition of entitlement to commission)

1. The agent shall acquire entitlement to commission when and to the extent that one of the following circumstances exists:

a) the principal has complied with the contract or should have done so by virtue of the agreement concluded with the third party;
b) the third party has complied with the contract.

2. Any agreement the parties may have entered into regarding entitlement to commission cannot prevent this arising at least when the third party complies with the contract or when that party should have complied with the contract, if the principal has already complied with his obligation.

3. The commission referred to in the preceding numbers shall be paid by the final day of the month following the quarter in which the right is acquired.

4. Should a Del Credere Agreement exist, the agent may nevertheless ask for the commission owing on entering into the contract.

ARTICLE 20
(Non-compliance)

The agent shall not forfeit the right to ask for the commission if non-compliance with the contract is due to the default of the principal.

ARTICLE 21
(Expenditure)

Unless otherwise agreed, the agent shall be entitled to a refund of the expenditure incurred in the normal pursuit of his activity on behalf of the principal.

SECTION III
Protection of Third Parties

ARTICLE 22
(Duty of information)

The agent shall have a duty to inform interested parties of the powers held by means in particular of notices displayed in his workplaces and in all documents in which he identifies himself as the agent of another party, such documents obligatorily stating whether he does or does not have powers of representation and whether he can or cannot recover amounts receivable.

ARTICLE 23
(Representation without powers)

1. Without prejudice to the provisions in the following Article, business the agent enters into on behalf of the other party without powers of representation shall have the effects provided for in Article 268(1) of the Civil Code.

2. In the cases referred to in the preceding number, the business shall be deemed to be ratified by the other party if, as soon as that party becomes aware that it has been entered into and aware of its essential content, fails to notify the third party in good faith that he is opposed to the business within five days of becoming aware of it.

ARTICLE 24
(Apparent representation)

1. Business concluded by an agent without powers of representation shall be effective vis-à-vis the principal if serious reasons assessed objectively exist, in the light of the relevant circumstances, which justify the third party's confidence in good faith of the agent's standing, provided the principal has also contributed

towards establishing that confidence.

2. The provision in the preceding number shall apply, mutatis mutandis, to the recovery of amounts receivable by an agent who is not authorised to do so.

SECTION IV
Cessation of the Contract

ARTICLE 25
(Forms of cessation)

An agency contract may cease due to:

a) agreement between the parties;
b) expiry;
c) termination;
d) rescission.

ARTICLE 26
(Mutual agreement)

An agreement whereby the parties decide to bring an end to the contractual relationship shall be set down in a written instrument.

ARTICLE 27
(Expiry)

An agency contract shall expire:

a) after the expiry of the time limit set, where applicable;
b) if the condition the parties made the contract conditional upon arises, or if it becomes certain that it cannot arise, according to whether the condition is resolutory or suspensory;
c) due to the death of the agent or, in the case of a legal person, its dissolution.

ARTICLE 28
(Contract duration)

1. If the parties have not agreed a time limit, the contract shall be deemed to be concluded for an indefinite period.

2. A fixed-term contract the content of which continues to be performed by the parties shall be deemed to have become an agency contract of indefinite duration, notwithstanding the expiry of the respective time limit.

ARTICLE 29
(Termination)

1. Termination shall be permitted only for contracts

concluded for an indefinite duration, provided the other party is notified in writing with the following minimum notice:

a) one month if the contract lasts for less than one year;
b) two months if the contract has already begun its second year;
c) three months in other cases.

2. Unless otherwise agreed in writing, termination of the time limit referred to in the preceding number must coincide with the last day of the month.

3. Should the parties stipulate longer time limits than those laid down in 1(a) to (c) of this Article, the time limit to be observed by the principal may not be less than that pertaining to the agent.

4. In the case provided for in 2 above, the time prior to the expiry of the time limit shall also be taken into account to determine the notice within which termination shall be communicated.

ARTICLE 30
(Failure to give notice)

1. The party that terminates the contract without observing the time limits referred to in the preceding Article shall compensate the other party for the damage caused by their failure to give notice.

2. Compensation shall be calculated on the basis of the average monthly remuneration earned during the preceding year, multiplied by the missing time, if the contract has lasted for less than one year, taking the average monthly remuneration earned during the contract into account.

ARTICLE 31
(Rescission)

1. An agency contract may be rescinded by any of the parties in the following cases:

a) if the other party fails to comply with their obligations when the gravity or repetition of breaches renders continuation of the contractual relationship impossible;
b) if circumstances arise which prevent or seriously hinder the achievement of the subject-matter of the contract, in terms of

there being no requirement to maintain the contract until the time limit agreed or imposed in the event of termination expires.

2. The contract shall be rescinded by means of written notification to the other party within one month of their becoming aware of the relevant facts, the grounds on which it is based being indicated therein.

ARTICLE 32
(Compensation)

1. Irrespective of the right to rescind the contract, either party shall be entitled to compensation in general terms for the damage arising out of the other party's failure to comply with its obligations.

2. Rescission of the contract on the basis of Article 30(1)(b) of this Law shall grant the right to compensation according to equity.

ARTICLE 33
(Clientele Compensation)

1. Regardless of any other compensation to which the terms of the foregoing provisions give rise, the agent shall have a right, after termination of the contract, to clientele compensation, as long as the following requirements, cumulatively, are met:

a) the agent has acquired new customers for the other party or substantially increased the business volume with the existing clientele;
b) the other party comes to benefit considerably, even after termination of the contract, from the activities developed by the agent;
c) the agent stops receiving any payment for contracts negotiated or executed, after termination of the contract, with the customers referred to in a) above.

2. If the agent dies, customer compensation may be required by the respective heirs.

3. No customer compensation is due if the contract has ended for reasons attributable to the agent or, by agreement with the other party, the agent has assigned

his contractual position to a third party.

4. The right to compensation shall be extinguished if the agent or his heirs do not inform the principal, within one year of contract termination that they are making a claim to it, and any action at law must be filed within the year following this communication.

ARTICLE 34

(Calculation of Clientele Compensation)

1. The clientele compensation shall be established on an equitable basis, but may not exceed an amount equivalent to the annual compensation, calculated from the average annual remuneration received by the agent over the past five years.

2. If the contract has lasted for a shorter period of time, the average of the actual period will be used.

ARTICLE 35

(Right of Retention)

From the credits resulting from his activities, the agent shall have the right to retain the objects and valuables he received and holds under the contract.

ARTICLE 36

(Obligation to Return)

Without prejudice to the terms of the previous article, each contracting party shall have the obligation to return objects, valuables, and other items belonging to the other party, at the end of the contract.

CHAPTER II

Franchise Agreements

SECTION 1

General Provisions

ARTICLE 37

(Concept)

1. A franchise is an agreement whereby a person, whether singular or plural (the franchisor or licensor) grants to another (the franchisee or licensee), for consideration, the marketing of its goods or services, by using the brand name and other distinctive signs of the franchisor and according to the plan, method, and guidelines prescribed thereby.

2. The Franchise Agreement may assign a

particular area or circle of customers to the agent.

ARTICLE 38

(Types of Franchise)

The following types of franchise are possible:

a) Distribution—when the franchisee is obligated to sell certain products manufactured or distributed by the franchisor, in an establishment with the image and the name of the franchisor;
b) Service— when the franchise renders a service with the brand name and technology of the franchisor;
c) Production or Industrial —when the franchisee manufactures certain products under the brand name of the franchisor, according to the instructions of the franchisor.

ARTICLE 39

(Form of Contract)

The Franchise Contract (Agreement) must be in the written form.

ARTICLE 40

(Exclusivity)

Unless there is a written agreement to the contrary, the franchisee may not carry out activities that compete with those of the principal and the latter may not use other franchisees for the activity sector in question, within the same area or circle of customers.

ARTICLE 41

(Good Faith)

In compliance with their contractual obligations, the franchisee and franchisor must proceed in good faith, for full accomplishment of the contractual goal

ARTICLE 42

(Subcontracting)

With the express authorization of the franchisor, the franchisee may enter into sub-franchise agreements.

SECTION II

Obligations and Rights of Parties

ARTICLE 43

(Obligations of Franchisee)

1. The obligations of the franchisee are as follows:

a) adopt and use the set of products and/or services presented by the franchisor;
b) in the manner agreed, pay for the services rendered by the franchisor;
c) maintain secrecy of all the information transmitted thereto by the franchisor, including manufacturing processes and knowhow, for the entire duration of the contract and after it ends;
d) not compete with the franchisor, under the terms of Article 11 of this Statute;
e) carry out his or its activities within the formats defined by the franchisor and under the latter's guidance, exhibiting the distinctive signs of the franchisor.

2. The Franchise Agreement may also include the obligation of the franchisee to acquire from the franchisor the products that it distributes.

3. The Franchise Agreement may also include franchisee obligations in the matter of supplies, prices, and accounting organization.

ARTICLE 44
(Remuneration)

The franchise remuneration is as established in the contract, and may include:

a) payment of a startup fee;
b) payment of royalties—periodic, fixed, or variable remuneration that may be calculated according to business volume, gross receipts, or quantity of goods supplied by the franchisor;
c) payment of an advertising rate.

ARTICLE 45
(Obligations of Franchisor)

The obligations of the franchisor are as follows:

a) give the franchisee a license to use its distinctive signs, manufacturing processes, and knowhow, under the agreed terms;

b) provide the franchisee with the products or services to which it is committed;
c) render technical assistance to the franchisee in carrying out his or its activities;
d) improve its methods, knowledge, and processes that are patented or secret and transmit innovations to the franchisee;
e) support the franchisee, particularly in the matter of training, advertising, studies, and projects.

ARTICLE 46

(Rights of Franchisee)

The following are the rights of the franchisee:

a) use of the brand names, names, and insignia of the franchisor;
b) use of any other distinctive signs of the franchisor, including, where applicable, the décor and colors of the facilities and personnel uniforms;
c) where applicable, using the knowhow of the franchisor;
d) using the technical assistance of the franchisor.

ARTICLE 47

(Organization of Business)

In the exercise of the franchisee's activities, the franchisor shall:

a) without prejudice to the responsibility of the franchisee himself or itself, be responsible to the consumers for the quality of the products supplied and the services rendered;
b) have the right, under reasonable conditions that do not adversely affect the business, to inspect the establishment and the exercise of the franchisee's activities;
c) have the obligation to compensate the franchisee for any damages caused thereto by reason of defective compliance with the contract.

SECTION III

Termination of Contract

ARTICLE 48

(Applicable Rules)

Without prejudice to the terms established in the contract regarding termination, the terms of Articles 25 through 36 of this Statute shall apply to Franchise Agreements, with the adjustments arising from the specific nature of the contract.

CHAPTER III

Commercial Concession Contracts

SECTION I

General Provisions

ARTICLE 49

(Concept)

1. A commercial concession is a contract whereby a person, singular or plural, the grantor, grants to the other, the grantee, the right to distribute, in its name and on its behalf, a certain product manufactured by the grantor, in a given area, and promote its resale, with both parties participating in the proceeds.

2. In performance of the contract, the grantor and grantee will enter into successive product purchase and sale agreements.

ARTICLE 50

(Purpose and Content of Contract)

1. The purpose of a commercial concession is the purchase and/or sale by the grantee of products manufactured, distributed, and/or acquired by the grantee.

2. The Commercial Concession Contract must include the following:

a) a description of the products covered by the contract;
b) the minimum quantities of products to be sold by the grantee for a given period of time, where applicable;
c) the duration of the contract and the conditions of its renewal;
d) establish the rules for setting the timing and conditions of product deliveries to the grantee, as well as the payment to the grantee;
e) establish the time after which the risk of perishing or deterioration of the products will transfer;
f) establish rules for ensuring product quality.

3. The grantor may retain ownership of the products

until the amounts due by the grantee are paid in full.

ARTICLE 51

(Form of Contract)

The Commercial Concession Contract must be in the written form.

ARTICLE 52

(Exclusivity)

In the absence of a written agreement to the contrary, the Commercial Concession Contract involves, for the grantor and for the grantee, the exclusivity obligation that entails the following:

a) the grantee may only buy from the grantor the products that are the subject of the contract and may only sell the products purchased from the grantor;
b) in the area covered by the contract, the grantor may only provide the grantee with the products that are the subject of the contract.

SECTION II

Rights and Obligations of Parties

ARTICLE 53

(Obligations of Grantee)

In addition to other obligations under law or contract, the obligations of the grantee are:

a) to do business to sell the products of the grantor;
b) to obey the orders and instructions of the grantor, particularly in the matter of prices, delivery periods, payments, insurance, guarantees, and business organization;
c) to acquire, where applicable, a minimum quantity of products from the grantor over a certain period and sell them to third parties in the area to which the contract refers;
d) to sell the products as received from the grantor, not making any changes to them without the express authorization of the grantor;
e) regularly report to the grantor on the progress of his or its activities and submit accounts on the activities performed;

f) make the payments due to the grantor.

ARTICLE 54

(Payments and Deductions)

1. In the payments to be made to the grantor, the grantee may only make the deductions allowed by the contract.

2. Retention by the grantee of any unapproved amounts will be an abuse of trust offence.

SECTION III

Obligations and Rights of Parties

ARTICLE 55

(Obligations of Grantor)

In addition to other obligations under law or contract, the obligations of the grantor are:

a) to make the goods under the contract available to the grantee within the periods of time and under the conditions established;
b) to provide the grantee with all the technical and business information needed for operating the concession;
c) within the established limits, pay the expenses incurred by the grantee such as negotiation, execution, and performance of contracts as well as advertising, promotion, and training of grantee personnel;
d) render technical assistance to the grantee.

ARTICLE 56

(Compliance Guarantee)

1. Unless agreed to in the contract, the grantee may, through an agreement reduced to writing, guarantee compliance with third-party obligations as long as they relate to the contract that it negotiated or executed.

2. The compliance guarantee shall be valid only if it specifies the contract or the persons covered by individually specified.

ARTICLE 57

(Instructions by Grantor)

1. Unless otherwise provided, the grantor may establish the rules and conditions, including payment periods, for the contracts to be entered into by the grantee

with third parties for goods supplied thereby.

2. If the grantee does not abide by these conditions, the grantee will be obliged to comply with them for the grantor, including payment periods.

3. If the grantor countermands any of the instructions referred to in 1. above, it must reimburse and compensate the grantee for the expenses incurred by the latter, as well as losses incurred.

4. It will be considered justified if, in the performance of its functions, the grantee exceeds the instructions of the grantor in the following cases:

a) when the steps he or it takes involve benefits to the grantor;
b) when the business deal is a rush matter.

5. In the cases referred to in the above paragraph, the excess shall be deemed to have been remedied if the deal is ratified by the grantor.

ARTICLE 58

(Rights of Grantee)

1. The following are rights of the grantee:

a) be paid under the agreed terms, usually a percentage of the value of the contracts entered into;
b) be reimbursed for expenses it has incurred in negotiating, executing, and performing the contracts;
c) be reimbursed and compensated if the contracts it executes cannot be performed for reasons attributable to the grantor.

2. Unless otherwise expressly agreed, the grantee may do business on its own account.

ARTICLE 59

(Right to Notice)

If there is a reduction in capacity on the part of the grantor, the grantee shall have the right to be immediately informed that the other party is only able to enter into a number of contracts that is considerably less than that agreed or that could be expected, depending on the circumstances.

SECTION IV

Termination of Contract

ARTICLE 60

(Applicable Rules)

Unless otherwise agreed by the parties in the contract regarding termination, the provisions of Articles 25 through 36 of this Statute, and the adjustments arising from the specific nature of this contract, shall apply to Commercial Concession Contracts.

CHAPTER IV

Final Provisions

ARTICLE 61

(Additional Law)

In all matters not specifically regulated, regarding the nature of these contracts, the provisions of Agency Contracts shall additionally be applicable to Franchise Agreements and Commercial Concession Contracts.

ARTICLE 62

(Applicable Law)

1. Unless otherwise provided by mandatory regulations, the parties may freely choose the law applicable to the contracts, provided that the choice falls on a law whose applicability corresponds to a serious interest of the parties or is connected to any of the elements of the legal business, namely the domiciles of the parties, the place of execution of the contract, or the place of performance of the contract.

2. If the parties have not chosen the applicable law, the Angolan rules of conflict under Civil Code Article 42 shall apply.

ARTICLE 63

(Jurisdiction)

1. Without prejudice to the rules of international competence of Angolan courts, the parties may freely choose the courts competent to resolve disputes emerging from the contracts.

2. If the parties opt for arbitration solutions, the contract must specify the law applicable to the process, the type of dispute that will be referred to the arbitral tribunal chosen, and the place of arbitration.

ARTICLE 64

(Questions and Omissions)

Questions regarding and omissions arising from interpretation and application of this Statute shall be resolved by the National Assembly.

ARTICLE 65

(Effective Date)

This Statute shall enter effect on the date published.

Seen and approved by the National Assembly in Luanda on July 5, 2002.

The President of the National Assembly, *Roberto António Víctor Francisco de Almeida.*

Enacted on February 27, 2003.
To be published.

The President of the Republic,
JOSÉ EDUARDO DOS SANTOS.

Appendix — Angola Law on Distribution, Agency, Franchise and Dealership Contracts (in Portuguese)

Angola

Terça-feira, 12 de Agosto de 2003 — I Série — N.º 63

DIÁRIO DA REPÚBLICA

ÓRGÃO OFICIAL DA REPÚBLICA DE ANGOLA

Preço deste número — Kz: 150,00

Toda a correspondência, quer oficial, quer relativa a anúncio e assinaturas do «Diário da República», deve ser dirigida à Imprensa Nacional — U.E.E., em Luanda, Caixa Postal 1306 — End. Teleg.: «Imprensa»

ASSINATURAS	Ano
As três séries	Kz: 165 000,00
A 1.ª série	Kz: 97 750,00
A 2.ª série	Kz: 55 250,00
A 3.ª série	Kz: 38 250,00

O preço de cada linha publicada nos Diários da República 1.ª e 2.ª séries é de Kz: 75,00 e para a 3.ª série Kz: 95,00, acrescido do respectivo imposto do selo, dependendo a publicação da 3.ª série de depósito prévio a efectuar na Tesouraria da Imprensa Nacional — U. E. E.

IMPRENSA NACIONAL-U.E.E.
Rua Henrique de Carvalho n.º 2
Caixa Postal n.º 1306

CIRCULAR

Excelentíssimos Senhores:

Havendo necessidade de se evitarem os inconvenientes que resultam para os nossos serviços do facto das respectivas assinaturas no *Diário da República* não serem feitas com a devida oportunidade.

Para que não haja interrupção no fornecimento do *Diário da República* aos estimados clientes, temos a honra de informá-los que estão abertas a partir desta data até 15 de Dezembro de 2003 as respectivas assinaturas para o ano de 2004 pelo que deverão providenciar a regularização dos seus pagamentos junto dos nossos serviços.

1. Os preços das assinaturas do *Diário da República* no território nacional passam a ser os seguintes:

As 3 séries	Kz: 300 750,00
1.ª série	Kz: 185 750,00
2.ª série	Kz: 96 250,00
3.ª série	Kz: 75 000,00

2. As assinaturas serão feitas apenas no regime anual.

3. Aos preços mencionados no n.º 1 acrescer-se-á um valor adicional para portes de correio por via normal das três séries, para todo o ano, no valor de Kz: 55 750,00 que poderá sofrer eventuais alterações em função da flutuação das taxas a praticar pela Empresa Nacional de Correios de Angola, E.P. no ano de 2004. Os clientes que optarem pela recepção das suas assinaturas através do correio deverão indicar o seu endereço completo, incluindo a Caixa Postal, a fim de se evitarem atrasos na sua entrega, devolução ou extravio.

Observações:

a) estes preços poderão ser alterados se houver uma desvalorização da moeda nacional, numa proporção superior à base que determinou o seu cálculo;

b) as assinaturas que forem feitas depois de 15 de Dezembro de 2003 sofrerão um acréscimo de uma taxa correspondente a 15%;

c) aos organismos do Estado que não regularizem os seus pagamentos até 15 de Dezembro do ano em curso não lhes serão concedidas a crédito as assinaturas do Diário da República para o ano de 2004;

d) aos Governos Provinciais que fizerem mais de 5 assinaturas das 3 séries faremos um desconto de 35% sobre o valor dos portes de correio.

SUMÁRIO

Assembleia Nacional

Lei n.º 18/03:

Sobre os contratos de distribuição, agência, franchising e concessão comercial.

Lei n.º 19/03:

Sobre os contratos de conta em participação, consórcios e agrupamentos de empresas. — Revoga os artigos 224.º a 229.º do Código Comercial relativos à conta em participação.

Ministério das Finanças

Despacho n.º 62/03:

Fixa o fundo permanente do Ministério dos Petróleos para o ano económico de 2003.

ASSEMBLEIA NACIONAL

Lei n.º 18/03
de 12 de Agosto

Os contratos de distribuição, agência e de franchising têm assumido uma importância crescente no domínio do comércio interno e internacional, como forma de desenvolver novos mercados, divulgar produtos e serviços e reduzir os custos. Embora menos utilizado, também o contrato de concessão comercial tem sido um importante instrumento na procura das empresas por novos mercados com custos reduzidos.

Também em Angola, apesar de não haver legislação específica para este tipo de contratos, os empresários têm, com alguma frequência, utilizado alguns destes mecanismos contratuais, especialmente nas áreas da agência e da comissão.

Embora, a nível nacional, os contratos de franchising não tenham, ainda, sido massivamente acolhidos, o desenvolvimento do País, num prazo curto, pode beneficiar com a utilização de contratos desta natureza.

Torna-se por isso necessário acolher estas modalidades de contratos no nosso regime jurídico, como forma de aumentar as garantias das partes e a segurança do comércio.

Nestes termos, ao abrigo da alínea *b*) do artigo 88.º da Lei Constitucional, a Assembleia Nacional aprova a seguinte:

Lei Sobre os Contratos de Distribuição, Agência, Franchising e Concessão Comercial

CAPÍTULO I
Contratos de Agência

SECÇÃO I
Disposições Gerais

ARTIGO 1.º
(Noção)

1. Contrato de Agência é o contrato pelo qual uma pessoa, singular ou colectiva, se obriga a promover, por conta de outra, a celebração de contratos, de modo autónomo, estável e mediante retribuição.
2. O Contrato de Agência pode atribuir ao agente certa zona ou determinado círculo de clientes.

ARTIGO 2.º
(Agência com representação)

O agente só pode celebrar contratos em nome da outra parte se esta lhe tiver conferido, por escrito, os necessários poderes.

ARTIGO 3.º
(Forma do contrato)

O Contrato de Agência está sujeito a forma escrita.

ARTIGO 4.º
(Reclamações e providências urgentes)

1. Independentemente de existirem ou não os poderes de representação previstos no artigo 2.º da presente lei, podem ser apresentadas ao agente as reclamações ou outras declarações respeitantes aos negócios concluídos por seu intermédio.
2. O agente tem legitimidade para requerer as providências urgentes que se mostrem indispensáveis em ordem a acautelar os direitos do principal.

ARTIGO 5.º
(Cobrança de créditos)

1. O agente só pode efectuar a cobrança de créditos quando para isso for expressamente autorizado, por escrito, pela outra parte.
2. Presume-se autorizado a cobrar os créditos resultantes dos contratos por si celebrados o agente a quem tenham sido conferidos poderes de representação.
3. Se o agente cobrar créditos sem a necessária autorização, sem prejuízo do regime consagrado no artigo 25.º da presente lei, é-lhe aplicável o disposto no artigo 770.º do Código Civil.

ARTIGO 6.º
(Exclusividade)

Na falta de convenção escrita em contrário, o agente não pode exercer actividades que estejam em concorrência com as do principal e este não pode utilizar outros agentes para o respectivo ramo de actividade, dentro da mesma zona ou do mesmo círculo de clientes.

ARTIGO 7.º
(Subagência)

1. Salvo convenção escrita em contrário, é permitido o recurso à subagentes.
2. À relação de subagência aplicam-se, com as necessárias adaptações, as normas da presente lei.

ARTIGO 8.º
(Boa-fé)

No cumprimento das suas obrigações contratuais, o agente e o principal devem proceder de boa-fé, em ordem à realização plena do fim contratual.

SECÇÃO II
Obrigações e Direitos das Partes

ARTIGO 9.º
(Obrigações do agente)

Constituem obrigações do agente, nomeadamente:

a) respeitar as instruções da outra parte que não ponham em causa a sua autonomia;
b) prestar as informações que lhe forem solicitadas ou que se mostrem necessárias a uma boa gestão, nomeadamente as respeitantes à solvabilidade e seriedade dos clientes;
c) informar a outra parte sobre a situação do mercado e perspectivas de evolução;
d) prestar contas nos termos acordados ou sempre que isso se justifique.

ARTIGO 10.º
(Obrigação de segredo)

1. É vedado ao agente, mesmo após o termo do contrato, utilizar ou revelar a terceiros segredos da outra parte que lhe hajam sido confiados ou de que ele tenha tomado conhecimento no exercício da sua actividade, salvo no caso de violação do contrato na medida em que as regras de deontologia profissional o permitam.

2. A violação do disposto no número anterior faz incorrer o agente em responsabilidade civil, nos termos gerais, nomeadamente do artigo 798.º e seguintes do Código Civil.

ARTIGO 11.º
(Obrigação de não concorrência)

1. As partes podem convencionar, no contrato, a obrigação de o agente não exercer, após a cessação do contrato, actividades que estejam em concorrência com as da outra parte.

2. A obrigação de não concorrência só pode ser convencionada por um período máximo de dois anos e circunscreve-se à zona ou círculo de clientes confiado ao agente.

ARTIGO 12.º
(Garantia de cumprimento)

1. O agente pode garantir, através de convenção reduzida a escrito, o cumprimento das obrigações de terceiro, desde que respeitantes ao contrato por si negociado ou concluído.

2. A garantia de cumprimento só é válida quando se especifique o contrato ou se individualizem as pessoas garantidas.

ARTIGO 13.º
(Impossibilidade temporária)

O agente que esteja temporariamente impossibilitado de cumprir o contrato, no todo ou em parte, deve avisar, de imediato e por escrito, o outro contraente.

ARTIGO 14.º
(Direitos do agente)

Constituem direitos do agente, nomeadamente:

a) obter da outra parte todas as informações e meios que, tendo em conta as circunstâncias, se mostrem necessários ao exercício da sua actividade;
b) ser imediatamente informado da aceitação ou recusa dos contratos negociados e dos que haja concluído sem os necessários poderes;
c) receber uma relação dos contratos celebrados e das comissões devidas, com a periodicidade estabelecida no contrato e o mais tardar até ao último dia do mês seguinte ao trimestre em que o direito à comissão tiver sido adquirido;
d) exigir que lhe sejam fornecidas todas as informações, nomeadamente um extracto dos livros de contabilidade da outra parte, que sejam necessárias para verificar o montante das comissões que lhe são devidas;
e) receber o pagamento da retribuição nos termos acordados;
f) receber comissões especiais, que podem acumular-se, relativas a encargos de cobrança de créditos e à Convenção *Del Credere*;
g) receber uma compensação pela obrigação de não concorrência após a cessação do contrato.

ARTIGO 15.º
(Direito ao aviso)

Em caso de redução de capacidade da outra parte, o agente tem o direito a ser imediatamente informado de que a outra parte só está em condições de concluir um número de contratos consideravelmente inferior ao que fora convencionado ou aquele que era de esperar, segundo as circunstâncias.

ARTIGO 16.º
(Retribuição)

Na ausência de convenção de partes, a retribuição do agente é calculada segundo os usos ou, na falta destes, de acordo com a equidade.

ARTIGO 17.º
(Direito à comissão)

1. O agente tem direito a receber uma comissão pelos contratos que tenha promovido, bem como pelos contratos celebrados com clientes por si angariados, desde que concluídos antes do termo da relação de agência.

2. Caso goze de um direito de exclusivo para uma zona geográfica ou um círculo de clientes, o agente tem,

igualmente, direito a receber uma comissão por actos concluídos, durante a vigência do contrato, com clientes pertencentes a essa zona ou círculo de clientes.

3. O agente só tem direito a receber comissões pelos contratos celebrados após o termo da relação de agência quando prove ter sido ele a negociá-los ou, tendo-os preparado, ficar a sua conclusão a dever-se, principalmente, à actividade por si desenvolvida, contanto que em ambos os casos sejam celebrados num período razoável subsequente ao termo do contrato de agência.

ARTIGO 18.º
(Sucessão de agentes no tempo)

Durante a vigência do contrato, o agente não tem direito à comissão prevista no n.º 1 do artigo anterior se a mesma for devida, por força do n.º 3 do artigo anterior, ao agente que o anteceder, sem prejuízo de a comissão poder ser repartida equitativamente entre ambos, quando se verifiquem circunstâncias que o justifiquem.

ARTIGO 19.º
(Aquisição do direito à comissão)

1. O agente adquire o direito à comissão quando e na medida em que se verifique uma das seguintes circunstâncias:

a) o principal haja cumprido o contrato ou devesse tê-lo cumprido por força do acordo concluído com o terceiro;
b) o terceiro haja cumprido o contrato.

2. Qualquer acordo que as partes hajam celebrado sobre o direito à comissão não pode impedir que este se constitua, pelo menos, quando o terceiro cumpra o contrato ou no momento em que devesse tê-lo cumprido, caso o principal tenha já cumprido a sua obrigação.

3. A comissão referida nos números anteriores deve ser paga até ao último dia do mês seguinte ao trimestre em que o direito tiver sido adquirido.

4. Existindo Convenção *Del Credere*, pode, porém, o agente exigir as comissões devidas no momento da celebração do contrato.

ARTIGO 20.º
(Falta de cumprimento)

O agente não perde o direito a exigir a comissão se o não cumprimento do contrato se ficar a dever a causa imputável ao principal.

ARTIGO 21.º
(Despesas)

Na falta de convenção em contrário, o agente tem direito ao reembolso das despesas que haja efectuado pelo exercício normal da sua actividade por conta do principal.

SECÇÃO III
Protecção de Terceiros

ARTIGO 22.º
(Dever de informação)

O agente tem o dever de informar os interessados sobre os poderes que possui, nomeadamente através de letreiros afixados nos seus locais de trabalho e em todos os documentos em que se identifica como agente de outrem, dos quais deve obrigatoriamente constar se tem ou não poderes de representação e se pode ou não efectuar a cobrança de créditos.

ARTIGO 23.º
(Representação sem poderes)

1. Sem prejuízo do disposto no artigo seguinte, o negócio que o agente celebre em nome da outra parte, sem poderes de representação, tem os efeitos previstos no n.º 1 do artigo 268.º do Código Civil.

2. Nos casos a que se refere o número anterior, considera-se o negócio ratificado pela outra parte se esta, logo que tenha conhecimento da sua celebração e do conteúdo essencial do mesmo, não manifestar ao terceiro de boa-fé, no prazo de cinco dias a contar daquele conhecimento, a sua oposição ao negócio.

ARTIGO 24.º
(Representação aparente)

1. O negócio celebrado por um agente sem poderes de representação é eficaz perante o principal se tiverem existido razões ponderosas, objectivamente apreciadas, tendo em conta as circunstâncias do caso, que justifiquem a confiança do terceiro de boa-fé na legitimidade do agente, desde que o principal tenha igualmente contribuído para fundar a confiança do terceiro.

2. À cobrança de créditos por agente não autorizado aplica-se, com as necessárias adaptações, o disposto no número anterior.

SECÇÃO IV
Cessação do Contrato

ARTIGO 25.º
(Formas de cessação)

O contrato de agência pode cessar por:

a) acordo entre as partes;
b) caducidade;
c) denúncia;
d) resolução.

ARTIGO 26.º
(Mútuo acordo)

O acordo pelo qual as partes decidem pôr termo à relação contratual deve constar de documento escrito.

ARTIGO 27.º
(Caducidade)

O Contrato de Agência caduca:

a) findo o prazo estabelecido, se o houver;
b) verificando-se a condição a que as partes o subordinaram ou tornando-se certo que não pode verificar-se, conforme a condição seja resolutiva ou suspensiva;
c) por morte do agente ou, tratando-se de pessoa colectiva, pela sua extinção.

ARTIGO 28.º
(Duração do contrato)

1. Se as partes não tiverem convencionado prazo, o contrato presume-se celebrado por tempo indeterminado.
2. Considera-se transformado em Contrato de Agência por tempo indeterminado o contrato por prazo determinado cujo conteúdo continue a ser executado pelas partes, não obstante o decurso do respectivo prazo.

ARTIGO 29.º
(Denúncia)

1. A denúncia só é permitida nos contratos celebrados por tempo indeterminado e desde que comunicada ao outro contraente, por escrito, com a seguinte antecedência mínima:

a) um mês, se o contrato durar há menos de um ano;
b) dois meses, se o contrato já tiver iniciado o segundo ano de vigência;
c) três meses, nos restantes casos.

2. Salvo convenção escrita em contrário, o termo do prazo a que se refere o número anterior deve coincidir com o último dia do mês.
3. Se as partes estipularem prazos mais longos do que os consagrados nas alíneas *a*) a *c*) do n.º 1 do presente artigo, o prazo a observar pelo principal não pode ser inferior ao do agente.
4. No caso previsto no n.º 2 do presente artigo, para a determinação da antecedência com que a denúncia deve ser comunicada, deve ter-se igualmente em conta o tempo anterior ao decurso do prazo.

ARTIGO 30.º
(Falta de pré-aviso)

1. A parte que denunciar o contrato sem respeitar os prazos referidos no artigo anterior é obrigada a indemnizar o outro contraente pelos danos causados pela falta de pré-aviso.

2. A indemnização deve ser calculada com base na remuneração média mensal auferida no decurso do ano precedente, multiplicada pelo tempo em falta, se o contrato durar há menos de um ano, atende-se à remuneração média mensal auferida durante a vigência do contrato.

ARTIGO 31.º
(Resolução)

1. O contrato de agência pode ser resolvido por qualquer das partes nos seguintes casos:

a) se a outra parte faltar ao cumprimento das suas obrigações, quando, pela gravidade ou reiteração dos incumprimentos, não seja exigível a subsistência do vínculo contratual;
b) se ocorrerem circunstâncias que tornem impossível ou prejudiquem gravemente a realização do objecto contratual, em termos de não ser exigível que o contrato se mantenha até expirar o prazo convencionado ou imposto em caso de denúncia.

2. A resolução do contrato é feita através de notificação escrita à outra parte, no prazo de um mês após o conhecimento dos factos que a justificam, devendo indicar as razões em que se fundamenta.

ARTIGO 32.º
(Indemnização)

1. Independentemente do direito de resolver o contrato, qualquer das partes tem o direito a ser indemnizada, nos termos gerais, pelos danos resultantes do não cumprimento das obrigações da outra.
2. A resolução do contrato com base na alínea *b*) do n.º 1 do artigo 30.º da presente lei confere o direito a uma indemnização segundo a equidade.

ARTIGO 33.º
(Indemnização de clientela)

1. Sem prejuízo de qualquer outra indemnização a que haja lugar nos termos das disposições anteriores, o agente tem direito, após a cessação do contrato, a uma indemnização de clientela, desde que sejam preenchidos, cumulativamente, os seguintes requisitos:

a) o agente tenha angariado novos clientes para a outra parte ou aumentado substancialmente o volume de negócios com a clientela já existente;
b) a outra parte venha a beneficiar consideravelmente, mesmo após a cessação do contrato, da actividade desenvolvida pelo agente;

c) o agente deixe de receber qualquer retribuição por contratos negociados ou concluídos, após a cessação do contrato, com os clientes referidos na alínea a).

2. Em caso de morte do agente, a indemnização de clientela pode ser exigida pelos respectivos herdeiros.

3. Não é devida indemnização de clientela se o contrato tiver cessado por razões imputáveis ao agente ou se este, por acordo com a outra parte, houver cedido a terceiro a sua posição contratual.

4. Extingue-se o direito à indemnização se o agente ou os seus herdeiros não comunicarem ao principal, no prazo de um ano a contar da data da cessação do contrato, que pretendem recebê-la, devendo a acção judicial ser proposta no ano subsequente a esta comunicação.

ARTIGO 34.º
(Cálculo da indemnização de clientela)

1. A indemnização de clientela é fixada em termos equitativos, mas não pode exceder um valor equivalente a uma indemnização anual, calculada a partir da média anual das remunerações recebidas pelo agente durante os últimos cinco anos.

2. Tendo o contrato durado menos tempo, atende-se à média do período em que esteve em vigor.

ARTIGO 35.º
(Direito de retenção)

Pelos créditos resultantes da sua actividade, o agente goza do direito de retenção sobre os objectos e valores que haja recebido e detenha em virtude do contrato.

ARTIGO 36.º
(Obrigação de restituir)

Sem prejuízo do disposto no número anterior, cada contraente tem a obrigação de restituir, no termo do contrato, os objectos, valores e demais elementos pertencentes ao outro.

CAPÍTULO II
Contratos de Franchising

SECÇÃO I
Disposições Gerais

ARTIGO 37.º
(Noção)

1. Franchising é o contrato pelo qual uma pessoa, singular ou colectiva (o franchisador ou licenciador) concede a outrem (o franchisado ou licenciado), mediante contrapartidas, a comercialização dos seus bens ou serviços, através da utilização da marca e demais sinais distintivos do franchisador e conforme o plano, método e directrizes prescritos por ele.

2. O Contrato de Franchising pode atribuir ao agente certa zona ou círculo de clientes.

ARTIGO 38.º
(Tipos de franchising)

O franchising pode revestir-se nos seguintes tipos:

a) de Distribuição – quando o franchisado se obriga a vender determinados produtos fabricados ou distribuídos pelo franchisador, num estabelecimento com a imagem e o nome do franchisador;
b) de Serviços – quando o franchisado presta um serviço com a marca e a técnica do franchisador;
c) de Produção ou Industrial – quando o franchisado fabrica, de acordo com as instruções do franchisador, determinados produtos fabricados sob a marca do franchisador.

ARTIGO 39.º
(Forma do contrato)

O Contrato de Franchising está sujeito a forma escrita.

ARTIGO 40.º
(Exclusividade)

Na falta de convenção escrita em contrário, o franchisado não pode exercer actividades que estejam em concorrência com as do principal e este não pode utilizar outros franchisados para o respectivo ramo de actividade, dentro da mesma zona ou do mesmo círculo de clientes.

ARTIGO 41.º
(Boa-fé)

No cumprimento das suas obrigações contratuais, o franchisado e franchisador devem proceder de boa-fé, em ordem à realização plena do fim contratual.

ARTIGO 42.º
(Sub-contratação)

Com a autorização expressa do franchisador, o franchisado pode celebrar contratos de sub-franchising.

SECÇÃO II
Obrigações e Direitos das Partes

ARTIGO 43.º
(Obrigações do franchisado)

1. Constituem obrigações do franchisado, nomeadamente:

a) adoptar e utilizar o conjunto de produtos e/ou serviços apresentados pelo franchisador;
b) remunerar, pela forma acordada, os serviços prestados pelo franchisador;
c) guardar segredo sobre toda a informação que lhe seja transmitida pelo franchisador, incluindo sobre processos de fabrico e *know-how*, durante todo o período de duração do contrato e após o seu termo
d) não fazer concorrência ao franchisador, nos termos do artigo 11.º da presente lei;
e) exercer a sua actividade nos moldes definidos pelo franchisador e sob a sua orientação e com a exibição dos sinais distintivos do franchisador.

2. O Contrato de Franchising pode, também, incluir a obrigação de o franchisado adquirir ao franchisador os produtos que distribui.

3. O Contrato de Franchising pode ainda incluir obrigações para o franchisado em matéria de fornecimentos, preços e organização contabilística.

ARTIGO 44.º
(Remuneração)

A remuneração da franquia é a estabelecida no contrato, podendo incluir:

a) o pagamento de um direito de entrada;
b) o pagamento de uma *royaltie*-remuneração periódica, fixa ou variável, que pode ser calculada em função do volume de negócios, das receitas brutas ou da quantidade de bens fornecidos pelo franchisador;
c) o pagamento de uma taxa de publicidade.

ARTIGO 45.º
(Obrigações do franchisador)

Constituem obrigações do franchisador, nomeadamente:

a) conceder ao franchisado licença para a exploração dos seus sinais distintivos, processos de fabrico e *know-how*, nos termos acordados;
b) fornecer ao franchisado os produtos ou serviços a que se obrigou;
c) prestar assistência técnica ao franchisado para a realização da sua actividade;
d) aperfeiçoar os seus métodos, conhecimentos e processos, patenteados ou secretos e transmitir as inovações ao franchisado;
e) apoiar o franchisado, nomeadamente em matéria de formação, publicidade, estudos e projectos.

ARTIGO 46.º
(Direitos do franchisado)

Constituem direitos do franchisado, nomeadamente:

a) uso das marcas, nomes e insígnias do franchisador;
b) uso de quaisquer outros sinais distintivos do franchisador, incluindo, se for caso disso, a decoração e cores das instalações e uniformes do pessoal;
c) utilização, se for caso disso, do *know-how* do franchisador;
d) utilização da assistência técnica do franchisador.

ARTIGO 47.º
(Organização do negócio)

No exercício da actividade do franchisado, compete ao franchisador:

a) sem prejuízo da responsabilidade do próprio franchisado, ser responsável, perante os consumidores, pela qualidade dos produtos fornecidos e dos serviços prestados;
b) ter o direito de, em condições razoáveis que não prejudiquem o negócio, fiscalizar o estabelecimento e o exercício das actividades do franchisado;
c) ter a obrigação de indemnizar o franchisado por quaisquer prejuízos que lhe cause, por motivos de cumprimento defeituoso do contrato.

SECÇÃO III
Cessação do Contrato

ARTIGO 48.º
(Normas aplicáveis)

Sem prejuízo do que as partes estabelecerem no contrato em matéria de cessação, são aplicáveis aos Contratos de Franchising as disposições constantes dos artigos 25.º a 36.º da presente lei, com as adaptações que decorram da natureza específica do contrato.

CAPÍTULO III
Contratos de Concessão Comercial

SECÇÃO I
Disposições Gerais

ARTIGO 49.º
(Noção)

1. Concessão comercial é o contrato pelo qual uma pessoa, singular ou colectiva, o concedente, concede a outra, o concessionário, o direito a distribuir, em seu nome

e por conta própria, certo produto fabricado pelo concedente, numa determinada área e a promover a sua revenda, participando ambas as partes nos resultados obtidos.

2. Na execução do contrato, o concedente e concessionário celebram sucessivos contratos de compra e venda de produtos.

ARTIGO 50.º
(Objecto e conteúdo do contrato)

1. A concessão comercial tem por objecto de compra e/ou venda pelo concessionário de produtos fabricados, distribuídos e/ou adquiridos pelo concedente.

2. O Contrato de Concessão deve incluir, nomeadamente:

a) a descrição dos produtos abrangidos no contrato;
b) as quantidades mínimas de produtos a comprar pelo concessionário durante determinado período, se for caso disso;
c) a duração do contrato e as condições da sua renovação;
d) estabelecer as regras para a fixação dos prazos e condições das entregas dos produtos ao concessionário, bem como do pagamento ao concedente;
e) estabelecer o momento a partir do qual se opera a transferência do risco pelo perecimento ou deterioração dos produtos;
f) estabelecer regras relativas à garantia da qualidade dos produtos.

3. O concedente pode reservar para si a propriedade dos produtos até ao pagamento integral das importâncias devidas pelo concessionário.

ARTIGO 51.º
(Forma do contrato)

O Contrato de Concessão Comercial está sujeito à forma escrita.

ARTIGO 52.º
(Exclusividade)

Na falta de convenção escrita em contrário, o Contrato de Concessão Comercial integra, para o concedente e para o concessionário, a obrigação de exclusividade, que implicam que:

a) o concessionário só possa comprar ao concedente os produtos que constituem objecto do contrato e que só possa vender os produtos comprados ao concedente;
b) na área abrangida pelo contrato, o concedente só possa fornecer ao concessionário os produtos que constituem objecto do contrato.

SECÇÃO II
Direitos e Obrigações das Partes

ARTIGO 53.º
(Obrigações do concessionário)

Para além de outras que resultam da lei ou do contrato, constituem obrigações do concessionário:

a) celebrar negócios para a venda dos produtos do concedente;
b) respeitar as ordens e instruções do concedente, nomeadamente em matéria de preços, prazos de entregas, pagamentos, seguros, garantias e organização do negócio;
c) adquirir, quando for esse o caso, uma quantidade mínima de produtos ao concedente durante certo período e proceder à sua venda a terceiros, na zona a que o contrato se refere;
d) vender os produtos tal como os recebeu do concedente, não devendo introduzir-lhes qualquer alteração sem autorização expressa do concedente;
e) informar regularmente o concedente sobre a forma como decorre a sua actividade e prestar-lhe contas da actividade realizada;
f) fazer ao comitente os pagamentos devidos.

ARTIGO 54.º
(Pagamentos e deduções)

1. Nos pagamentos a efectuar ao comitente, o concessionário apenas pode proceder às deduções autorizadas pelo contrato.

2. A retenção pelo concessionário de quaisquer quantias não autorizadas constitui crime de abuso de confiança.

SECÇÃO III
Obrigações e Direitos das Partes

ARTIGO 55.º
(Obrigações do concedente)

Para além de outras que resultem da lei ou do contrato, constituem obrigações do concedente, nomeadamente:

a) pôr à disposição do concessionário, nos prazos e condições estabelecidos, as mercadorias que constituem objecto do contrato;
b) prestar ao concessionário todas as informações técnicas e comerciais necessárias à exploração da concessão;
c) suportar, dentro dos limites estabelecidos, as despesas efectuadas pelo concessionário com a

negociação, celebração e execução dos contratos, bem como com publicidade, promoção e formação do pessoal do concessionário;

d) prestar assistência técnica ao concessionário.

ARTIGO 56.º
(Garantia de cumprimento)

1. Salvo convenção em contrário, o concessionário pode garantir, através de convenção reduzida a escrito, o cumprimento das obrigações de terceiro, desde que respeitantes ao contrato por si negociado ou concluído.

2. A garantia de cumprimento só é válida quando se especifique o contrato ou se individualizem as pessoas garantidas.

ARTIGO 57.º
(Instruções do concedente)

1. Salvo disposição em contrário, o concedente pode estabelecer as regras e condições, incluindo prazos de pagamento, dos contratos a celebrar pelo concessionário com terceiros para mercadorias que aquele forneça.

2. Caso o concessionário não respeite essas condições, o concessionário é obrigado a cumpri-las para com o concedente incluindo os prazos de pagamento.

3. Se o concedente revogar algumas das instruções referidas no n.º 1, é obrigado a reembolsar e indemnizar o concessionário pelas despesas que este haja efectuado, bem como pelos prejuízos sofridos.

4. Considera-se justificado que, no exercício das suas funções, o concessionário exceda as instruções do comitente nos seguintes casos:

a) quando os actos que pratique acarretem vantagens para o concedente;

b) quando haja urgência na celebração do negócio.

5. Nos casos a que se refere o número anterior, considera-se sanado o excesso em caso de ratificação do negócio pelo concedente.

ARTIGO 58.º
(Direitos do concessionário)

1. Constituem direitos do concessionário, nomeadamente:

a) ser remunerado nos termos acordados, em regra uma percentagem sobre o valor dos contratos que celebra;

b) ser reembolsado das despesas que haja efectuado por motivo da negociação, celebração e execução dos contratos;

c) ser reembolsado e indemnizado no caso de os contratos por ele celebrados não poderem ser realizados por motivo imputável ao concedente.

2. Salvo convenção expressa em contrário, o concessionário pode fazer negócio consigo próprio.

ARTIGO 59.º
(Direito ao aviso)

Em caso de redução de capacidade do concedente, o concessionário tem o direito a ser imediatamente informado de que a outra parte só está em condições de concluir um número de contratos, consideravelmente inferior ao que fora convencionado ou aquele que era de esperar, segundo as circunstâncias.

SECÇÃO IV
Cessação do Contrato

ARTIGO 60.º
(Normas aplicáveis)

Sem prejuízo do que as partes estabelecerem no contrato em matéria de cessação, são aplicáveis aos Contratos de Concessão Comercial as disposições constantes dos artigos 25.º a 36.º da presente lei, com as adaptações que decorram da natureza específica deste contrato.

CAPÍTULO IV
Disposições Finais

ARTIGO 61.º
(Direito supletivo)

Em tudo o que não estiver especialmente regulado e respeitando a natureza desses contratos, são supletivamente aplicáveis aos Contratos de Franchising e de Concessão Comercial as disposições dos Contratos de Agência.

ARTIGO 62.º
(Lei aplicável)

1. Sem prejuízo de disposições imperativas em contrário, as partes podem escolher livremente a lei aplicável aos contratos, desde que a escolha recaia sobre uma lei cuja aplicabilidade corresponda a um interesse sério das partes ou esteja em conexão com algum dos elementos do negócio jurídico, nomeadamente o domicílio das partes, o lugar da celebração do contrato ou o lugar da execução do contrato.

2. No caso de as partes não terem escolhido a lei aplicável, aplica-se as normas angolanas de conflitos, nos termos do artigo 42.º do Código Civil.

ARTIGO 63.º
(Jurisdição)

1. Sem prejuízo das regras de competência internacional dos tribunais angolanos, as partes podem escolher livremente os tribunais competentes para a solução dos litígios emergentes dos contratos.

2. Caso as partes optem por soluções arbitrais, o contrato deve especificar a lei aplicável ao processo, o tipo de litígios que lhe são submetidos, a câmara arbitral escolhida e o local da arbitragem.

ARTIGO 64.º
(Dúvidas e omissões)

As dúvidas e omissões que se suscitarem da interpretação e aplicação da presente lei são resolvidas pela Assembleia Nacional.

ARTIGO 65.º
(Entrada em vigor)

A presente lei entra em vigor à data da sua publicação.

Vista e aprovada pela Assembleia Nacional, em Luanda, aos 5 de Julho de 2002.

O Presidente da Assembleia Nacional, *Roberto António Victor Francisco de Almeida.*

Promulgada em 27 de Fevereiro de 2003.

Publique-se.

O Presidente da República, José Eduardo dos Santos.

Lei n.º 19/03
de 12 de Agosto

Os contratos de cooperação entre empresas vêm assumindo uma particular importância desde a segunda metade do século passado e nomeadamente desde finais da segunda guerra mundial.

Com efeito, a aproximação entre empresas, face a uma concorrência cada vez maior, é frequentemente uma condição da sua sobrevivência no mercado. Razões de ordem técnica, de inovação tecnológica, de racionalização de meios humanos e financeiros e de ordem comercial, bem como factores de ordem política, induzem à associação cada vez mais frequente e economicamente cada vez mais importante entre empresas, quer ao nível interno quer internacional.

No nosso País, tendo em conta o facto de a legislação comercial não ter sido alterada desde a independência nacional, não existe, ao nível do direito positivo, regulamentação para a maior parte dos novos contratos de associação entre empresas, embora pela dinâmica da actividade económica, tenham sido celebrados vários desses contratos.

Contudo, a inexistência de definições legais e de regulamentação sobre essas figuras gerava grandes dificuldades na sua interpretação e utilização.

De entre essas formas de associação, para além de muitas outras inominadas, revestem-se de particular importância as figuras da conta em participação, do consórcio e do agrupamento de empresas.

A conta em participação, regulada pelos artigos 224.º a 229.º do Código Comercial, é um instituto que foi objecto de várias controvérsias na doutrina e na jurisprudência, quer quanto à sua definição e natureza, quer quanto às regras aplicáveis ao seu funcionamento.

Discutia-se, nomeadamente, se tratava-se de um contrato associativo ou de um contrato de sociedade (em comandita), se dava ou não origem a novo ente dotado de personalidade jurídica, que forma deveria adoptar e se gerava ou não bens comuns.

Por outro lado e uma vez que a sua regulamentação enferma de muitas lacunas, era frequentemente difícil caracterizá-la e determinar que disposições lhe eram supletivamente aplicáveis. Neste momento, o regime jurídico estabelecido pelo Código Comercial encontra-se já bastante desactualizado, pelo que urge modernizá-lo, atendendo à importância prática de que pode revestir-se.

Quanto ao consórcio e ao agrupamento de empresas, são figuras ainda não reguladas no nosso direito positivo, sobre as quais urge legislar, como forma, quer de actualizar o nosso sistema jurídico, quer de estimular a sua utilização e aumentar a segurança das partes.

Convém, por isso, consagrar legalmente estas figuras e estabelecer o seu regime legal, por forma a que possam ser mais um instrumento no aprofundamento da cooperação, interna e internacional, entre as empresas.

Nestes termos, ao abrigo da alínea *b)* do artigo 88.º da Lei Constitucional, a Assembleia Nacional aprova a seguinte:

Franchising in Botswana

Bonzo Makgalemele

Chibanda, Makgalemele & Company

Gaborone, Botswana

Botswana

I. Introduction

A. Historical Background of Country

Formerly the British protectorate of Bechuanaland, Botswana adopted its new name upon independence in 1966. Four decades of uninterrupted civilian leadership, progressive social policies, and significant capital investment have created one of the most dynamic economies in Africa. Mineral extraction, principally diamond mining, dominates economic activity, though tourism is a growing sector due to the country's conservation practices and extensive nature preserves.

B. Economy of the Country

Botswana has maintained one of the world's highest economic growth rates since independence in 1966, though growth fell below 5% in 2007–08, and turned sharply negative in 2009, with industry falling nearly 30%. Although the economy recovered in 2010, growth has remained flat. Through fiscal discipline and sound management, Botswana transformed itself into a middle-income country with a per capita GDP of US13,100 in 2010. Two major investment services rank Botswana as the best credit risk in Africa. Diamond mining has fueled much of the expansion and currently accounts for more than one-third of GDP, 70–80% of export earnings, and about one-third of the government's revenues. Botswana's heavy reliance on a single luxury export was a critical factor in the sharp economic contraction of 2009. Tourism, financial services, subsistence farming, and cattle raising are other key sectors. Although unemployment was 17.8% in 2009 according to official reports, unofficial estimates place it as much as double the official estimate. The prevalence of HIV/AIDS that remains second highest in the world and an expected leveling off in diamond mining production within the next two decades overshadow long-term prospects. A major international diamond company signed a 10-year deal with Botswana in 2013 to move its rough stone sorting and trading division from London to Gaborone by the end of 2013. This move may support Botswana's downstream diamond industry.

C. Franchise Legal Overview

Under the Botswana law, there is no specific law that regulates franchise agreements and/or transactions. The franchise agreement is seen as a contractual agreement between the parties and thus contract law will govern such an agreement.

II. Regulatory Requirements

A. Pre-Sale Disclosure

Please describe any pre-sale franchise disclosure or similar requirements that may apply to franchise transactions.

No pre-sale franchise disclosure or similar requirements apply to franchise transactions under the laws of Botswana.

Botswana does not have specific legislation on franchising. In many instances, the contracting parties simply enter into a franchise agreement to set the terms and conditions that will govern their conduct with respect to the franchise. If any dispute arises, the common law principles can be invoked by the courts to resolve matters.

B. Governmental Approvals, Registrations, Filing Requirements

Please describe any necessary government approvals, registrations, or filing requirements that may apply to franchise transactions.

Botswana law does not provide that the effectiveness of a franchise transaction is dependent on any formalities beyond the execution of a written contract, such as government approvals, registration or filing requirements.

See, however, Section V (Trademarks) of this chapter relating to the registration of licenses with trademark authorities.

Under the Companies Act of Botswana, there is a requirement that every company and/or trade name to be used within the jurisdiction must be registered with the Registrar of Companies, Trademarks and Patents ("RGTP").

C. Limits of Fees and Typical Term of Franchise Agreement

Please describe any limits upon the nature and extent of fees and the term of a typical franchise agreement.

There are no limits to fees. As stated, a franchise agreement is a contractual agreement between parties. They are free to agree on terms and conditions and to be bound by the terms to which they agree. However, the terms and conditions should fully comply with the principles of public policy.

III. Currency

If all payments under a franchise agreement must be made in immediately available U.S. Dollars, please advise as to any restrictions, reporting requirements, or regulations concerning the exchange, repatriation, or remittance of U.S. Dollars.

There are no specific restrictions on payments made available in U.S. Dollars. It will depend on the parties' contractual agreement.

IV. Taxes, Tariffs, and Duties

Please do not provide any in-depth comments on tax structuring. However, please provide your general comments on the typical amount of withholding tax that would apply and whether a "gross-up" provision contained in a franchise agreement would be enforceable in your country.

Botswana

The *Value Added Tax Act* (*Cap 50:03* of the Laws of Botswana), provides for a value added tax (VAT) on any activity that is carried on in Botswana (or partly therein) involving the supply of goods or services for consideration. Corporate income tax is levied on all Botswana-sourced taxable income of all companies other than tax exempt bodies.

A. Applicable Rate

In Botswana, withholding tax is mainly a three (3) tier system.

1. Dividends.

A withholding tax of 15% is levied on all dividends paid by a resident company to a resident or a non-resident.

2. Interest.

A 15% withholding tax is levied on interest paid to non-residents and 10% on interest paid to residents. This tax may not be offset against corporate liability.

3. Royalties.

The withholding tax on royalty payments made to non-residents is 15%. The withholding tax on royalties may not be offset against the corporate liability.

STATUTORY AND DOUBLE TAXATION AGREEMENT WITHHOLDING TAX RATES

	Construction contracts payments	Interest	Dividends	Commercial Royalties	Management or Consultancy Fees	Payments to Entertainers and Sports persons	Rent	Commission/ brokerage fees	Surplus mine rehabilitation funds
	Statutory Rates								
Residents	3%	10%	7.5%	-	-	-	5%	10%	10%
Non-Residents	3%	15%	7.5%	15%	15%	10%	5%	10%	10%
Treaty Countries	**Treaty rates**								
Barbados	3%	10%	5%/12%	10%	10%	10%	5%	10%	-
France	3%	10%	5%/12%	10%	7.5%	10%	5%	7.5%	-
India	3%	10%	7.5%/10%	10%	10%	10%	5%	10%	-

	Construction contracts payments	Interest	Dividends	Commercial Royalties	Management or Consultancy Fees	Payments to Entertainers and Sports persons	Rent	Commission/ brokerage fees	Surplus mine rehabilitation funds
Lesotho	3%	10%	10%/15%	10%	10%	10%	5%	10%	-
Mauritius	3%	12%	5%/10%	12.5%	15%	10%	5%	15%	-
Namibia	3%	10%	10%	10%	15%	10%	5%	15%	-
Russia	3%	10%	5%/10%	10%	10%	10%	5%	10%	-
Seychelles	3%	7.5%	5%/10%	10%	10%	10%	5%	10%	-
South Africa	3%	10%	10%/15%	10%	10%	10%	5%	10%	-
Swaziland	3%	10%	10%/15%	10%	10%	10%	5%	10%	-
Sweden	3%	7.5%	5%/10%	10%	15%	10%	5%	15%	-
UK	3%	10%	5%/12%	10%	7.5%	10%	5%	7.5%	-
Zimbabwe	3%	10%	5%/10%	10%	10%	10%	5%	10%	-

B. Gross-up Clauses

Gross-up provisions may be permissible depending on the agreement made between the parties to a contractual agreement.

V. Trademarks

Please advise us as to whether there are any special requirements for granting a valid trademark license, including the use of a registered user agreement or a short trademark license agreement and any required filing of such an agreement with the trademark authorities.

Intellectual property rights in Botswana are governed by the *Industrial Property Act Chapter 68:03*. Under *Section 67 of the Act*, owners of trademarks are entitled to enter into contracts to license the use of trademarks by others. Section 67 provides for effective control by the licensor of the quality of the goods or services under which such trademark is being licensed.

Section 71 of the same Act stipulates that a license contract concerning a registered trademark has to be filed and recorded by the Registrar in the appropriate register.

In Botswana, the registration of trademarks is regulated under the *Industrial Property Act, 2010*. Under *Section 76*, provision is made for registration of a trademark. This process involves the filing of a written application plus the prescribed fee. This fee can be revised by the Minister of Trade and Industry from time to time. For every application for registration of a trademark, *Article 4 of the Paris Convention* shall apply (right of priority).

After filing, the Registrar of Trademarks shall assess the application to verify that it meets the standard requirements under the Act.

Section 92 of the Act deals with licensing for the use of the trademark by the registered proprietor, to the effect that any license so issued shall provide for the effective control by the licensor of the quality of the goods or services of the license in connection with which the mark is used.

The regulatory authority reserves the right to reject registration of a trademark if it fails to meet the specified standards of the definition of a "mark" under *Section 74(1)*.

Section 74(1) provides that a mark is not capable of registration if (i) it fails to distinguish the goods or services of one business from the other, (ii) is contrary to public policy or morality, (iii) is likely to mislead the public with regard to geographical origin or identical to a mark already in existence, (iv) the mark has acquired status of custom to be used in the particular trade, or (v) it is similar to what can be referred to as national emblems, flags, or any official government mark.

VI. Restrictions on Transfer

Please advise as to whether there are any restrictions on (1) a franchisor to restrict transfers by a master franchisee, any interest in a master franchisee, or the assets of the master franchisee or (2) the ability of a master franchisee to control and/or restrict transfers of a subfranchisee's rights under a master franchise agreement, interest in the subfranchisee, or the assets of the subfranchisee.

Botswana

A. In Relation to Master Franchisee

Under Botswana Law there is no specific regime governing the franchise agreement. The parties may agree on any provision that is not against the law or public policy.

1. Assignment

Generally, neither party may assign its contractual position without the prior consent of the other party. While it is common for franchise agreements to subject the franchisee's right to assign its contractual position to the consent of the franchisor, this also applies automatically per direct operation of the law, if the agreement does not expressly provide for such a rule.

2. Change of Control

It is permissible under Botswana law to subject to the franchisor's consent the right of the franchisee's shareholders to transfer their interest in the share capital of a franchisee.

3. Transfer of Assets

A clause by virtue of which the franchisee becomes obliged, upon termination of the franchise agreement, to transfer to the franchisor (or to another entity designated by the franchisor) all assets used in the franchise is permissible and also common in franchise agreements. The parties are free to determine whether such provision shall be included in the agreement and, if so, the mechanism to calculate the value of these assets.

B. In Relation to Subfranchisees.

4. Assignment

Neither party may assign its contractual position without the prior consent of the other. Therefore, although it may not be expressly provided for in the subfranchise agreement, a party may not assign its contractual position without the other's approval.

Moreover, the parties may also agree to subject the subfranchisee's right to assign its contractual position to the consent of the franchisor.

5. Change of Control

It is permissible under Botswana law to subject to the franchisor's consent the right of the franchisee's shareholders to transfer their interest in the share capital of a franchisee.

6. Transfer of Assets

The parties may agree on any terms as to how the assets may be transferred upon termination of the franchise. The parties are also at liberty to include any other clauses in the franchise agreement relating to transfer of such assets and how to value the assets upon such transfer.

VII. Termination

Please advise us as to any laws relating to termination in your country, such as agency laws, required indemnity provisions, notice or "good cause" requirements, or other laws affecting termination of a franchise agreement. Please describe.

A franchise agreement will terminate in the same manner as any other contract. Termination will arise upon the mutual agreement or by breach of performance of material contractual obligation by either of the parties. A franchise agreement may also be terminated due to unforeseen occurrence or other conditions.

VIII. Governing Law, Jurisdiction, and Dispute Resolution

A. Choice of Law of Foreign Jurisdiction

Please confirm whether the choice of law of a foreign jurisdiction would likely to be upheld under the law of the country, except for certain matters such as trademarks, bankruptcy, and competition matters, which we assume would be governed by the law in your country.

The choice of law designated by the parties will be upheld in Botswana as long as the parties agreed upon it. However, the choice of law should not be against the public policy of Botswana. If there is no choice of law assigned and chosen by the parties, the jurisdiction of Botswana law will take precedence.

B. International Arbitration Dispute Resolution

Please confirm that a court in your country would honor an election of international arbitration dispute resolution, and therefore refuse to hear any disputes arising under a franchise agreement.

The law in Botswana regulating and governing arbitration is set out in the *Arbitration Act Chapter 06.01* of the *Botswana Laws*. Upon a dispute arising, parties are free to choose their arbitrators or mediators. They are also free to choose their seat of arbitration resolution.

The recognition and enforcement of *Foreign Arbitral Award Act, Chapter 06:02 of Botswana Laws* ("FAA") governs foreign arbitral awards made somewhere other than in Botswana. It also gives effect to some provisions of the *Convention on the Recognition and Enforcement of Foreign Arbitral Awards* (the "New York Convention"). Botswana is a signatory to the convention.

Botswana

Section 3(2) of the FAA provides that the provisions of the act shall apply to awards arising under legal relationships whether contractual or not as long as they are considered commercial relationships under the laws of Botswana.

Section 3(3) of the FAA provides that no arbitral award made in any country that is party to the New York Convention shall be enforceable in Botswana, unless similar awards made in Botswana would be enforceable in such country. Local courts can intervene or challenge the award only if the following has occurred:

- the subject matter of the dispute is not capable of settlement by arbitration under the law of that country;
- recognition of such award would be contrary to the public policy of that country;
- one of the parties was under some incapacity;
- the agreement is not valid under the law to which the parties have subjected it or under the law of the country where the award was made;
- the party against whom the award is invoked was not given proper notice of the appointment of the arbitrator or notice of arbitration proceedings to present his case;
- the award deals with a dispute not contemplated by or not falling within the terms of the submission;
- the composition of the arbitral authority is not in accordance with the agreement of the parties; and
- the award has not yet become binding on the parties, and has been set aside or suspended by a competent authority of the country in which or under the law of which that award was made.

Finally, obtaining recognition of a foreign arbitral award under the laws of Botswana entails following the procedure set out in the New York Convention.

IX. Non-Competition Provisions

If the franchise agreement prohibits the master franchisee from engaging in certain competitive activities during the term of the agreement, and for a 12-month period after the termination or expiration of the agreement, please comment on the enforceability of non-competition covenants in your country.

Generally, since there is no specific legal regime governing franchise agreements, the parties themselves may agree on competition provisions. However, such provisions shall not be against public policy of Botswana law and should also not hinder others from engaging in and competing in the particular market.

X. Language Requirements

Does the law in your country require that a franchise agreement be translated into the local language in order to be enforceable between the parties?

The English language is predominantly used in commercial transactions. There is no requirement for an agreement to be translated into Setswana, the national language of Botswana.

XI. Other Significant Matters

Please advise as to whether there are any significant matters not addressed above of which a franchisor should be aware in connection with its entering into a franchise agreement in your country.

There are no other significant matters to be addressed.

Franchising in Burundi

Gilbert Nyatanyi

ENSafrica | Burundi

Bujumbura, Burundi

Burundi

I. Introduction

A. Historical Background of Country

Burundi's first democratically elected president was assassinated in October 1993 after only 100 days in office, triggering widespread ethnic violence between Hutu and Tutsi factions. More than 200,000 Burundians perished during the conflict that spanned almost a dozen years. Hundreds of thousands of Burundians were internally displaced or became refugees in neighboring countries. An internationally brokered power-sharing agreement between the Tutsi-dominated government and the Hutu rebels in 2003 paved the way for a transition process that led to an integrated defense force, established a new constitution in 2005, and elected a majority Hutu government in 2005. The government of President Pierre Nkurunziza, who was reelected in 2010, continues to face many political and economic challenges.

B. Economy of the Country

Burundi's economy is predominantly agricultural; agriculture accounts for just over 30% of GDP and employs more than 90% of the population. Burundi's primary exports are coffee and tea, which account for 90% of foreign exchange earnings, though exports are a relatively small share of GDP. Burundi's export earnings—and its ability to pay for imports—rests primarily on weather conditions and international coffee and tea prices. Burundi will remain heavily dependent on aid from bilateral and multilateral donors—foreign aid represents 42% of Burundi's national income, the second highest rate in Sub-Saharan Africa. Burundi joined the East African Community in 2009, which should boost Burundi's regional trade ties, and also in 2009 received $700 million in debt relief.

C. Franchise Legal Overview

Under Burundian law, there is no specific law that regulates franchise agreements and/or transactions. The franchise agreement is seen as a contractual agreement between the parties and thus contract law will govern such an agreement.

II. Regulatory Requirements

A. Pre-Sale Disclosure

Please describe any pre-sale franchise disclosure or similar requirements that may apply to franchise transactions.

No pre-sale franchise disclosure or similar requirements apply to franchise transactions under the laws of Burundi.

B. Governmental Approvals, Registrations, Filing Requirements

Please describe any necessary government approvals, registrations, or filing requirements that may apply to franchise transactions.

Local law does not provide that the effectiveness of a franchise transaction is dependent on any formalities beyond the execution of a written contract, such as government approvals, registration, or filing requirements.

C. Limits of Fees and Typical Term of Franchise Agreement

Please describe any limits upon the nature and extent of fees and the term of a typical franchise agreement.

There are no limits upon the nature and extent of fees and the term of a typical franchise agreement.

III. Currency

If all payments under a franchise agreement must be made in immediately available U.S. Dollars, please advise as to any restrictions, reporting requirements, or regulations concerning the exchange, repatriation, or remittance of U.S. Dollars.

Pursuant to local regulations and exchange rules, such as Articles 61-63 of the *Rules of Exchange of June 2010*, repatriation by a non-resident of investment is free. To repatriate funds, a request must be submitted to the bank for transmission to the Central Bank (*Banque de la République du Burundi*) with the following information and/or documents:

- the amount to be repatriated,
- the sales contract or any other document showing the origin of the amount to be transferred, and
- a certificate of non-indebtedness issued by the Burundi Revenue Authority (*Office Burundais des Recettes*).

Capital transfers, investments in financial markets, and investments abroad by residents are subject to the approval of the Central Bank. The entry of foreign currency in the form of investment is free but must be registered.

IV. Taxes, Tariffs, and Duties

Please do not provide any in-depth comments on tax structuring. However, please provide your general comments on the typical amount of withholding tax that would apply and whether a "gross-up" provision contained in a franchise agreement would be enforceable in your country.

Burundians tax rates are as follows:

A. Corporate Income Tax.

The general corporate tax rate is 30%.

B. Dividends.

A withholding tax of 15% is levied on all dividends paid by a resident company to a resident or a non-resident.

C. Management Fees.

A 15% withholding tax is levied on management fees.

D. Royalties.

Any professional income earned in Burundi is taxable per month according to the following table:

Tax Bands (in Burundian Francs)		Tax rate
From	To	
0	150,000	0%
150,001	300,000	20% of the amount that exceeds BIF 150,000
300,001	more	30% of the amount that exceeds BIF 300,000

The rate of the Value Added Tax, including rent for offices is 18%.

Burundi has signed a double taxation agreement within the East African Community, which includes Rwanda, Tanzania, Uganda, and Kenya. However, please note that the agreement is not yet in force. Burundi does not have a double taxation agreement with the United States.

V. Trademarks

Please advise us as to whether there are any special requirements for granting a valid trademark license, including the use of a registered user agreement or a short trademark license agreement and any required filing of such an agreement with the trademark authorities.

The license agreement must provide for control by the licensor over the services and products of the licensee. Otherwise, according to Article 334 of *Law no. 1/13 of July 28, 2009 relating to Industrial Property in Burundi*, the Court may declare that the trademark has been abandoned by its holder. The aforementioned law does not provide that the Department of Industrial Property must validate the contract to make it applicable.

While Burundian law does not specifically provide for contractual licensing, it is possible that a license agreement containing quality-control provisions will not jeopardize rights under a trademark registration.[258]

VI. Restrictions on Transfer

Please advise as to whether there are any restrictions on (1) a franchisor to restrict transfers in a master franchisee, any interest in a master franchisee, or the assets of the master franchisee or (2) the ability of a master franchisee to control and/or restrict transfers of a subfranchisee's rights under a master franchise agreement, interest in the subfranchisee, or the assets of the subfranchisee.

[258] Edward Fennessy and International Contributors, *Trademarks Throughout the World, Fifth Edition, Release #18 28-5*, THOMAS REUTERS/WEST (2012).

Since there is no legal framework specific to franchise agreements in Burundi, the parties may freely contract regarding provisions on restrictions on transfer in the franchise agreement.

VII. Termination

Please advise us as to any laws relating to termination in your country, such as agency laws, required indemnity provisions, notice or "good cause" requirements, or other laws affecting termination of a franchise agreement. Please describe.

While there are no specific laws governing termination of franchise agreements, various provisions of Burundian law govern termination in the commercial setting including under the local labor law, and commercial law. For example, certain provisions of *Law no 1/07 of April 26, 2010 on Commercial Act* provides for an indemnity in the event of termination of an agency agreement.

Pursuant to Article 225 of *Law no 1/07 of April 26, 2010 on Commercial Act* in the following instances the indemnity will not apply:

- when the breach is provoked by the gross negligence of the commercial agent;
- when the termination is the result of the commercial agent, unless it can be justified by circumstances attributable to the mandator or if it is due to the impossibility for the agent to continue its activity because of his age, infirmity, or illness;
- when after agreeing, the commercial agent cedes to a third party its rights and contractual obligations.

Local practice indicates that the parties may avoid a franchise agreement being defined as an agency agreement in Burundi by waiving any agency relationship in the franchise agreement.

Burundi

VIII. Governing Law, Jurisdiction, and Dispute Resolution

A. Choice of Law of Foreign Jurisdiction

Please confirm whether the choice of law of a foreign jurisdiction would likely to be upheld under the law of the country, except for certain matters such as trademarks, bankruptcy, and competition matters, which we assume would be governed by the law in your country.

The choice of a law of a foreign jurisdiction law can be upheld under the laws of Burundi provided that it is not contrary to public policy principles or public law in Burundi.

Under Trademarks Article 478 of *Law no 1/13 of July 28, 2009 relating to Industrial Property in Burundi* provisions of the international industrial property treaties to which Burundi is a party shall apply to the matters governed by the law and prevail in the event of conflict with the provisions of this law.

B. International Arbitration Dispute Resolution

Please confirm that a court in your country would honor an election of international arbitration dispute resolution, and therefore refuse to hear any disputes arising under a franchise agreement.

In order to enforce a foreign judgment or arbitral award in Burundi, an exequatur of such foreign judgment or arbitral award should be applied for. The exequatur will be granted if the foreign judgment or arbitral award fulfills the following conditions:

- the judgment or arbitral award does not contain any element that is contrary to public policy principles or public law in Burundi;

- the judgment or arbitral award is final;
- the court or tribunal that rendered the judgment or arbitral award did not obtain jurisdiction solely by reason of the plaintiff's nationality;
- due process has been observed and the defendant was given an opportunity to defend itself in the proceedings resulting in the judgment or arbitral award; and
- a copy of the judgment or arbitral award is submitted which satisfies the conditions necessary for its authenticity.

Burundi is not a signatory to the *Convention on the Recognition and Enforcement of Foreign Arbitral Awards* (the "New York Convention") but has initiated procedures to become a signatory.

IX. Non-Competition Provisions

If the franchise agreement prohibits the master franchisee from engaging in certain competitive activities during the term of the agreement, and for a 12-month period after the termination or expiration of the agreement, please comment on the enforceability of non-competition covenants in your country.

Pursuant to Article 22 of *Law no 1/06 of March 25, 2010 on the Legal Regime of Competition* a non-competition provision is valid if it is limited in scope and in time and space.

X. Language Requirements

Does the law in your country require that a franchise agreement be translated into the local language in order to be enforceable between the parties?

It is not required that the franchise agreement be translated into the local language in order to be enforceable between parties. However, please note that it should be translated into Kirundi (national language) or French (official language) before instituting legal action.

XI. Other Significant Matters

Please advise as to whether there are any significant matters not addressed above of which a franchisor should be aware in connection with its entering into a franchise agreement in your country.

Brassieres et Limonaderies de Burundi S.A. - Brarudi S.A. is operating under license of the Coca-Cola Company. The agreement includes use of Coca-Cola trademarks. Landline number of Brarudi S.A. is: + 257 22215360. Web site: www.brarudi.net.

Hilton Worldwide signed a license agreement with the Opulent Group as franchisee who will operate the former Novotel as a DoubleTree by Hilton in Bujumbura, Burundi, Tel: +25722222600; +25722227606.

Franchising in Cape Verde

João Afonso Fialho

Miranda Correia Amendoeira & Associados

Lisbon, Portugal

Cape Verde

I. Introduction

A. Historical Background of Country

Following independence in 1975, and a tentative interest in unification with Guinea-Bissau, a one-party system was established and maintained until multi-party elections were held in 1990. Cape Verde continues to exhibit one of Africa's most stable democratic governments. Repeated droughts during the second half of the 20th century caused significant hardship and prompted heavy emigration. As a result, Cape Verde's expatriate population is greater than its domestic one.

B. Economy of the Country

This island economy suffers from a poor natural resource base, including serious water shortages exacerbated by cycles of long-term drought. The economy is service-oriented with commerce, transport, tourism, and public services accounting for about three-fourths of GDP. Although nearly 70% of the population lives in rural areas, the share of food production in GDP is low. About 82% of food must be imported. The fishing potential, mostly lobster and tuna, is not fully exploited. Cape Verde annually runs a high trade deficit financed by foreign aid and remittances from emigrants; remittances supplement GDP by more than 20%. Economic reforms are aimed at developing the private sector and attracting foreign investment to diversify the economy. Future prospects depend heavily on the maintenance of aid flows, the encouragement of tourism, remittances, and the momentum of the government's development program. Cape Verde became a member of the WTO in July 2008.

C. Franchise Legal Overview

Cape Verde has a civil law legal system. Most of the provisions governing contracts are established in the Civil Code or in other statutes.

Cape Verde

Cape Verdean contract law is governed by the principle of contractual freedom. Within the limits set forth in the law, parties may freely agree on the terms of a contract. This principle is expressly contained in the Civil Code, approved by *Decree-law 47344, of November 25, 1966*, as amended ("Civil Code").

In relation to the franchise agreements, there is no specific statute governing franchising in Cape Verde. Thus, the contractual relationship (rights and obligations) established between the parties in a franchise agreement must be construed in accordance with the provisions of the Civil Code or other statutes that may also be applicable.

In the absence of a specific statute, a franchise agreement is simply an agreement aimed at governing a relationship between two business parties, and therefore qualifies as a non-standard commercial agreement. The legal regime for this type of agreement is set forth in the Commercial Code, approved by *Letter of Law dated June 28, 1888*, as amended ("Commercial Code").

II. Regulatory Requirements

A. Pre-Sale Disclosure

Please describe any pre-sale franchise disclosure or similar requirements that may apply to franchise transactions.

No pre-sale franchise disclosure or similar requirements apply to franchise transactions under the laws of Cape Verde.

B. Governmental Approvals, Registrations, Filing Requirements

Please describe any necessary government approvals, registrations, or filing requirements that may apply to franchise transactions.

Other than the registration referred to below—*see* Section III (Currency)—no other government approval, registration, or filing requirements shall apply to franchise agreements.

Notwithstanding the above, a Cape Verdean franchisor or franchisee will be subject to the regular registration procedures and filing requirements required for performing business activities in Cape Verde, such as, inter alia, commercial registration with the Companies Registrar, if applicable; tax registration with the Tax Office; obtaining a commercial operations permit from the Ministry of Commerce; and an import/export license.

C. Limits of Fees and Typical Term of Franchise Agreement

Please describe any limits upon the nature and extent of fees and the term of a typical franchise agreement.

As there is no specific legal framework governing the franchise agreement, the parties are free to agree on the terms and conditions of a franchise agreement as long as they keep within certain general public policy principles established in the Constitution, the Commercial Code, and/or the Civil Code, and are in compliance with the general principles of law and justice. There are no other limits on the nature and extent of fees and the term that shall apply.

III. Currency

If all payments under a franchise agreement must be made in immediately available U.S. Dollars, please advise as to any restrictions, reporting requirements, or regulations concerning the exchange, repatriation, or remittance of U.S. Dollars.

Transfer of foreign currency into or out of Cape Verde is subject to the controls and prior authorization of the Central Bank ("*Banco de Cabo Verde*"). However, this is not a particularly restrictive regime and a relevant party is simply required to submit relevant documentation to the Central Bank prior to requesting a transfer.

In order to obtain the Central Bank's authorization, the interested party must submit a request to a commercial local bank attaching all documentation evidencing and explaining the relevant transaction. To that end, a Portuguese language translation of the agreement will most likely be necessary. The commercial bank will then liaise with the Central Bank to obtain the necessary authorization. The Bank's authorization is granted in almost all cases, particularly since there has not been an instance of a shortage of foreign currency in the last 15 years.

IV. Taxes, Tariffs, and Duties

Please do not provide any in-depth comments on tax structuring. However, please provide your general comments on the typical amount of withholding tax that would apply and whether a "gross-up" provision contained in a franchise agreement would be enforceable in your country.

A. Applicable Rate

From a Cape Verdean tax standpoint, payments as consideration for the rendering of management services, advertising, publicity, as well as royalty fees paid under a franchising agreement may trigger income tax withholding.

Cape Verde at present has only two international double taxation treaties on income tax in force, with Portugal and Macau. Apart from these treaties, there is no other available mechanism to reduce or eliminate the assessment of withholding tax in Cape Verde, thus, international tax relief for non-resident investors (besides Portuguese and Macau based investors) can only be obtained in their home jurisdiction.

Pursuant to the *Single Tax on Income Code* as approved by the *Law 127/IV/95*, of June 26, 1995 and *Decree-Law 1/96* of January 15, 1996, as amended (*Imposto Único sobre os*

Rendimentos), income, as defined in the several categories of taxable income, obtained by a non-resident franchisor from a Cape Verdean source (i.e., paid by a resident franchisee), is subject to withholding tax, depending on the nature of the payment.[259]

Given the above, according to the Cape Verde State Budget for 2010, income obtained as a consideration for the rendering of services by a non-resident franchisor is subject to a withholding of 20% of the gross income.

The term royalties, as defined under the Single Tax on Income Code, includes payments arising from the use or the right to use industrial and commercial equipment, the granting of information concerning industrial, commercial, or scientific experience and technical assistance, and, thus, royalty fees paid under a franchising agreement to a non-resident franchisor will be subject to 15% withholding.

Payments made between Cape Verde taxpayers are not subject to income tax withholding, and will be considered as business profits subject to the annual 25% Single Tax on Income.

B. Gross-up Clauses

Tax gross-up clauses are valid and contractually binding pursuant to Cape Verdean tax law and should preclude any economic loss in the event that any tax is due to the Cape Verdean tax authorities on any payments made under a franchising agreement. Notwithstanding, such clauses, from a tax standpoint, are not binding for the tax authorities since legally it is not possible to assign responsibility for the payment of any taxes in Cape Verde.

---

[259] Non-resident franchisors with no permanent establishment in Cape Verde are only subject to tax on income from Cape Verdean sources.

V. Trademarks

Please advise us as to whether there are any special requirements for granting a valid trademark license, including the use of a registered user agreement or a short trademark license agreement and any required filing of such an agreement with the trademark authorities.

Intellectual property in Cape Verde is regulated by the *Cape Verdean Industrial Property Code* (*Código de Propriedade Industrial*), as approved by the *Council of Ministers' Decree 4/2007* of August 20, 2007. This Code allows one party to license a registered trademark to a third party. Article 173 of that Code is the specific provision governing the relationship between licensee and licensor. Under this Article, the trademark owner is entitled to claim its rights as owner of the trademark against the licensee. This would apply in particular when the licensee has breached any clause or provision of the licensing agreement, particularly those that deal with its term, the distinctiveness of a trademark, the nature or quality of the goods or services for which the license was granted, or any geographic limitations to the use of the licensed trademark.

The law does not establish any particular requirement or formalities to enter into a trademark license agreement or to file the licensing agreement with the trademark office.

VI. Restrictions on Transfer

Please advise as to whether there are any restrictions on (1) a franchisor to restrict transfers by a master franchisee, any interest in a master franchisee, or the assets of the master franchisee or (2) the ability of a master franchisee to control and/or restrict transfers of a subfranchisee's rights under a master franchise agreement, interest in the subfranchisee, or the assets of the subfranchisee.

Cape Verdean law does not set forth any specific restrictions on the franchisor's ability to restrict the (i) transfers by a master franchisee, (ii) transfers of an interest in a master franchisee, or (iii) transfers of assets of the master franchisee, nor does it do so on the master's franchisee's ability to control and/or restrict (i) transfers of a subfranchisee's rights under a master franchise agreement, (ii) transfers of an interest in the subfranchisee, or (iii) transfers of assets of the subfranchisee.

Considering the private nature of a franchise agreement, the parties may, within the scope of their contractual freedom, introduce such clauses as they see fit, provided they are not unlawful or against public order.

In relation to the assignment of a party's contractual position, the Civil Code sets forth that neither party may assign its contractual position without the prior consent of the other.

In relation to the subfranchise agreement, the same principles apply. In other words, the assignment by one of the parties is subject to the consent of the other and it may also be subject to the prior consent of a third party, unless the relevant consent is previously agreed in the contract. The law allows for general, non-specific consent without the name of the assignee being set.

Under Cape Verdean law, it is permissible to subject to the consent of the franchisor the right of the franchisee's shareholders to transfer their (direct and/or indirect) interests in the share capital of the franchisee. Also, the parties may further agree that the subfranchisee's shareholders may only transfer their (direct and/or indirect) interests in the subfranchisee's share capital upon the franchisor's approval. However, in both cases, the shareholders accepting these restrictions must execute the relevant agreement.

Under the law, the parties may agree on a clause by virtue of which the franchisee/subfranchisee becomes obliged, upon termination of the franchise/subfranchise agreement, to transfer to the franchisor/franchisee (or to other entity nominated by the franchisor) all the assets used in the franchise/subfranchise. On the other hand, the same provision may be agreed between the parties, but in respect of the franchisor, (i.e., obliging the subfranchisee to transfer to the franchisor the relevant assets upon termination of the subfranchise agreement), the franchisor must also be part of the relevant agreement.

The parties must determine whether such provisions must be included in the agreement and, if so, the mechanism to calculate the value of these assets.

VII. Termination

Please advise us as to any laws relating to termination in your country, such as agency laws, required indemnity provisions, notice or "good cause" requirements, or other laws affecting termination of a franchise agreement. Please describe.

As mentioned above in Section I, in the absence of a specific regime governing the franchise agreement, the Civil Code rules apply. Causes for termination are those that are commonly accepted, such as (i) mutual agreement, (ii) unilateral termination, and (iii) the occurrence of any of the events as may be agreed between the parties. In the event of termination by one of the parties, compensation for damages must be paid.

VIII. Governing Law, Jurisdiction, and Dispute Resolution

A. Choice of Law of Foreign Jurisdiction

Please confirm whether the choice of law of a foreign jurisdiction would likely to be upheld under the law of the country, except for certain matters such as trademarks, bankruptcy, and competition matters, which we assume would be governed by the law in your country.

The Civil Code sets out the general principle that the parties may freely choose the law governing their agreements provided that such choice of law corresponds to a serious interest of the parties and has a relevant connection with an element of the contract. A foreign law is deemed to have a connection with the underlying contract if it is the law of: (i) the domicile of the parties (or of one of them); (ii) the place of performance of the contractual obligations (place of shipment of the goods or acceptance of orders, place of payment, etc.); or (iii) the place where the contract was executed.

In the absence of such a relevant connection, the other party may claim that the choice of law and the election of a certain court do not serve any serious legally protected interest and the Cape Verdean courts may consider themselves as having competence to rule on the case.

The abovementioned choice of law principle is limited by the conflict of laws principles included in Cape Verdean law. In accordance with such principles, the law of a foreign jurisdiction shall not be applicable if deemed contrary to (i) the public policy principles of Cape Verdean Law (which will always apply, even if the governing law chosen by the parties is not Cape Verdean law), and (ii) the mandatory provisions of Cape Verdean law. A provision qualifies as mandatory whenever the law expressly states so.

In the absence of a treaty or convention between Cape Verde and the relevant country on the recognition and enforcement of foreign awards, a judgment passed by a foreign court would have to be confirmed by the Cape Verdean Supreme Court[260] to be enforceable in Cape Verde. This confirmation process is purely formal and the Supreme Court limits its intervention to the verification of the compliance with the principles of due process of law and little more to issue the "exequatur" and allow the enforcements of the judgment before the lower courts (no decision on the merits involved).

---

[260] Pursuant to the Cape Verdean Civil Procedure Code, the Courts of Appeals are the courts with jurisdiction to entertain procedures for the recognition and confirmation of foreign decisions. The Courts of Appeals, however, have not yet been installed, therefore according to *Law 88/VII/2011, February 14, 2011 on the organization, operation and jurisdiction of the law courts*, the Supreme Court shall remain the court with jurisdiction for such procedures until they come into operation for the Courts of Appeals.

Cape Verde

B. International Arbitration Dispute Resolution

Please confirm that a court in your country would honor an election of international arbitration dispute resolution, and therefore refuse to hear any disputes arising under a franchise agreement.

As to the choice of a foreign venue for any arbitral proceedings, *Cape Verdean Arbitration Law* (*Law 76/VI/2005, of August 16, 2005*) recognizes the concept of "international arbitration" and allows the parties to choose the venue at which the arbitral proceedings are to take place.

Cape Verde is not a signatory of the *Convention on the Recognition and Enforcement of Foreign Arbitral Awards* (the "New York Convention"). This does not, however, mean that Cape Verde will not recognize and enforce foreign arbitral awards.

In accordance with the Cape Verdean Civil Procedure Code, (approved by *Legislative Decree 7/2010, July 1, 2010*, and rectified on September 27, 2010) and the Arbitration Law, to be enforceable in Cape Verde foreign arbitral awards are subject to recognition and confirmation by the Supreme Court. This procedure consists of a formal review of the relevant foreign arbitral award and does not imply a rehearing or any other decision on the merits of the case.

Foreign arbitral awards will be recognized and enforced in Cape Verde, unless:

- the arbitration agreement is not valid under the governing law thereof;
- the party against which the enforcement is sought was not given proper notice of the appointment of the arbitrator or of the arbitration proceedings, or its procedural rights were otherwise denied;

- the award concerns a dispute not comprised in the arbitration clause, or contains matters beyond the scope of the arbitration. In such case the award may only be enforced to the extent that it contains decisions on matters validly submitted to arbitration;

- the constitution of the arbitral court or the arbitral was not in accordance with agreement of the parties or, failing such agreement, with the law of the place where the hearing took place (the "lex loci arbitri");

- the award has not yet become enforceable upon the parties, or has been set aside or suspended by a court of competent jurisdiction, either in the country where the award was issued or pursuant to the law of the arbitration agreement;

- the matter under dispute could not be referred to arbitration;

- the recognition or the enforcement of the awards would contravene Cape Verdean public order; or

- the country where the award was issued would not recognize or enforce an arbitral award issued in Cape Verde.

IX. Non-Competition Provisions

If the franchise agreement prohibits the master franchisee from engaging in certain competitive activities during the term of the agreement, and for a 12-month period after the termination or expiration of the agreement, please comment on the enforceability of non-competition covenants in your country.

It is common practice to include non-competition provisions in commercial agreements. Therefore, the parties in a franchise agreement may freely agree on non-competition provisions, such as the prohibition of the franchisee from engaging in certain competitive activities during the term of the agreement and for a 12-month period after the termination or expiration of the agreement, and such agreed rules would be considered enforceable.

In any case, it is common to extend the prohibition of competition (i) to affiliates and related persons/entities of the franchisee and (ii) for a certain period after termination of the franchise agreement. However, as previously noted, as a non-regulated agreement, the parties are free to agree on the existence of a non-competition provision and its terms, always in compliance with the general principles of the law.

X. Language Requirements

Does the law in your country require that a franchise agreement be translated into the local language in order to be enforceable between the parties?

The civil law allows private agreements to be executed in a foreign language. However, if an agreement is to be filed with any public authority in a foreign language, a Portuguese sworn translation is required.

By way of *Decree 1/2009, January 19, 2009*, the Cape Verdean government approved *The Hague Convention of October 5, 1961* ("Convention"), which waives the requirement of legalizing public documents from countries that are signatories to the Convention. The Convention entered into force in Cape Verde on February 10, 2010.

For the purposes of the Convention, public documents include (i) documents originated from an authority or official of a state, including the attorney general and the courts; (ii) administrative documents; (iii) acts carried out before or by a public notary; and (iv) official certificates that are placed on documents signed by persons in their private capacity, such as authentication of signatures by a notary.

Cape Verde

XI. Other Significant Matters

Please advise as to whether there are any significant matters not addressed above of which a franchisor should be aware in connection with its entering into a franchise agreement in your country.

There are no other significant matters to be addressed.

Franchising in Democratic Republic of the Congo

Emery Mukendi Wafwana, Nady Mayifuila Dina, Jonathan van Kempen, Edouard Laddy Tshishimbi Mpamba, Emmanuel Otshudiema Bengu and Dr. Sancy Lenoble Matschinga

Emery Mukendi Wafwana & Associates

Kinshasa/Gombe, DRC

Democratic Republic of the Congo

I. Introduction

A. Historical Background of Country

The Democratic Republic of the Congo ("DRC"), formerly known as Zaire, is located in central Africa, surrounded by nine neighboring countries.

The DRC is a civil law country, whose private law is based on the *1804 Napoleonic Civil Code*. The general characteristics of the DRC legal system are very similar to legal systems in force in other French-speaking African countries. At the apex of the legal system, the *DRC Constitution of February 18, 2006,* is the first source of law.

Since September 12, 2012, all provisions of the *Organization for Business Law in Africa* ("OHADA") Treaty[261] as well as *OHADA Uniform Acts* are applicable in the DRC.[262] This set of applicable laws brings increased modernity and reliability to the domestic legal system, as well as a new court, the Common Court of Justice and Arbitration ("CCJA"). It is the highest competent court in the DRC for matters covered by the OHADA Uniform Acts.

Various legal areas not covered by the *OHADA Uniform Acts* are also being reformed. For example, reforms in the insurance and electricity sectors are planned to end the state's monopoly in these sectors. The DRC, notably through the creation of the national agency for the investment promotion (*Agence Nationale pour la Promotion de l'Investissement* "ANAPI") and the

261 OHADA is an African organization, established on October 17, 1993, which currently counts 17 member states, including Benin, Burkina Faso, Cameroon, Central African Republic, Chad, the Republic of Congo, Comoros, Cote d'Ivoire, the DRC, Equatorial Guinea, Gabon, Guinea, Guinea Bissau, Mali, Niger, Senegal, and Togo.

262 There are currently nine uniform acts promulgated by OHADA, including a uniform act on commercial law and a uniform act on agreements of transportation of goods by road.

steering committee for the improvement of the business and investment climate (*Comité de Pilotage pour l'Amélioration du Climat des Affaires et des Investissements* "CPCAI") as well as its legal reforms, has shown a willingness to facilitate and increase investments. Such a desire is confirmed by the DRC's imminent accession to the *New York Convention on the Recognition and Enforcement of Foreign Arbitral Awards* of June 10, 1958 (the "New York Convention").

B. Economy of the Country

The DRC is immensely rich in natural resources and holds some of the world's largest mineral deposits, which play an important role in the DRC economy. DRC's economy grew 7.2% in 2012 and as agriculture and extractive industries remain pillars of the DRC economy, increasing global demands in minerals and investments in the sector should keep the economy growing. The mining industry contributes about 28% to the country's GDP.

C. Franchise Legal Overview

Under DRC law, there is no specific law that regulates franchise agreements and/or transactions. The franchise agreement is seen as a contractual agreement between parties and thus contract law will govern such an agreement.

However, specific laws or regulations governing certain areas, such as labor law or laws regulating commercial leases may have an impact on a particular franchise agreement.

II. Regulatory Requirements

A. Pre-Sale Disclosure

Please describe any pre-sale franchise disclosure or similar requirements that may apply to franchise transactions.

No pre-sale franchise disclosure or similar requirements apply to franchise transactions under the DRC law.

B. Governmental Approvals, Registrations, Filing Requirements

Please describe any necessary government approvals, registrations, or filing requirements that may apply to franchise transactions.

There is no specific requirement under the DRC law for government approvals, registrations, or filing requirements for franchise transactions. However, see Section V of this chapter on trademark licenses regulated under *Law n°82-001 of January 7, 1982 on Industrial Property* (the "Industrial Property Law").

C. Limits of Fees and Typical Term of Franchise Agreement

Please describe any limits upon the nature and extent of fees and the term of a typical franchise agreement.

As stated, a franchise agreement is a contractual agreement between parties. According to the DRC law, parties are free to enter into any contractual agreement, to agree on any terms and conditions and to be bound by the terms to which they agree. There are no specific guidelines on term limits applicable to franchise agreements; therefore, parties are free to indicate the duration of the agreement. Nevertheless, the agreement must not be contrary to mandatory rules and/or DRC public policy law.

III. Currency

If all payments under a franchise agreement must be made in immediately available U.S. Dollars, please advise as to any restrictions, reporting requirements, or regulations concerning the exchange, repatriation, or remittance of U.S. Dollars.

There are no specific restrictions on parties transacting in U.S. Dollars. All repatriation or remittance must be made through an approved DRC bank. The following fees and restrictions apply to remittances. First, the Central Bank of Congo ("BCC") levies a change royalty of 2% on any payment to or from a foreign country regardless of the status of the transferor or transferee; second, cross-border transfers to and from the DRC, with a value equal to or greater than US$ 10,000 must be made through an approved credit institution or intermediary and has to be made on a specific form, known as RC declaration; third, revenues (remuneration, income, dividends, leasehold, interests, etc.) can only be received or transferred through an approved DRC bank.

Repayments of loans, principal, and interests are made in accordance with the terms of the agreement, and require the use of an RC declaration to be issued by a DRC-approved bank.

There is generally no obligation to repatriate foreign earnings to the DRC, except amounts received in payment for the export of goods or services. These must be repatriated through an approved bank within the time frame specified in the BCC's exchange regulations.

IV. Taxes, Tariffs, and Duties

Please do not provide any in-depth comments on tax structuring. However, please provide your general comments on the typical amount of withholding tax that would apply and whether a "gross-up" provision contained in a franchise agreement would be enforceable in your country.

The DRC general tax system provides for direct and indirect taxes. Direct taxes are subdivided between asset-based taxes, which include taxes on real property and on vehicles, and income-based taxes, which include taxes on rental income, taxes on interests and dividends, and professional taxes, which comprise taxes on profits and taxes on salaries. Indirect taxes include Value Added Tax ("VAT"). The DRC tax system provides for a withholding obligation for dividends and interests which are annually taxed at the rate of 22%. Net profits made through activities undertaken in the DRC are taxed at the rate of 40%. The DRC tax system also provides for VAT payable on the gross amount of sales of products or services. Standard VAT rate is 16%.

The DRC entered into a double tax treaty with Belgium, which came into force on December 24, 2011, and with South Africa, which came into force on July 18, 2012.

Gross-up provisions may be permissible depending on the agreement made between the parties to a contractual agreement.

V. Trademarks

Please advise us as to whether there are any special requirements for granting a valid trademark license, including the use of a registered user agreement or a short trademark license agreement and any required filing of such an agreement with the trademark authorities.

In the DRC, industrial and intellectual properties are primarily governed by the Industrial Property Law and *Ordinance-law n°86-033 of April 5, 1986 on the Protection of Copyrights and Neighboring Rights*.

Owners of trademark rights are entitled to enter into license agreements to license the use of trademarks to other parties. A Trademark license agreement needs to be in writing and an original of the license trademark must be filed and registered with the Ministry of Intellectual Property along with registration fees.

VI. Restrictions on Transfer

Please advise as to whether there are any restrictions on (1) a franchisor to restrict transfers by a master franchisee, any interest in a master franchisee, or the assets of the master franchisee or (2) the ability of a master franchisee to control and/or restrict transfers of a subfranchisee's rights under a master franchise agreement, interest in the subfranchisee, or the assets of the subfranchisee.

Under the DRC law there are no restrictions on a franchisor to restrict transfers by a master franchisee, any interest in a master franchisee, or the assets of the master franchisee; or on the ability of a master franchisee to control and/or restrict transfers of a subfranchisee's rights under a master franchise agreement, interest in the subfranchisee, or the assets of the subfranchisee.

Since franchising is generally regulated by contract law, most of the obligations of the parties are usually governed by the terms of the parties' agreement, thus everything depends on the will of the respective parties. The parties may agree on any provision that is not against the law or public policy.

VII. Termination

Please advise us as to any laws relating to termination in your country, such as agency laws, required indemnity provisions, notice or "good cause" requirements, or other laws affecting termination of a franchise agreement. Please describe.

In the DRC, there is currently no specific law on agency or distributorship agreements. Agreements such as franchise agreements are governed by general contract law rules set in the DRC *Civil Law Code*. According to Article 33 of the *Civil Law Code*, terms and conditions set in contracts form the law between the parties. It is, however, worth mentioning that commercial leases and their termination clauses are regulated by specific laws. Notice to terminate a commercial lease is six months. Notice for termination of an employment contract is also regulated in the DRC. Congolese labor law provides that duration of notice is increased with seven working days for each full year of continuous employment.

Franchise agreement may also be terminated due to an unforeseen occurrence or good cause.

VIII. Governing Law, Jurisdiction, and Dispute Resolution

A. Choice of Law of Foreign Jurisdiction

Please confirm whether the choice of law of a foreign jurisdiction would likely to be upheld under the law of the country, except for certain matters such as trademarks, bankruptcy, and competition matters, which we assume would be governed by the law in your country.

The choice of law of a foreign jurisdiction would be upheld under the law of the DRC. The DRC judges will, in principle, enforce franchise agreements governed by foreign law, subject to their compliance with mandatory or public order rules. Matters relating to real estate law, incorporation of companies and creation of security interests, tax and customs law, trademarks, bankruptcy, and labor law will necessarily be subject to the DRC law.

B. International Arbitration Dispute Resolution

Please confirm that a court in your country would honor an election of international arbitration dispute resolution, and therefore refuse to hear any disputes arising under a franchise agreement.

The choice of an international arbitration dispute resolution clause by the parties is authorized by the DRC law as long as the parties agreed upon it. Currently, foreign arbitral awards rendered outside of OHADA member states are recognized and enforced in the DRC after a tribunal of competent authority has rendered an enforcement decision.

Nevertheless, this situation will soon change because a law authorizing the ratification of the New York Convention was recently promulgated. The New York Convention will enter into force in the DRC on the ninetieth day following the date of deposit by the DRC of its instrument of ratification or accession. It should be noted, however, that the DRC made four reservations to the New York Convention.[263] Foreign arbitral awards rendered in other OHADA member states are recognized and enforced in the DRC according to the rules established in the OHADA Uniform Act on Arbitration.

IX. Non-Competition Provisions

If the franchise agreement prohibits the master franchisee from engaging in certain competitive activities during the term of the agreement, and for a 12-month period after the termination or expiration of the agreement, please comment on the enforceability of non-competition covenants in your country.

As previously stated, since franchise is a non-regulated agreement, parties are free to agree on the existence of a non-competition provision and its terms, but always in compliance with general principles of the law.

Non-competition clauses are common in practice. Some guidance may be found in labor law where non-competition clauses are regulated. When such clauses are permissible, they may not exceed one year after the termination of the employment contract and their scope must be limited to the activities covered under the employment contract.

---

[263] A first reservation, based on the principle of reciprocity, provides that arbitral awards made in the territory of states that have not ratified or acceded to the convention are not eligible for the enforcement of arbitral awards on DRC territory. A second reservation provides that only awards on matters considered "commercial" under national law will be recognized and enforced in the DRC. A third reservation notes that only arbitral awards made after the accession of the DRC to the New York Convention may be enforced under it. This reservation confirms the principle of non-retroactivity. Finally, the last reservation provides that the New York Convention does not apply to disputes related to real estate property located in the considered state or on a right related to such property.

Furthermore, the Industrial Property Law provides that clauses contained in the licensing contracts relating to these contracts shall be null and void if they impose limitations on the licensee, which do not arise from the rights conferred by the license. Nevertheless, the following shall not be considered unlawful limitations: (i) limitations concerning the measurement, scope, quantity, territory or term of the exploitation of the subject of the license; (ii) limitations imposed by the licensor to ensure the best possible technical working of the license; (iii) the obligation imposed upon the licensee to refrain from any act likely to infringe the rights of the licensor.

Therefore, a non-competition clause shall be, in principle, acceptable under the Industrial Property Law, provided that they are not in contrary with mandatory rules or public policy rules.

X. Language Requirements

Does the law in your country require that a franchise agreement be translated into the local language in order to be enforceable between the parties?

The DRC law does not require that a franchise agreement be translated into the local language to be enforceable between the parties. However, it must be translated into French, which is the DRC official language, if the franchise agreement is presented to DRC courts or administration.

XI. Other Significant Matters

Please advise as to whether there are any significant matters not addressed above of which a franchisor should be aware in connection with its entering into a franchise agreement in your country.

There are no other significant matters to be addressed.

Franchising in Egypt

Girgis Abd El-Shahid

Sarwat A. Shahid Law Firm

Cairo, Egypt

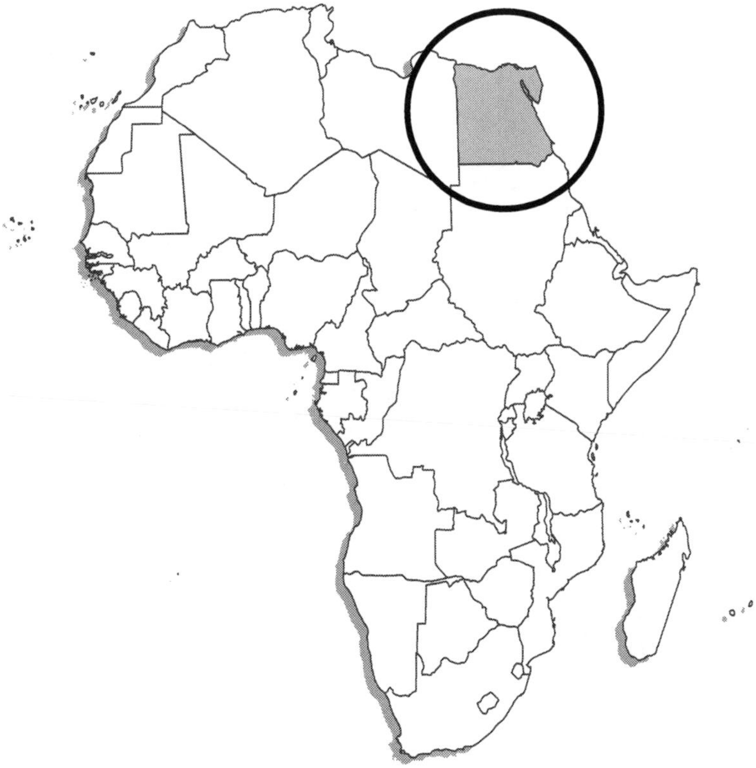

Egypt

I. Introduction

A. Historical Background of Country

Partially independent from the United Kingdom in 1922, Egypt acquired full sovereignty with the overthrow of the British-backed monarchy in 1952. The completion of the Aswan High Dam in 1971 and the resultant Lake Nasser have altered the time-honored place of the Nile River in the agriculture and ecology of Egypt. A rapidly growing population, limited arable land, and dependence on the Nile all continue to overtax resources and stress society. The government has struggled to meet the demands of Egypt's population through economic reform and massive investment in communications and physical infrastructure. Inspired by the 2010 Tunisian revolution, Egyptian opposition groups led demonstrations and labor strikes countrywide, culminating in President Hosni Mubarak's ouster. Egypt's military assumed national leadership until a new parliament was in place in early 2012. The same year candidate, Mohammed Mursi, won the presidential election and a new constitution was affirmed. In July 2013, the military ousted Mursi and he was replaced by interim president Adly Mansour.

B. Economy of the Country

Occupying the northeast corner of the African continent, Egypt is bisected by the highly fertile Nile valley, where most economic activity takes place. Egypt's economy was highly centralized during the rule of former President Gamal Abdel Nasser but opened up considerably under former Presidents Anwar El-Sadat and Mohamed Hosni Mubarak. Cairo from 2004 to 2008 aggressively pursued economic reforms to attract foreign investment and facilitate GDP growth; however, the global financial crisis slowed reform efforts. In 2010, the government spent more on infrastructure and public projects, and exports drove GDP growth to more than 5%.

After unrest erupted in January 2011, the Egyptian government backtracked on economic reforms, drastically increasing social spending to address public dissatisfaction but political uncertainty at the same time caused economic growth to slow significantly, reducing the government's revenues. Tourism, manufacturing, and construction were among the hardest hit sectors of the Egyptian economy and economic growth is likely to remain slow during the next several years.

C. Franchise Legal Overview

The *Egyptian Civil Code of 1948* (the "Civil Code") and *Commercial Code of 1999 (Law No. 17)* (the "Commercial Code") govern commercial activities in Egypt since there are no specific laws regarding franchising and distribution in the country. Consequently, the rights and obligations of parties to a franchise agreement will be construed according to the provisions of Egypt's general commercial laws, which are the main sources of legal rules regarding contracts. A franchise agreement may, however, be governed by the Commercial Code, if it is construed as a transfer of technology.

II. Regulatory Requirements

A. Pre-Sale Disclosure

Please describe any pre-sale franchise disclosure or similar requirements that may apply to franchise transactions.

No pre-sale franchise disclosure or similar requirements apply to franchise transactions under the laws of Egypt.

B. Governmental Approvals, Registrations, Filing Requirements

Please describe any necessary government approvals, registrations, or filing requirements that may apply to franchise transactions.

There are no government approvals, registrations, or filing requirements that apply to franchise transactions.

See, however, Section V (Trademarks) of this chapter relating to the registration of trademark licenses under the *Egyptian Intellectual Property Rights Law*.

C. Limits of Fees and Typical Term of Franchise Agreement

Please describe any limits upon the nature and extent of fees and the term of a typical franchise agreement.

There are no set provisions related to the nature and extent of fees and the term of a franchise agreement.

III. Currency

If all payments under a franchise agreement must be made in immediately available U.S. Dollars, please advise as to any restrictions, reporting requirements, or regulations concerning the exchange, repatriation, or remittance of U.S. Dollars.

Previously, there were no restrictions, reporting requirements, or regulations concerning the exchange, repatriation, or remittance of U.S. Dollars imposed by the Central Bank of Egypt or any other competent authority of the Arab Republic of Egypt, except that currency transfers must be made through a local bank or an institution permitted to deal with foreign currencies.[264] Since the events that took place in Egypt in January 2011, the Central Bank of Egypt has set certain rules limiting and/or regulating persons' ability to transfer foreign funds outside of Egypt.

[264] *See The Banking Sector and the Money Law No. 88* for the year 2003 and its Executive Regulations. According to Article 5 of the *Treaty between the United States of America and the Arab Republic of Egypt concerning the Reciprocal Encouragement and Protection of Investments*, Egypt and the United States shall grant the "free transfer of … royalties and other payments deriving from licenses, franchises and other similar grants of rights."

IV. Taxes, Tariffs, and Duties

Please do not provide any in-depth comments on tax structuring. However, please provide your general comments on the typical amount of withholding tax that would apply and whether a "gross-up" provision contained in a franchise agreement would be enforceable in your country.

The Egyptian Tax Law stipulates that payments of service fees or royalties made to non-residents of Egypt are subject to a 20% withholding tax.

A "gross up" provision contained in a franchise agreement would be enforceable in Egypt.

Egypt has entered into double taxation treaties with a number of countries, including the United States.[265]

V. Trademarks

Please advise us as to whether there are any special requirements for granting a valid trademark license, including the use of a registered user agreement or a short trademark license agreement and any required filing of such an agreement with the trademark authorities.

In strict compliance with the *Egyptian Intellectual Property Rights Law* ("IPR Law"), trademark licenses should be registered at the Trademark Office to make them enforceable vis-à-vis third parties. The trademark license, whether taking a form

[265] Egypt has double taxation treaties with: Albania, Algeria, Austria, Bahrain, Belarus, Belgium, Bulgaria, Canada, China, Cyprus, Czech Republic, Denmark, Finland, France, Germany, Greece, Holland, Hungary, India, Indonesia, Iraq, Italy, Japan, Jordan, Kuwait, Lebanon, Libya, Malaysia, Malta, Montenegro, Morocco, North Korea, Norway, Pakistan, Palestine, Poland, Romania, Russia, Serbia, Singapore, South Africa, Spain, Sudan, Sweden, Switzerland, Syria, Tunisia, Turkey, Ukraine, United Arab Emirates, United Kingdom, United States, and Yemen.

of a normal trademark license agreement, or a registered user agreement, must be duly notarized, consularized, and legalized by the appropriate Egyptian consulate.

Notwithstanding any registration requirements under the IPR Law, it is highly recommended that parties not register any trademark license agreements for the following reasons:

- The Trademark Office takes a very passive attitude when requested to deregister any license, especially in case of a dispute between the parties;
- The second paragraph of Article 95 of the IPR Law stipulates that the "mark owner may only terminate or choose not to renew [a] license based on a legitimate reason." It is not clear whether the lapse or expiration of the term of an agreement is deemed to be legitimate. Local practitioners are contesting the constitutionality of this clause in the hope of striking it from the IPR Law; and
- The lack of registration does not affect the enforceability of any agreement between the parties.

VI. Restrictions on Transfer

Please advise as to whether there are any restrictions on (1) a franchisor to restrict transfers by a master franchisee, any interest in a master franchisee, or the assets of the master franchisee or (2) the ability of a master franchisee to control and/or restrict transfers of a subfranchisee's rights under a master franchise agreement, interest in the subfranchisee, or the assets of the subfranchisee.

There are no definite transfer restrictions on a franchisor towards the master franchisee as it depends on the franchise transaction. Further, the master franchisee can impose reciprocal transfer restrictions on the subfranchisees.

VII. Termination

Please advise us as to any laws relating to termination in your country, such as agency laws, required indemnity provisions, notice or "good cause" requirements, or other laws affecting termination of a franchise agreement. Please describe.

The Egyptian law allows parties to terminate a franchise agreement, provided one of the parties commits an act of breach and such defaulting party is obliged to indemnify the non-defaulting party for the loss suffered as a result for such termination. Further, the law allows the contracting parties to fix in advance the amount of damages in the franchise agreement to be paid in the event of a contractual breach.[266]

VIII. Governing Law, Jurisdiction, and Dispute Resolution

A. Choice of Law of Foreign Jurisdiction

Please confirm whether the choice of law of a foreign jurisdiction would likely to be upheld under the law of the country, except for certain matters such as trademarks, bankruptcy, and competition matters, which we assume would be governed by the law in your country.

---

[266] *Editor's note:* Egyptian practitioners are divided on whether the *Commercial Agency Law* (*Law No. 120 of 1982*) applies to the franchisor-franchisee relationship. This law regulates the licensing and operation of commercial agents. If this law were applied to franchise arrangements, the application of local law would be mandatory with respect to: (1) notice and opportunity to cure prior to termination, (2) notice prior to non-renewal, and (3) compensation for breaches. It is difficult to predict how a judge in Egypt may interpret the compensation requirement, because there is no compensation formula in the law. Regardless, providing for waivers of agency law rights in the franchise agreement is advisable. *See* Mazero and Maisonneuve, *supra* note 110, at 15. Recently, the Egyptian Constitutional Court rendered a provision allowing for compensation in case of the non-renewal of a fixed term agency null and void.

In the event that a franchise agreement is construed as a "transfer of technology" agreement under the Commercial Code, then it will be mandatorily subject to Egyptian law.

The Commercial Code does not contain a definition of "technology" and the Egyptian Court of Cassation (the Supreme Court Equivalent in Egypt) has not yet issued any judgments further interpreting its provisions. Most local practitioners are of the opinion that a technology transfer was meant to capture franchise arrangements. Other practitioners are of the opinion that franchise arrangements are only deemed to be captured by technology transfer if a great deal of "know-how" is transferred from the franchisor to the franchisee.

If a franchise agreement is not construed as a "transfer of technology" agreement, the parties may choose the governing law, and their choice will be upheld under Egyptian law. Egyptian law recognizes the choice of the parties, except for those provisions conflicting with Egyptian public policy.

B. International Arbitration Dispute Resolution

Please confirm that a court in your country would honor an election of international arbitration dispute resolution, and therefore refuse to hear any disputes arising under a franchise agreement.

Egypt is a signatory to the *Convention on the Recognition and Enforcement of Foreign Arbitral Awards* (the "New York Convention"). Therefore, an arbitral award under international rules, such as the *ICC Rules of Conciliation and Arbitration* or the like would be recognized and enforced by the Egyptian courts without re-examination of the merits.

In order to enforce a foreign arbitral award in Egypt, the award must first be deposited with a special expert office at the Ministry of Justice. This expert office then determines whether to accept such deposit based on certain thresholds, mainly related to whether such award infringes any Egyptian public policy or mandatory rules. Once the award is deposited at this expert office, the depositor may file a case before the Courts of Appeal for execution.

If the franchise agreement is construed as a "transfer of technology" agreement under the Commercial Code, the venue of arbitration must be in Egypt. Otherwise, the venue will be honored by an Egyptian court.

IX. Non-Competition Provisions

If the franchise agreement prohibits the master franchisee from engaging in certain competitive activities during the term of the agreement, and for a 12-month period after the termination or expiration of the agreement, please comment on the enforceability of non-competition covenants in your country.

The Egyptian law respects the importance of the protection of the know-how. Accordingly, it allows the parties to any agreement to protect it in the way they deem appropriate.

If the franchise arrangement is deemed to be captured by the notion of technology transfer, Egyptian law restricts the technology provider from imposing any condition in the technology transfer contract, which restricts the freedom of the transferee in using the technology. The foregoing, however, shall not apply if these conditions are provided in the technology transfer contract for the protection of consumers or for safeguarding a legitimate interest of the supplier of technology.

Egyptian jurisprudence does not provide clear guidance as to what can be deemed to be a "legitimate interest of the supplier of technology."

X. Language Requirements

Does the law in your country require that a franchise agreement be translated into the local language in order to be enforceable between the parties?

There is no requirement that a franchise agreement be translated into local language in order to be enforceable between the parties.

XI. Other Significant Matters

Please advise as to whether there are any significant matters not addressed above of which a franchisor should be aware in connection with its entering into a franchise agreement in your country.

Depending on the magnitude of the know-how transferred, a franchise agreement may or may not be construed as an agreement involving a "transfer of technology" and thereby subjecting the agreement to specific rules stipulated in the Egyptian Commercial Code, which in spirit favors the franchisee.[267]

---

[267] *Editor's note*: Certain practitioners in Egypt believe that franchise agreements would be subject to the provisions of the Commercial Code (*Law No. 17 of 1999*) governing transfer of technology agreements (the "Technology Transfer Provisions"). If so, as previously noted, the agreements would be subject to mandatory Egyptian choice-of-law and choice-of-forum provisions. It might also be more difficult for a franchisor to terminate the agreements pursuant to their terms. The Technology Transfer Provisions may not apply to franchise agreements because the Commercial Code exempts franchise agreements authorizing the use of trademarks or trade names, unless such use includes a transfer of "technical data." Most franchise agreements would not likely contemplate such a transfer. Disclaimers that the Technology Transfer Provisions do not apply have not been tested in Egyptian courts. As a result, they are of uncertain enforceability in Egypt. However, an express disclaimer of the Technology Transfer Provisions would still mitigate the risk that a foreign court or arbitral tribunal might itself determine that the mandatory choice-of-forum

(Footnote continued on next page)

provisions in the Technology Transfer Provisions would deprive it of jurisdiction over a given dispute. *See* Mazero and Maisonneuve, *supra* note 110, at 15.

Franchising in Ethiopia

Yohannes Assefa and Biset Beyene Molla

Pioneer International Legal Consulting

Addis Ababa, Ethiopia

Ethiopia

I. Introduction

A. Historical Background of Country

Ethiopia adopted its current constitution in 1994 and the country's first multiparty elections were held in 1995. A border war with Eritrea late in the 1990s ended with a peace treaty in December 2000. In November 2007, the Eritrea-Ethiopia Border Commission (EEBC) issued specific coordinates as virtually demarcating the border and pronounced its work finished. Alleging that the EEBC acted beyond its mandate in issuing the coordinates, Ethiopia has not accepted them and has not withdrawn troops from previously contested areas pronounced by the EEBC as belonging to Eritrea.

B. Economy of the Country

Ethiopia's economy is based on agriculture, which accounts for 41% of GDP and 85% of total employment. Coffee has been a major export crop. The agricultural sector suffers from poor cultivation practices and frequent drought, but recent joint efforts by the Government of Ethiopia and donors have strengthened Ethiopia's agricultural resilience, contributing to an increased food security and a reduction in the poverty rate of the country. The five-year *Growth and Transformation Plan* that Ethiopia unveiled in October 2010 presents a government-led effort to achieve the country's ambitious development goals. The banking, insurance, and micro-credit industries are restricted to domestic investors, but Ethiopia has attracted significant foreign investment in textiles, leather, commercial agriculture, and manufacturing. Under Ethiopia's constitution, the state owns all land and provides long-term leases to the tenants. Land use certificates are now being issued in some areas so that tenants have more recognizable rights to continued occupancy and hence make more concerted efforts to improve their leaseholds. While the economy has grown by an average of 10.6% over the past 10 years, per capita income of $410 per year is among the lowest in the world.

Ethiopia

C. Franchise Legal Overview

In 2012, the *Economist* identified Ethiopia as the fastest growing non-oil based economy in Africa, growing by double digits over the past seven years. While Ethiopia's economy is mostly agrarian, the recent expansion of the country's middle class and urban population and its per capita income has made the country ripe for international franchising businesses, especially those involved in the consumer retail business. Yet, few international franchisors have entered the Ethiopian market.

The reasons for the stagnation of the franchising market are many but the most important cause was the 1974 military coup and the subsequent adoption of Soviet-style communist economic policies that wiped out the private sector in Ethiopia. Commercial laws governing businesses and, to some degree, franchise arrangements, changed very little during this period and business activity in Ethiopia continued, to a large degree, to be governed by the *Commercial Code of the Empire of Ethiopia,*[268] 1960 (the "Commercial Code"). Consequently, any review of current Ethiopian law governing franchising activity will have to include aspects of both the Commercial Code and new additions and modifications introduced since 1991.

Ethiopia currently does not have per se a body of law specifically governing business franchising. In fact, the term "franchise" or "franchise law" does not appear in the Commercial Code. A review of published legal commentaries on the Commercial Code and contract law also reveals no reference to franchise law. However, there are patchworks of disparate laws that collectively affect the activities of franchisors in Ethiopia.

---

[268] *Commercial Code of the Empire of Ethiopia, Proclamation No. 166/1960. Federal Negarit Gazeta* Extraordinary Issue, Year, 19, No 3, May 5, 1960.

Ethiopia

II. Regulatory Requirements

A. Pre-Sale Disclosure

Please describe any pre-sale franchise disclosure or similar requirements that may apply to franchise transactions.

No pre-sale disclosure or similar requirements apply to any franchise transactions under the laws of Ethiopia.

B. Governmental Approvals, Registrations, Filing Requirements

Please describe any necessary government approvals, registrations, or filing requirements that may apply to franchise transactions.

Generally, franchise agreements are not required to be registered. They also do not require approval from any governmental or regulatory body under Ethiopian law. Certain aspects of a franchise agreement may, however, be required to be registered at the Ethiopia Investment Agency ("Agency")[269] under legislation regarding technology transfers. Determining what comprises a transfer of technology agreement within the context of a franchise agreement requires a close review of each franchise agreement by local counsel familiar with the regulatory structures of Ethiopian commercial and investment laws.

The Ethiopian Parliament adopted *Investment Reenactment Proclamation 769/2012* (the "2012 Investment Proclamation"). Under this Proclamation, Parliament reaffirmed the Agency's jurisdiction in the registration and regulation of technology

---

[269] The Ethiopian Investment Agency is a government agency established in 1992 to promote private investment, primarily foreign direct investment. The activities of the Agency are supervised by an Investment Board, which is chaired by the Minister of Industry. *See* http://www.eia.gov.et/english (last visited March 7, 2014).

transfer agreements[270] and mandated that all technology transfer agreements be submitted to the Agency for "approval and registration."[271]

The 2012 Investment Proclamation refined the definition of "transfer of technology" to mean "the transfer of systemic knowledge for the manufacture of a product, for the application of improvement of a process, or for the rendering of a service, including management and marketing technologies."[272] The definition does not extend to transactions involving the mere sale or lease of goods.[273] Franchise agreements may fall under the purview of the Investment Proclamations if a franchise agreement includes, for example, a marketing technology, proprietary business processes, and/or specified machines that could be used for the production of goods or for rendition of a service. In these instances, the franchise agreement may require registration with the Agency.

See also Section V (Trademarks) of this chapter relating to the registration of licenses with the Ethiopian Intellectual Property Office and Section III (Currency) of this chapter relating to potential requirements for the remittance of foreign currency.

C. Limits of Fees and Typical Term of Franchise Agreement

Please describe any limits upon the nature and extent of fees and the term of a typical franchise agreement.

---

[270] *Investment Proclamation No. 769/2012, Federal Nagarit Gazeta*, Year 18, No. 63, September 17, 2012, Article 21. This Article reiterated what was provided in *Proclamation No. 280/2002 Article 18* (renumbered Article 20, Amendment Proclamation 375/2003), without, however, affecting the jurisdiction of the Ethiopian Investment Agency with regard to registration and approval of transfers of technology.

[271] *Id.*

[272] *Id.* Article 2 (10).

[273] *Id.*

Ethiopia

1. Limits on Nature of Fees

For the most part, the 2012 Investment Proclamation replaced an earlier regulatory regime. However, it is unclear what aspects of the repealed regulations remain in effect and applicable to transfer of technology agreements. For those franchise agreements deemed to be technology transfers, the repealed regulations regulated fees and payments. While payments could be made on the basis of lump-sum, royalties, or a combination of the two,[274] the procedure and currency of payment as well as the price indexation could be freely determined by the parties to the agreement.[275] However, the repealed regulations prohibited any fixed minimum royalty payments to the supplier of technology. If provisions of accessories, components, and spare parts were to be made available by the supplier of technology, the agreement had to provide that the prices of these articles should not be higher than the current international prices. It is unclear on what basis and standards the Agency will justify an approval or denial of certain aspects of transfer of technology agreements but the repealed regulations may provide some insight.

III. Currency

If all payments under a franchise agreement must be made in immediately available U.S. Dollars, please advise as to any restrictions, reporting requirements, or regulations concerning the exchange, repatriation, or remittance of U.S. Dollars.

There is no legal restriction on the payment of money in foreign currency to a franchisor that, under a franchise agreement, provides technology, proprietary business process, or other vital business services to a local franchisee. While the details are left to the National Bank of Ethiopia ("NBE"), the free transfer of

---

274 *Transfer of Technology Council of Ministers Regulation No. 121/93* ("TOT Regulation") 20 (2).

275 *Id.*

funds in foreign currency has been clearly reaffirmed in the 2012 Investment Proclamation.

The *National Bank Directives* provide for remittance of foreign currency by a resident business to foreign suppliers of technology and other services necessary for conducting of their business.[276] A franchisee that has evidence of debt due to a franchisor under the franchise agreement normally has the right to obtain foreign currency to effect payments to the franchisor.

Once a foreign investor is recognized by the NBE, an application may be made for remittance. To do so, one is required to provide evidence of payment of the business tax (under the *Income Tax Proclamation*). If the foreign investor is a business organization, the applicant must show evidence of payment of taxes on dividends from the tax authority as well as minutes of the meetings of partners or shareholders, as the case may be, showing the amount of profit declared as a dividend by the shareholders or partners.

The foreign investor or an agent must then file the application for grant of remittance through a commercial bank in which he or she holds a savings account in foreign or local currencies. Given the scarcity of hard currency available to the nation's foreign trade, it is always subject to prioritization. The franchisee may not have hard currency to readily pay its foreign franchisor.

There are areas designated by regulations as priority areas through which the government gives investors incentives including making available foreign currency for financing any debt they may contract including royalties, etc. If the area of investment is one the government considers by law a priority area for investment because of its potential to attract tourism, job opportunities, or increase foreign currency earnings in return, it

---

[276] *The National Foreign Exchange Regulation Directives* provide the details of how remittances may be made. As far as transfer of technology is concerned, the Investment Agency registered certificate is one requirement for remittance.

may be easy to obtain the permission of NBE for the required hard currency.

In case the franchisor is not a partner in the business of the franchisee but entitled only to a royalty under the franchise agreement, the NBE will require the franchisee to present the franchise agreement under which the royalty is due to the franchisor. It is important to exercise caution in drafting franchise agreements to avoid any risk of rejection on the basis of exorbitant prices.

IV. Taxes, Tariffs, and Duties

Please do not provide any in-depth comments on tax structuring. However, please provide your general comments on the typical amount of withholding tax that would apply and whether a "gross-up" provision contained in a franchise agreement would be enforceable in your country.

The *Income Tax Proclamation* provides for withholding of taxes on royalties payable to nonresident licensors[277] and on dividends.[278] The legislation calls for a 5% withholding for royalties and a 10% withholding for dividends.[279] It is also important to note the *Value Added Tax ("VAT") Proclamation No. 286/2002*. Under this proclamation, a VAT registered person who receives service from a nonresident person and has to pay for such service is bound to withhold a 15% VAT from the amount payable, unless the transaction is exempted[280] from

[277] Income Tax Proclamation No. 286/2002; *Federal Negarit Gazeta*, Year 8, No. 34 4th July 2002; Article 31/3.

[278] *Id.* Article 34/1.

[279] Ethiopia has agreements on avoidance of double taxation with the Czech Republic, France, Tunisia, Algeria, Israel, Turkey, South Africa, Yemen, Russia, Kuwait, Italy, and Romania.

[280] Exemptions under Article 8 (2) include (a) the sale or transfer of a used dwelling, or the lease of a dwelling; (b) the rendering of financial services; (c) the supply or import of national or foreign currency (except for that

(Footnote continued on next page)

payment of VAT under Article 8 of the Proclamation.[281] This is irrespective of whether the customer receiving the services from the nonresident is registered for VAT or not.

There is nothing stated, expressed, or implied, in Ethiopian tax law prohibiting provisions related to gross-ups. Therefore, the general view among tax authorities is that the amount of withholding tax grossed-up may be, in the worst case scenario, considered earnings by the non-resident/recipient and earnings on which the same rate of tax applies.

V. Trademarks

Please advise us as to whether there are any special requirements for granting a valid trademark license, including

used for numismatic purposes), and securities; (d) the import of gold to be transferred to the National Bank of Ethiopia; (e) the rendering by religious organizations of religious or church related services; (f) the import or supply of prescription drugs specified in directives issued by the Minister of Health, and the rendering of medical services; (g) the rendering of educational services provided by educational institutions, as well as child care services for children at pre-school institutions; (h) the supply of goods and rendering of services in the form of humanitarian aid, as well as import of goods transferred to state agencies of Ethiopia and public organizations for the purpose of rehabilitation after natural disasters, industrial accidents, and catastrophes; (i) the supply of electricity, kerosene, and water; (j) goods imported by the government, organizations, institutions or projects exempted from duties and other import taxes to the extent provided by law or by agreement; (k) supplies by the post office authorized under the Ethiopian Postal Services Proclamation, other than services rendered for a fee or commission; (l) the provision of transport; (m) permits and license fees; (n) the import of goods to the extent provided under Schedule 2 of the Customs Tariffs Regulations; (o) the supply of goods or services by a workshop employing disabled individuals if more than 60 percent of the employees are disabled; and (p) the import or supply of books and other printed materials to the extent provided in regulations. The Ministry of Finance and Economic Development has been authorized to exempt, by directives, other goods and services not listed under Article 8 of the Proclamation.

[281] *Value Added Tax Proclamation No. 285/2002, Article 23/1, Federal Negarit Gazeta*, Year 8, No 33, July 4, 2002.

the use of a registered user agreement or a short trademark license agreement and any required filing of such an agreement with the trademark authorities.

Under Ethiopian law, a right relating to a registered trademark may be assigned or licensed in whole or in part. The Trademark Registration and Protection Proclamation No. 501/2006 ("Trademark Proclamation") provides that a license contract must be made in writing and submitted to the Ethiopian Intellectual Property Office ("EIPO") for registration. Subsequent modifications or cancellations are also subject to registration with EIPO.[282] The contract should indicate whether the license extends to all or part of the goods or services for which the trademark is registered.[283] If it does not contain any references to the scope of the license, the effect is that the licensee is free to use it for all products for which the trademark is registered. The license contract will have no effect on third parties until it is registered by EIPO and publicized by a designated intellectual property gazette (which does not exist to date) or a paper with nationwide circulation, such as the state-owned, Amharic daily paper, *Addis Zemen* and the English daily *Ethiopian Herald*. In its publication of the license contract for a public announcement, EIPO is bound to keep the details confidential.[284]

The trademark owner may grant a license for the use of the trademark by the franchisee within a limited territory or with respect to limited products that the trademark normally covers in its registration.[285]

---

[282] *Trademark Registration and Protection Proclamation No. 501/2006, Federal Negarit Gazeta*, Year 12, No. 37, July 7, 2006. Article 29/2.

[283] *Id.* Article 29/1.

[284] *Id.* Article 29/2.

[285] *Id.* Article 31/2/a. Though the practice has yet to evolve, any limitation concerning the territory in which the trademark may be used by the franchisee/licensee may constitute market segmentation for the purpose of the *Trade Practice and Consumer Protection Proclamation No. 685/2010.*
(Footnote continued on next page)

Ethiopia

A long awaited implementing directive of the Trademark Proclamation became effective February 2013. The EIPO regulation and the directive deal with a number of trademark law issues and requirements, but there are still some concerns for franchisors and other businesses, even those that have previously registered marks.[286] For example, marks registered in Ethiopia prior to enactment of the Trademark Proclamation, as well as certain marks registered under the Trademark Proclamation, must be re-registered, even if the current term of validity of the marks has not expired.[287] In sum, a new application must be filed with the EIPO and the filer must adhere to the registration requirements in the directive and implementing regulation. Marks registered after the Trademark Proclamation became effective must be amended so that their registration certificates reflect a new term of validity.[288]

Despite positive changes to the law as a result of the directive, some potentially burdensome filing requirements remain.[289] For example, a foreign trademark application must be filed together with an authenticated power of attorney.[290] Moreover, a foreign trademark application must be accompanied by a copy of the home registration certificate—a certificate issued in any country

This issue has yet to be decided. In the opinion of these authors, as *Article 13/1/a/iii of the Trade Practice and Consumer Protection Proclamation* states in general terms that "agreements as to market or consumer segmentation" are deemed to be anticompetitive, segmentation of the market by territory based on trademarks is acceptable because the trademark law should prevail over a law that is general in character.

286 Kendal H. Tyre, Jr., Yohannes Assefa, & Getachew Mengistie *New Intellectual Property Regulation Requires Scramble to Protect Marks in Ethiopia*, NIXON PEABODY FRANCHISE LAW ALERT (October 2013).

287 *Id.*

288 *Id.*

289 *Id.*

290 *Id.*

outside of Ethiopia—or a copy of a certificate of business license.[291]

VI. Restrictions on Transfer

Please advise as to whether there are any restrictions on (1) a franchisor to restrict transfers by a master franchisee, any interest in a master franchisee, or the assets of the master franchisee or (2) the ability of a master franchisee to control and/or restrict transfers of a subfranchisee's rights under a master franchise agreement, interest in the subfranchisee, or the assets of the subfranchisee.

Any restrictions on the franchisor, vis à vis its interests and assets in the master franchisee (or the master franchisee vis à vis its interests and assets in the subfranchisee), depends on the terms of the contract. However, Article 201 of the Commercial Code provides a clear restriction on any assignment without the written consent of the lessor, which, in this case, is the franchisor. The law restricts the lessee because, under the law, "a contract of lease is made on the basis of the personal qualification of the lessee." Franchisor relies on the personal and/or organizational qualification of the franchisee when determining whether the franchisee will maintain the goodwill and standards of the business. Accordingly, assigning or sub-franchising the franchise without the prior consent of the franchisor (or the master franchisee, as applicable) is prohibited.

VII. Termination

Please advise us as to any laws relating to termination in your country, such as agency laws, required indemnity provisions, notice or "good cause" requirements, or other laws affecting termination of a franchise agreement. Please describe.

---

291 *Id.*

The law of contracts stipulates that contracting parties, and only they, may determine the contents of their contract, subject to the mandatory provisions of the law.[292] A franchise agreement is no different. As long as there is no specific law to which it has to be subjected, the parties are free to determine the terms of the contract and advance their interests.

VIII. Governing Law, Jurisdiction, and Dispute Resolution

A. Choice of Law of Foreign Jurisdiction

Please confirm whether the choice of law of a foreign jurisdiction would likely to be upheld under the law of the country, except for certain matters such as trademarks, bankruptcy, and competition matters, which we assume would be governed by the law in your country.

Recent draft legislation for consideration by the Federal House of People's Representatives provides contractual parties may, in the absence of specific law to the contrary, stipulate in advance to choice of law provisions.[293] The parties, however, must choose from among a list of choices expressly provided in the draft rules which are:

> *"...the law of nationality, the law of domicile, the law of the place where the transaction was made, the law of the place where the subject matter is situated, the law of the place where the transaction is to be performed, or the law of the place which is reasonably connected to the matter."*[294]

---

[292] Article 1731/2.

[293] *Draft Proclamation to Provide for Federal Rules of Private International Law*, Article 21/1.

[294] *Id.*

As it now stands, the parties may not opt for any other law that cannot be identified as one of the above. Thus, assuming the draft legislation passes, franchising parties may agree on any one of the available choices to govern the substance of the franchise agreement in the event of a dispute. However, the choice of law must be explicit or clearly evident from the agreement or from the circumstances of the case.[295]

Please note that currently the 2012 Investment Proclamation provides that transfer of technology agreements are subject to Ethiopian law except where the parties agree to settle their disputes through negotiation, conciliation, or arbitration. Although untested in practice, there are no restrictions on choice of law clauses as long as the choice has no objective of bypassing the application of laws with important public policy bearings.

B. International Arbitration Dispute Resolution

Please confirm that a court in your country would honor an election of international arbitration dispute resolution, and therefore refuse to hear any disputes arising under a franchise agreement.

The *Civil Code* (Articles 3307 to 3346) and the *Civil Procedure Code* (Article 244/2/g, Articles 274 to 277 and 315 through 319) recognize out of court settlement of disputes be it by arbitration, conciliation, or mediation. Contracting parties who have a dispute settlement provision in their contract or those who agree later to arbitrate or conciliate are bound by the terms of their agreement and must submit any dispute to these mechanisms for resolution. Most international transactions with Ethiopian parties provide for international arbitration. The courts uphold such

[295] *Id.* Article 72/3

provisions and have procedures for their enforcement in the *Civil Procedure Code of the Empire of Ethiopia, 1965*.[296]

Ethiopia is not a signatory to the *Convention on the Recognition and Enforcement of Foreign Arbitral Awards* (the "New York Convention").

IX. Non-Competition Provisions

If the franchise agreement prohibits the master franchisee from engaging in certain competitive activities during the term of the agreement, and for a 12-month period after the termination or expiration of the agreement, please comment on the enforceability of non-competition covenants in your country.

Non-competition provisions are well-known to Ethiopian law. Under the Commercial Code, the seller of a business has to refrain, for a duration of five years from the time of sale, from any act of competition that is likely to injure the buyer.[297] The seller may not carry on a trade similar to the one he sold in the vicinity where the sold business is operated by the buyer. Furthermore, the contract of sale may provide the extent of the prohibition and fix the duration in which the non-competition restriction should last, which, in any case, cannot be for more than five years. It is also stipulated under Article 55 of the Commercial Code that a commercial agent may be bound by the contract of agency not to carry on a private trade similar to that of the principal upon the termination of the agreement. Contractual restrictions on the agent, however, may not be effective for more than five years notwithstanding any provision to the contrary.[298] Given these legal standards currently recognized by Ethiopian law, it is reasonable to conclude that

---

[296] *Civil Procedure Code Decree No. 52/1965. Federal Negarit Gazeta,* Extraordinary Issue, Year, 25, No. 3. Article 461.

[297] Article 158.

[298] Article 55/2.

reasonable non-competition provisions in a franchise agreement will be enforceable.

X. Language Requirements

Does the law in your country require that a franchise agreement be translated into the local language in order to be enforceable between the parties?

There is no requirement that franchise agreements be translated into the local language to be enforceable. English is acceptable. Generally, however, if the franchise agreement is disputed in court, the party introducing the franchise agreement as evidence is required to provide an official translation of the document in the official working language of the court. Federal courts require translation to Amharic while state courts require translation to their respective working languages.

XI. Other Significant Matters

Please advise as to whether there are any significant matters not addressed above of which a franchisor should be aware in connection with its entering into a franchise agreement in your country.

The *Commercial Registration and Business Licensing Proclamation*[299] issued in June 2010 by the Federal legislative body has provided strict requirements for applicants to produce a valid certificate of professional competence issued by the relevant sectoral public body for an effective business license to be issued by the Ministry of Trade or the relevant regional bureau. Thus, a franchisee who may want to commence business under a license granted by a franchise agreement will likely need

[299] *Proclamation to Provide for Commercial Registration and Business Licensing* No. 686/2010. *Federal Negarit Gazeta* 16th, Year No. 42. 24th July 2010, Article 32/8.

to seek approval of the public body in charge of issuing certificates of competence for the business in question.

Franchising in Ghana

Divine K.D. Letsa and Elizabeth Ashun

Bentsi-Enchill, Letsa & Ankomah

Accra, Ghana

Ghana

I. Introduction

A. Historical Background of Country

Formed from the merger of the British colony of the Gold Coast and the Togoland trust territory, Ghana on March 6, 1957, became the first sub-Saharan country in colonial Africa to gain its independence. Ghana endured a long series of coups before Lt. Jerry Rawlings took power in 1981 and banned political parties. After approving a new constitution and restoring multiparty politics in 1992, Rawlings won presidential elections for the New Democratic Congress (NDC) in 1992 and 1996, but was constitutionally prevented from running for a third term in 2000. John Kufuor of the New Patriotic Party (NPP) succeeded him and was re-elected in 2004.

John Atta Mills took over as head of state in early 2009. However, he did not complete his term in office due to his untimely death in July 2012 and John Dramani Mahama became the incumbent president.

In the December 2012 elections, the candidates competing for presidency were incumbent president Mahama, his main challenger Nana Akufo-Addo of the NPP, and six other candidates. The Electoral Commission declared President Mahama as the winner. On August 19, 2013, the Supreme Court of Ghana dismissed a petition filed by the NPP challenging the results of the 2012 presidential election, therefore affirming President Mahama as the validly elected president.

B. Economy of the Country

Ghana's economy has been strengthened by a quarter century of relatively sound political stability and management, a competitive business environment and sustained reductions in poverty levels. Ghana is well endowed with natural resources, and agriculture accounts for roughly one-quarter of GDP and employs more than half of the workforce, mainly small landholders. The services sector and manufacturing sector account for 48% and 26% of GDP respectively. Gold and cocoa production and individual remittances are major sources of foreign exchange.

Ghana opted for debt relief under the IMF Heavily Indebted Poor Country (HIPC) program in 2002, and is also benefiting from the Multilateral Debt Relief Initiative that took effect in 2006. In 2009, Ghana signed a three-year Extended Credit Facility Program (previously the Poverty Reduction and Growth Facility) with the IMF to improve macroeconomic stability, private sector competitiveness, human resource development, and good governance and civic responsibility. Sound macro-economic management along with high prices for gold and cocoa helped sustain GDP growth between 2008 and 2012.

Ghana successfully completed a five-year compact with Millennium Challenge Corporation (MCC), which it signed in 2006. Its goal was to assist in transforming Ghana's infrastructure and agricultural sectors. Ghana is currently in the process of developing a second MCC compact that will focus on the power sector.

Oil production at Ghana's offshore Jubilee field began in mid-December 2010 and has boosted economic growth and crude oil is now Ghana's third main export. President Mahama faces challenges in managing new oil revenue while maintaining fiscal discipline and resisting debt accumulation.

C. Franchise Legal Overview

There is no specific legislation governing franchising in Ghana and there are also no franchise industry associations in Ghana. Franchise agreements are generally entered into as a result of contractual negotiations between the parties and are therefore regulated by the general principles of contract law. In cases where the franchise will include the provision of specific services such as banking, etc., such enterprises will be subject to the regulatory requirements pertaining to that sector.

Ghana

Certain aspects of a franchising agreement may be construed as a transfer of technology and any agreement relating to such a transfer must be submitted for approval and registered with the Ghana Investment Promotion Centre (the "GIPC") pursuant to the *Ghana Investment Promotion Centre Act, 1994 (Act 478)* (the "GIPC Act") and will be governed by the terms of the *Technology Transfer Regulations, 1992 (LI 1547)* ("the TT Regulations").

In July 2013, Ghana's Parliament passed the amended Ghana Investment Promotion Centre (GIPC) Bill 2013 (the "GIPC Bill"), revising the country's investment laws to guarantee optimum business opportunities and incentives for Ghanaian enterprises. The GIPC Bill proposes minor changes to the management of technology transfer agreements. As the GIPC Bill has not yet received Presidential Assent, it is possible amendments to the GIPC Bill may be introduced, debated, and agreed to and further amendments may be made that may affect franchising agreements construed as a transfer of technology.

II. Regulatory Requirements

A. Pre-Sale Disclosure

Please describe any pre-sale franchise disclosure or similar requirements that may apply to franchise transactions.

No pre-sale franchise disclosure requirements or similar requirements apply to franchise transactions under the laws of Ghana.

B. Governmental Approvals, Registrations, Filing Requirements

Please describe any necessary government approvals, registrations, or filing requirements that may apply to franchise transactions.

Ghana

There is no specific legislation under Ghanaian law that requires any government approvals, registrations, or filing requirements for franchise transactions. However, as certain aspects of a franchising agreement may be construed as a transfer of technology, the agreement will be required to be registered with the GIPC[300] and the TT Regulations will apply. Where there is a breach of any of the provisions of the TT Regulations, the GIPC may not register the agreement and the agreement will be considered unenforceable.

Under Section 40 of the GIPC Act, a technology transfer agreement is defined as an agreement relating to an enterprise to which the GIPC Act applies and that involves:

- the assignment, sale, or use of foreign patents, trademarks or any other industrial property rights;
- the supply of foreign technical know-how or technological knowledge;
- foreign technical assistance, design and engineering, consultancy, or any other technical services in whatever form they may be supplied; and
- foreign managerial, marketing, or other services.

However, an agreement will not be regarded as a technology transfer agreement if its duration does not exceed a period of eighteen months.

An enterprise is defined under the GIPC Act as including an industry, a project, an undertaking, or a business to which the GIPC Act applies or an expansion of that industry, undertaking,

---

[300] The GIPC Bill is proposing that the GIPC shall maintain a record of technology transfer agreements and on receipt of a technology transfer agreement intended for registration shall review the agreement and following registration shall monitor and ensure compliance with the terms and conditions of the agreement.

project, or business or a part of that industry, undertaking, project, or business and an enterprise duly registered with the GIPC where there is foreign participation.

For a technology transfer agreement to qualify for registration and not be rendered unenforceable, Regulation 4 of the TT Regulations provides that it must not contain any of the following clauses or contain any clause the effect of which is the same or similar which:

- permit the transfer of technology which is freely and easily available in Ghana; or
- restrict the volume of production or the sale of the franchisee's products in the franchisee's country; or
- completely prohibit the exportation of the franchisee's products or the right to export to specific geographical areas other than to areas where the franchisor has previously granted exclusive rights to third parties; or which require:
    - the franchisee to export exclusively through the franchisor or on unfavorable terms; or
    - the franchisor's prior permission before any export transaction is made; or
    - the franchisee to pay additional royalty on export sales; or
    - which impose an obligation on the franchisee to acquire or procure its inputs including equipment, tools, parts, raw materials, or intermediate products exclusively from the franchisor or any other person or a specific source except where such inputs are not commercially available elsewhere or such inputs are special to the technology supplied or are required to meet the specifications of products to

be produced either under license or trademark; or

- which impose on the franchisee an obligation to employ personnel to be appointed by the franchisor whose remunerations shall be provided by the franchisee unless in the opinion of the GIPC the obligation is considered indispensable, taking into account the transferred technology; the remuneration for it compares favorably with what prevails in the international market for similar services to be performed by the personnel; and in any such case the provisions of the service is supported by a properly drawn-up management or technical services agreement; or

- which provide for the obligatory transfer by the franchisee of improvements or innovations introduced or developed, or patents acquired by the franchisee in respect of the licensed technology to the franchisor, except that such a clause, excluding patents acquired by the franchisee, may be permissible where they are mutual or reciprocal; or

- which require payment for patent and other industrial property rights after their expiration, termination, or invalidation; or

- which prohibit the manufacture or sale or both of products based on the technology transferred on the expiration of the agreement, or prohibit the use of licensed technical know-how acquired from the use of the licensed technology after the expiry of the agreement; or

- which are designed to prevent the franchisee from contesting or assisting in determining, either administratively or by means of judicial proceedings, the validity of industrial property rights claimed or secured in Ghana by the franchisor; or

- which restrict research and development activities of the franchisee to improve and adapt the licensed technology or restrict the franchisee access to continue improvements in techniques and processes related to the licensed technology; or

- which forbid the use of the franchisee of complementary technologies; prevent the manufacture of products different from those covered by the agreement or prevent the manufacture of products similar to those covered by the technology transfer agreement; or

- which require the consent of the franchisor before any modifications to products, processes, or plants can be effected by the franchisee or which impose on the franchisee obligations to introduce unnecessary designs, except where the licensed technology is used to manufacture specific products under a license or trademark; or

- which limit the scope, volume of production or the sale or resale prices of the products manufactured by the franchisee; or

- which impose on the franchisee an obligation to sell all its manufactured products to the franchisor at a price fixed by the latter or to any other person or enterprise designated by the franchisor; except that this provision shall not apply where:

    - the franchisee is engaged exclusively in the manufacture of intermediate products, parts, or components for subsequent transformation, assembly, or finishing by the franchisor, and the franchisor is the sole potential buyer of such intermediate goods; or

- o the requirement is related exclusively to certain export markets; or
- o the franchisor can prove that it possesses an adequate distribution system or enjoys sufficient prestige in the trade to be able to market the products covered by the agreement more efficiently than the franchisee provided always that the franchisee shall at all times not be coerced into any such transaction.

It would be advisable that prior to concluding an agreement that bears characteristics of a franchising agreement to seek confirmation from the GIPC whether it constitutes a technology transfer.

C. Limits on Fees and Typical Term of Franchise Agreement

Please describe any limits upon the nature and extent of fees and the term of a typical franchise agreement.

The franchise agreement is a contractual agreement and under Ghanaian law parties are free to enter into any contractual agreement to the extent that the applicable terms and conditions of the agreement are not contrary to Ghanaian law and public policy. There are no specific Ghanaian guidelines on term limits applicable to franchise agreements; therefore, parties are free to indicate the duration of the agreement.

However for those franchise agreements deemed to be technology transfers the following applies:

Limits on Nature of Fees

1. Payment for Technology

Royalties in respect of know-how patents and other industrial property rights shall range from 0% to 6% of net sales of the technology recipient.

2. Technical Service/Assistance

The fees for technical services or assistance (including know-how) ranges between 0% to 5% of net sales. The fee for know-how must not exceed 2% of net sales. The parties have the option of allowing running or lump sum fees considering the nature of the technical service, its duration, and dependence of the franchisee on continued foreign technical expertise—where continuing service is deemed to be required running fees are to be favored.

3. Management Service Fees

Management fees range between 0% and 2% of profit before tax. The fees for management services of projects for which profit is not anticipated during the early years can range from 0% and 2% of net sales during the first 3–5 years. The level of these fees is reduced pro-rata if the franchisor has 60% or more of the equity share capital of the franchisee company. Where a franchisor provides management/technical services in addition to patent, know-how, and trademarks, the total fee shall not exceed 8% of net sales.

Any request for fees higher than the upper levels specified above must be approved by the GIPC.

4. Taxes on Royalties

Every technology transfer agreement shall provide that taxes due on royalties shall be paid by the franchisor.

5. Incentive Royalties

Incentive royalties shall be available for sale of licensed products in overseas territories if marketed under the trademarks of the franchisor and any such approvals shall extend to subsidiaries of overseas firms.

Term of Typical Franchise Agreement

Regulation 9 of the TT Regulations provides that the duration of a technology transfer agreement shall not exceed ten years but it is renewable if required by the parties for subsequent terms each not exceeding five years.[301]

III. Currency

If all payments under a franchise agreement must be made in immediately available U.S. Dollars, please advise as to any restrictions, reporting requirements, or regulations concerning the exchange, repatriation, or remittance of U.S. Dollars.

There are no restrictions on the remittance of foreign exchange to or from Ghana; however, all remittances must be made through a person licensed by the Bank of Ghana to carry out the business of money transfers.[302]

Where the franchise is granted to a foreign enterprise, remittance of freely convertible currency is guaranteed and unconditional and can be done though any authorized dealer bank. Section 27(c) of the GIPC Act specifically provides for this in relation to fees and charges in respect of a technology transfer agreement registered under the GIPC Act. Where the franchise agreement relates to operating as a bank, as a non-banking institution engaged in the business of micro-finance etc., or as a credit bureau business, such institutions may be subject to reporting requirements or regulations prescribed by the Bank of Ghana.

---

[301] The GIPC Bill proposes that a technology transfer agreement may be renewed without the approval of the GIPC and the regulator of the relevant sector but a renewed agreement is subject to registration by the GIPC.

[302] Part III of the *Foreign Exchange Control Act, 2006 (Act 723)*.

IV. Taxes, Tariffs, and Duties

Please do not provide any in-depth comments on tax structuring. However, please provide your general comments on the typical amount of withholding tax that would apply and whether a "gross-up" provision contained in a franchise agreement would be enforceable in your country.

Withholding tax is currently levied as follows for non-residents:

1. Dividend and Interest—8%[303]
2. Royalties—15%[304]
3. Management and Technical Service Fees—15%[305]
4. Payments for goods and services—15%[306]

This tax exposure can be minimized if the party receiving the payments is incorporated in a country with which Ghana has a double taxation agreement. Currently, double taxation treaties exist between Ghana and the United Kingdom, France, Germany, South Africa, Italy, the Netherlands, Belgium, Switzerland, and Nigeria.

Since a franchise agreement is contractual, the rules of contract will apply to any gross-up provision in a franchise agreement and therefore will be enforceable in Ghana in the absence of any contrary intention by the parties.

V. Trademarks

Please advise us as to whether there are any special requirements for granting a valid trademark license, including the use of a registered user agreement or a short trademark

303 Section 85 of Internal Revenue Act, 2000 (Act 592).

304 *Id.*

305 *Id.*

306 *Id.*

license agreement and any required filing of such an agreement with the trademark authorities.

Aside from the requirement under the *Trademarks Act*[307] for registration of trademarks, no special requirements are necessary for the issuance of a valid trademark license. To that extent, there are no requirements for registered user agreements or short trademark license agreements.

VI. Restrictions on Transfer

Please advise as to whether there are any restrictions on (1) a franchisor to restrict transfers by a master franchisee, any interest in a master franchisee, or the assets of the master franchisee or (2) the ability of a master franchisee to control and/or restrict transfers of a subfranchisee's rights under a master franchise agreement, interest in the subfranchisee, or the assets of the subfranchisee.

A. In Relation to Master Franchisee

Under Ghanaian law, a person may by contract assign a legal right to another person, subject to any contrary intention (express or otherwise) of the parties in the agreement. There is thus no limitation on a franchisor to restrict transfers by a master franchisee, any interest in a master franchisee, or the assets of the master franchisee. The Ghanaian courts have held that an attempt by a third party to interfere with the contractual relations between franchisor and franchisee constitutes the tort of interference with contractual relations.

B. In Relation to Subfranchisees

A person may assign a legal right to another person, subject to any contrary agreement of the parties.[308] The ability of a master

---

[307] Trademarks Act 2004 (Act 664).

[308] Section 7 of the *Contracts Act, 1960 (Act 25)*.

franchisee to control and/or restrict transfers of a subfranchisee's rights under a master franchise agreement, transfers of an interest in the subfranchisee, or transfer of the assets of the subfranchisee is therefore not prohibited under Ghanaian law.

VII. Termination

Please advise us as to any laws relating to termination in your country, such as agency laws, required indemnity provisions, notice or "good cause" requirements, or other laws affecting termination of a franchise agreement. Please describe.

Given that there is no specific legislation governing franchise agreements in Ghana, a franchise agreement will be governed by the terms and conditions of the franchise agreement. The parties are therefore at liberty to include whatever termination clauses they deem applicable to the contract.

VIII. Governing Law, Jurisdiction, and Dispute Resolution

A. Choice of Law of Foreign Jurisdiction

Please confirm whether the choice of law of a foreign jurisdiction would likely to be upheld under the law of the country, except for certain matters such as trademarks, bankruptcy, and competition matters, which we assume would be governed by the law in your country.

Under Ghanaian law, an issue arising out of a transaction is determined according to the system of law intended by the parties to the transaction to govern the issue. The Ghanaian courts have held that not only will the choice of law of a foreign jurisdiction be upheld, but consideration will be given to a foreign system of law which the parties may, from the nature or form of the transaction, have intended to govern the issue.[309] However, the Ghanaian courts would also not decline jurisdiction in a matter despite the existence of a choice of law provision if the courts determine that the subject of dispute is closely connected to Ghana.

However, where the agreement is registered with the GIPC as a technology transfer agreement, the laws of Ghana shall govern the agreement[310] and any clause in the agreement that is designed to prevent the franchisee from contesting or assisting in determining, whether administratively or by means of judicial proceedings, the validity of industrial property rights claimed or secured in Ghana by the franchisor shall be unenforceable.[311]

Where the agreement is registered with the GIPC as a technology transfer agreement, Regulation 11 of the TT Regulations provide that if any dispute cannot be settled amicably, it may be submitted to arbitration:

a) in accordance with the rules of procedure for arbitration of the United Nations Commission on International Trade Law; or
b) within the framework of any bilateral and multilateral agreement on investment protection to which the governments of the franchisor and franchisee are parties; or
c) in accordance with any other international machinery for the settlement of investment disputes agreed to by the parties.

---

[309] *C.I.L.E v. Black Star Line and Another* [1967] GLR 744.

[310] Regulation 10 of the Technology Transfer Regulations, 1992 (LI 1547).

[311] Regulation 4(j) of the Technology Transfer Regulations 1992 (LI 1574).

B. International Arbitration Dispute Resolution

Please confirm that a court in your country would honor an election of international arbitration dispute resolution, and therefore refuse to hear any disputes arising under a franchise agreement.

The courts in Ghana will honor an international arbitration agreement. Under Ghanaian law, where a party to an arbitration agreement commences legal proceedings against another party to the agreement in any court, an application may be made to the court to stay the proceedings and the court, if satisfied that there is no sufficient reason why the matter should not be referred in accordance with the agreement, may make an order staying the proceedings. In other words, the determination of whether a stay should be granted is subject to the discretion of the court.[312]

Ghana is a signatory to the *Convention on the Recognition and Enforcement of Foreign Arbitral Awards* (the "New York Convention").

IX. Non-Competition Provisions

If the franchise agreement prohibits the franchisee from engaging in certain competitive activities during the term of the agreement, and for a 12-month period after the termination or expiration of the agreement, please comment on the enforceability of non-competition covenants in your country.

It is common practice to include non-competition provisions in commercial agreements. The parties in a franchise agreement may freely agree on non-competition provisions, such as the prohibition of the franchise from engaging in certain competitive activities during the term of the agreement and for such

[312] *Khoury v Khoury 1* [1962] GLR 98 at 101 and *C.I.L.E v. Black Star Line and Another* [1967] GLR 744 at 747.

reasonable time as the parties may agree after the termination or expiration of the agreement. These prohibitions would be considered enforceable. It is also common to extend the prohibition of competition to affiliates and related persons/ entities of the franchisee. However, as previously noted, as a non-regulated agreement, the parties are free to agree on the existence of a non-competition provision and its terms, always in compliance with general principles of the law.

It is common practice to include non-competition provisions in commercial agreements. The parties in a franchise agreement may freely agree on non-competition provisions, such as the prohibition of the franchise from engaging in certain competitive activities during the term of the agreement and for such reasonable time as the parties may agree after the termination or expiration of the agreement. These prohibitions would be considered enforceable. It is also common to extend the competition to affiliates and related persons/entitles of the franchisee. However, as previously noted, as a non-regulated agreement, the parties are free to agree on the existence of a non-competition provision and its terms, always in compliance with the general principles of the law.

The competition legislation in Ghana is the Protection Against Unfair Competition Act, 2000 (Act 589) (the "Unfair Competition Act") and the general principle, under the Unfair Competition Act, is that a conduct or activity in the ordinary course of industry or commercial activities which is contrary to honest practices is anti-competitive or unfair competition. An activity or conduct includes an act, practice, or an omission to act. However, the Unfair Competition Act does not provide a definition of "honest practices."

The Unfair Competition Act does not create any regulatory body or administrative process for the purpose of enforcement. It rather provides that an aggrieved person may seek common law remedies in court. The court may award injunctive or other equitable remedies, compensatory damages, or any other remedy that it deems fit.

Competition is regulated on an industry specific basis and the laws pertaining to some specific industries contain some specific regulations on anti-competitive practices.

However, if the franchise agreement is deemed to be captured by the TT Regulations, the GIPC will not register any agreement that contains any of the anti-competitive clauses referred to in Regulation 4 of the TT Regulations and as mentioned in part II. B above.

X. Language Requirements

Does the law in your country require that a franchise agreement be translated into the local language in order to be enforceable between the parties?

Ghanaian legislation does not require that a franchise agreement be translated into local language for purposes of enforceability; however, in certain instances the parties may be required to produce a certified copy in English, if the franchise agreement is in a language other than English.

Regulation 7 (1) of the TT Regulations provides that it is the duty of the franchisor to give full description of the technology and to supply all necessary documentation and information in English.

XI. Other Significant Matters

Please advise as to whether there are any significant matters not addressed above of which a franchisor should be aware in connection with its entering into a franchise agreement in your country.

It is likely that most franchise agreements exceeding 18 months in duration may be caught by the provisions of the TT Regulations, which in essence favors the franchisee unless suitable contractual alternatives are agreed. Under the TT Regulations, it will be the duty of the franchisor to provide process performance warranties in agreements covering large projects that involve considerable technical complexity not explained to the franchisee at the time of negotiations or before the franchisee makes front-end payments,[313] guarantee the efficient performance of the technology and the continuous availability of essential spare parts during the tenure of the agreement,[314] and inform the franchisee of improvements and innovations relating to the technology and shall supply them on terms mutually acceptable to the parties.[315]

---

[313] Regulation 13 of the Technology Transfer Regulations 1992 (LI 1574).

[314] Regulation 7(2) of the Technology Transfer Regulations 1992 (LI 1574).

[315] *Id.* at 7(3).

Franchising in Kenya

John Syekei and Joseph Githaiga

Coulson Harney

Nairobi, Kenya

Kenya

I. Introduction

A. Historical Background of Country

Founding President Jomo Kenyatta led Kenya from independence in 1963 until his death in 1978, when President Daniel Toroitich arap Moi took power in constitutional succession. Kenya was a de facto one-party state from 1969 until 1982. Close to 30 years later, in August 2010, Kenyans overwhelmingly adopted a new constitution in a national referendum. The new constitution introduced additional checks and balances to executive power and significant devolution of power and resources to 47 newly created counties. The first presidential election under the new constitution occurred on March 4, 2013. Uhuru Kenyatta, the son of founding President Jomo Kenyatta, won the March elections in the first round by a close margin and was sworn into office on April 9, 2013.

B. Economy of the Country

Kenya is the leading economy in East Africa and the hub for a majority of the foreign investment into the region. The growth of Kenya's economy has traditionally been underpinned by the tourism and agricultural industries (primarily exports of tea, coffee, and horticultural produce). However, over the last decade there has been a sustained government effort to diversify the economy, which, combined with investments from an active and engaged private sector, have resulted in remarkable developments in areas such as the telecommunications and IT sectors and the banking and insurance services industries. In addition, heavy annual remittances from the Kenyan diaspora have helped to further spur economic growth. Kenya now boasts some of the fastest growing urban centers on the continent, with Nairobi, the capital, being a showcase for this phenomenon—with its new malls, new roads, new hotels, and new gated communities. Recent discoveries in oil and gas as well as rare minerals are set to further boost the Kenyan growth story and cement its position as the regional powerhouse in East Africa. To effectively do so though, Kenya will also have to tackle key economic challenges such as high youth unemployment, spiraling budget deficits, inflationary pressures, and exchange rate fluctuations.

C. Franchise Legal Overview

There are no specific laws in Kenya governing franchise agreements. Franchise agreements are generally regulated by the law of contract as applicable in Kenya.[316]

II. Regulatory Requirements

A. Pre-Sale Disclosure

Please describe any pre-sale franchise disclosure or similar requirements that may apply to franchise transactions.

---

316 There are two sources of laws in Kenya—statutory law and non-statutory law. Kenyan statutory law is contained in statutes that were adopted from British colonial times and statutes that have been passed since December 12, 1963 (the date of independence). The pre-independence acts that were adopted subsequent to the date of independence are very similar to, if not identical to, acts dealing with similar subjects in other former British colonies such as Uganda, Tanzania, Zambia, Malawi, and Zimbabwe. The post-independence acts are largely derived from English acts on similar subjects with appropriate modifications for local circumstances. The adoption of a new Constitution for Kenya in August 2010 has brought, and will continue to bring, significant changes to the political, judicial, and administrative systems of Kenya. It also requires a large number of new laws to be enacted, either to replace current statutes, or to legislate for new aspects. This is likely to take several years to complete, notwithstanding that the process has begun.

Most of the non-statutory law in Kenya is based on English common law and equitable principles, but in addition, a section of common law has also developed from decisions of the Kenyan courts since the date of independence. Much of this latter section of law is based on the decisions of English courts and the courts of other countries in the commonwealth. Kenyan courts are not bound by these decisions, but they regard them to be highly persuasive if similar facts and law are involved and they are clearly not repugnant to the interests and circumstances of Kenya and its inhabitants. Consequently, most of the commercial law that is not specifically covered by Kenyan statutes is based on English common law.

Kenyan law does not prescribe any pre-sale disclosure requirements to franchise transactions.

B. Governmental Approvals, Registrations, Filing Requirements

Please describe any necessary government approvals, registrations, or filing requirements that may apply to franchise transactions.

There are no specific approval, registration, or filing requirements for franchise agreements. Nonetheless, particular franchise agreements or arrangements may fall within the ambit of the *Competition Act, 2010* ("Act") if they are determined to be restrictive trade practices, that is,

> *"agreements between undertakings, decisions by associations of undertakings, decisions by undertakings or concerted practices by undertakings which have as their object or effect the prevention, distortion or lessening of competition in trade in goods or services in Kenya, or a part of Kenya."*

Examples of restricted practices under the Act include:

a) directly or indirectly fixing purchase or sales prices or any other trading conditions;

b) dividing markets by allocating customers, suppliers, areas, or specific types of goods or services;

c) involving a practice of minimum resale price maintenance;

d) limiting or controlling production, market outlets, or access, technical development or investment; or

e) otherwise preventing, distorting, or restricting competition.

The foregoing practices are prohibited unless they have been specifically exempted under the Act by the Competition

Authority ("Authority"). The application for exemption must be in the prescribed manner and accompanied by such information as may be prescribed or as the Authority may reasonably require.

The Authority in determining the application for exemption may:

a) grant the exemption;

b) refuse to grant the exemption, and notify the applicant accordingly with a statement of the reasons for the refusal; or

c) issue a certificate of clearance stating that in its opinion, on the basis of the facts in its possession, the agreement, decision or concerted practice or the category of agreements, decisions, or concerted practices does not constitute a restricted trade practice.

The nature of the franchise business may also require the franchisor to seek a license if it operates or proposes to operate in a regulated industry, for example, telecommunications, insurance, banking, and so on.

C. Limits of Fees and Typical Term of Franchise Agreement

Please describe any limits upon the nature and extent of fees and the term of a typical franchise agreement.

There are no term limits that apply specifically to franchise agreements and, generally, the parties to the agreement are free to agree on the nature and extent of fees.

III. Currency

If all payments under a franchise agreement must be made in immediately available U.S. Dollars, please advise as to any restrictions, reporting requirements, or regulations concerning the exchange, repatriation, or remittance of U.S. Dollars.

There are currently no exchange controls applicable in Kenya that restrict the repatriation or remittance of foreign currency.

The *Central Bank Act, Cap 491 of the Laws of Kenya,*[317] states that, except with the permission of the Central Bank, the following transactions must be effected through an authorized bank:

a) payments in Kenya, to or for the credit of a person outside Kenya;

b) payments outside Kenya, to or for the credit of a person in Kenya; or

c) payments in Kenya (other than a payment for a current transaction[318]) between a resident and non-resident.

Accordingly, under the Central Bank Act, a person may seek the permission of the Central Bank of Kenya to exempt one of the types of transactions listed above from transfer through an authorized bank. A person who contravenes the above provisions commits an offence and shall be liable on conviction to a fine not exceeding five hundred thousand shillings (approximately US$5,786) or to imprisonment for a term not exceeding three years, or to both.

IV. Taxes, Tariffs, and Duties

Please do not provide any in-depth comments on tax structuring. However, please provide your general comments on the typical amount of withholding tax that would apply and whether a

[317] Section 33H of the Central Bank Act.

[318] According to Section 2 of the Central Bank Act, a "payment for a current transaction" is a payment other than a payment for transferring capital. It includes: (1) a payment due in connection with trade, (2) a payment due as interest or as net income or return from other investment, (3) a payment for amortization of a loan or for depreciation of direct investment, or (4) a remittance for family living expenses.

"gross-up" provision contained in a franchise agreement would be enforceable in your country.

In Kenya, withholding tax is applicable to dividends, interest, royalties, and technical services fees.

With regard to dividends, no withholding tax is imposed if the recipient is a qualifying Kenyan financial institution or the resident recipient company controls 12.5% or more of the capital of the payer. Otherwise, the rate is 5% for dividends paid to residents of Kenya and on listed shares for citizens of the East African Community. A rate of 10% applies for other nonresidents.

With regard to interest, there are different categories for withholding tax on interest. Interest received from financial institutions is subject to a 15% tax, while the withholding tax on interest on bearer certificates is 25%. Withholding tax on interest from bearer bonds is 10%.

Royalties paid to a resident are subject to a 5% withholding tax whereas the rate of 20% applies if royalties are paid to a nonresident.

A withholding tax of 10% is levied on the payment of technical service fees (as well as professional/management fees) where the services are provided by a resident. The rate is 20% where the service provider is nonresident.

Kenya is a party to double taxation treaties with a number of countries including Zambia, Norway, Denmark, Sweden, the United Kingdom, Germany, Canada, and India. Kenya has also signed double taxation treaties with Italy, Tanzania, and Uganda but they are not in force as they have not been ratified.

Gross-up provisions are recognized under Kenyan law and are common in agreements entered into in Kenya.

Kenya

V. Trademarks

Please advise us as to whether there are any special requirements for granting a valid trademark license, including the use of a registered user agreement or a short trademark license agreement and any required filing of such an agreement with the trademark authorities.

Any trademarks that are the subject of a franchise agreement need to be registered. The registration of trademarks in Kenya is similar to the procedure in most common law jurisdictions.

The *Trade Marks Act, Cap 506 of the Laws of Kenya* ("TMA"), allows for a person other than the proprietor of a trademark to be registered as a licensee thereof.

For a person to be registered as a licensee of a trademark, the proprietor and the proposed licensee are required to apply in writing to the Registrar of Trade Marks in the prescribed manner and furnish him or her with a statutory declaration made by the proprietor, or by some person authorized to act on his or her behalf and approved by the Registrar stating:

a) particulars of the relationship, existing or proposed, between the proprietor and the proposed licensee, including particulars showing the degree of control by the proprietor over the permitted use that their relationship will confer and whether it is a term of their relationship that the proposed licensee shall be the sole licensee or that there shall be any other restriction as to persons for whose registration as licensees application may be made;

b) the goods or services in respect of which registration is proposed;

c) any conditions or restrictions proposed with respect to the characteristics of the goods or services, to the mode or place of permitted use or to any other matter; and

d) whether the permitted use is to be for a period or without limit of period, and if for a period the duration thereof.

The Registrar should also be provided with such further documents, information or evidence as he or she may be require or as may be required under rules made pursuant to the TMA.

The TMA allows the Registrar to refuse registration as described above if it appears to him or her that such a grant would tend to facilitate trafficking in a trade mark.

The TMA does not prescribe the time it would take for the registration of a license with respect to a trademark. However, based on our experience we estimate that the registration process would approximately take two months.

VI. Restrictions on Transfer

Please advise as to whether there are any restrictions on (1) a franchisor to restrict transfers by a master franchisee, any interest in a master franchisee, or the assets of the master franchisee or (2) the ability of a master franchisee to control and/or restrict transfers of a subfranchisee's rights under a master franchise agreement, interest in the subfranchisee, or the assets of the subfranchisee.

Since there is no specific law in Kenya governing franchise arrangements, the provisions applicable to a franchise arrangement are dependent on the agreement reached between the franchisor and the franchisee and are therefore governed by the *Law of Contract Act, Cap 23 of the Laws of Kenya*, and the common law principles on contract.

Parties to a franchise agreement are free to incorporate transfer restrictions into the franchise agreement.

The inclusion of such restrictions in a particular franchise agreement and their enforceability may nonetheless be affected by other agreements entered into by a party to the franchise agreement with a third party. Such third party agreements may prohibit the exercise of the restrictions in the franchise agreement without the consent of the third party (for example a third-party agreement with a bank may prohibit an assignment of the franchise agreement or the transfer of the franchise business without the prior written consent of the bank).

VII. Termination

Please advise us as to any laws relating to termination in your country, such as agency laws, required indemnity provisions, notice or "good cause" requirements, or other laws affecting termination of a franchise agreement. Please describe.

Generally, the termination of a contract is a matter typically governed by the contract between the parties and is not prescribed in statute. English common law principles on agency and contract apply in Kenya in construing such provisions in a contract.

VIII. Governing Law, Jurisdiction, and Dispute Resolution

A. Choice of Law of Foreign Jurisdiction

Please confirm whether the choice of law of a foreign jurisdiction would likely to be upheld under the law of the country, except for certain matters such as trademarks, bankruptcy, and competition matters, which we assume would be governed by the law in your country.

Kenyan courts generally observe choice of law and forum clauses. A contract is governed by the law chosen by the parties. The choice can be expressed or demonstrated with reasonable certainty by the terms of the contract. Kenyan courts will disregard the application of a rule of foreign law where its application would be contrary to public policy.

B. International Arbitration Dispute Resolution

Please confirm that a court in your country would honor an election of international arbitration dispute resolution, and therefore refuse to hear any disputes arising under a franchise agreement.

Kenyan Courts would honor and uphold an election of international dispute resolution, if the parties have by agreement agreed to such submission. Therefore, if a franchise agreement provides that a dispute is to be submitted to arbitration in a foreign country, Kenyan courts will refuse to entertain a claim and would direct the parties to resolve the dispute through arbitration as provided for in the franchise agreement.

Kenya is a signatory to the 1958 New York Convention on the Recognition and Enforcement of Foreign Arbitral Awards (the "New York Convention"). The Arbitration Act provides that an international arbitration award shall be recognized as binding and enforced in accordance with the provisions of the New York Convention or any other convention to which Kenya is signatory and relating to arbitral awards.

IX. Non-Competition Provisions

If the franchise agreement prohibits the master franchisee from engaging in certain competitive activities during the term of the agreement, and for a 12-month period after the termination or expiration of the agreement, please comment on the enforceability of non-competition covenants in your country.

Non-competition covenants in Kenya are governed by the *Contracts in Restraint of Trade Act, Cap 24 of the Laws of Kenya* ("CRTA"). Such covenants may be included in contracts but the court may strike them out where a party to an agreement challenging the clause proves that they are unreasonable.

The CRTA specifically provides that any agreement or contract that contains a provision or covenant whereby a party to the agreement is restrained from exercising any lawful profession, trade, business, or occupation shall not be void only on the ground that the provision or covenant is contained in the agreement. However, the High Court shall have power to declare the provision or covenant to be void where the court is satisfied that, having regard to the nature of the profession, trade, business, or occupation concerned, and the period of time and the area within which it is expressed to apply, and to all the circumstances of the case, the provision or covenant is not reasonable either:

- in the interests of the parties (in that it affords more than adequate protection to the party in whose favor it is imposed); or

- in the interests of the public (in that it is not injurious to the public interest).

X. Language Requirements

Does the law in your country require that a franchise agreement be translated into the local language in order to be enforceable between the parties?

There is no specific provision in Kenyan law requiring that a franchise agreement be translated for it to be enforceable between the parties.

XI. Other Significant Matters

Please advise as to whether there are any significant matters not addressed above of which a franchisor should be aware in connection with its entering into a franchise agreement in your country.

Since there is no specific legislation governing franchise agreements in Kenya, there are no comprehensive legal requirements applicable to franchise agreements other than the ones discussed herein.

There is no franchise association in Kenya, which may be as a result of the fact that franchise arrangements involving Kenyan entities are not common and are mainly used by multinational brands. Examples of franchise brands in Kenya include the Hilton Hotel, Intercontinental Hotel, Crown Plaza, and Kentucky Fried Chicken (KFC).

Franchising in Mozambique

Diogo Xavier da Cunha

Miranda Correia Amendoeira & Associados

Lisbon, Portugal

Mozambique

I. Introduction

A. Historical Background of Country

Almost five centuries as a Portuguese colony came to a close for Mozambique when it became independent in 1975. Large-scale emigration, economic dependence on South Africa, a severe drought, and a prolonged civil war hindered the country's development until the mid-1990s. The ruling party, the Front for the Liberation of Mozambique (FRELIMO) formally abandoned Marxism in 1989, and the new constitution provided for multiparty elections and a free market economy. In 1992, a United Nations-negotiated peace agreement between FRELIMO and rebel Mozambique National Resistance forces ended the civil war. In December 2004, Mozambique underwent a delicate transition when Joaquim Chissano stepped down after being in office for 18 years. His successor Armando Emilio Guebuza, promised to continue the sound economic policies that have encouraged foreign investment.

B. Economy of the Country

Soon after its independence in 1975, Mozambique was one of the world's poorest countries. The mismanagement of the country and a brutal civil war (1977–1992) worsened the situation. In 1987, the government embraced a series of macroeconomic reforms designed to stabilize the economy. These reforms, combined with monetary assistance and political stability (since the multi-party elections in 1994) have drastically improved the country's growth rate. Monetary reforms have reduced inflation. Fiscal reforms, the introduction of a value-added tax, and the reform of the customs service, have improved the revenue collection abilities of the government. A substantial trade imbalance persists, although the opening of the Mozal aluminum smelter (the country's largest foreign investment project to date) has increased export earnings.

At the end of 2007, and after years of negotiations, the government took over Portugal's majority share of the Cahora

Bassa Hydroelectricity Company (CBHC). CBHC was a dam, which was not transferred to Mozambique after independence because of the ensuing civil war and its unpaid debts. More energy power is needed for additional investment projects in titanium extraction, processing, and garment manufacturing. These projects could further close the import/export gap. Mozambique's substantial foreign debt has been reduced through forgiveness and rescheduling under the IMF's Heavily Indebted Poor Countries (HIPC) and Enhanced HIPC initiatives, and it is now at a manageable level.

In July 2007, the Millennium Challenge Corporation signed a Compact with Mozambique. The Compact entered into force in September 2008 and will continue for five years. Compact projects will continue to focus on improving sanitation, roads, agriculture, and the business regulation environment in an effort to spur economic growth in the four northern provinces of the country. Mozambique grew at an average annual rate of 9% for most of the past decade. It is one of Africa's strongest performances. However, heavy reliance on aluminum, which accounts for about one-third of exports, subjects the economy to volatile international prices. The sharp decline in aluminum prices during the global economic crisis lowered the GDP growth by several percentage points.

In an attempt to maintain the cost of living low, the government implemented subsidies, decreased taxes and tariffs, and instituted other fiscal measures. Real growth of 7.2% was achieved in 2011.

C. Franchise Legal Overview

Despite some scattered provisions, there is no specific legal regime for franchising under Mozambican law.

In the absence of a specific regime, a franchise agreement is seen as an agreement between two parties in the exercise of a commercial activity, albeit an atypical commercial agreement. See the legal regime for which is set forth in the Mozambican

Commercial Code (approved by *Decree-law No. 2/2005, of December 27, 2005, as amended*) ("Commercial Code").

The contractual relationship (i.e., the rights and obligations) established between the parties in a franchise agreement is construed in accordance with the provisions of the Mozambican Civil Code (approved by *Decree-law No. 47344, of November 25, 1966, as amended*) ("Civil Code").

II. Regulatory Requirements

A. Pre-Sale Disclosure

Please describe any pre-sale franchise disclosure or similar requirements that may apply to franchise transactions.

No pre-sale disclosure or similar requirements apply to franchise transactions under the laws of Mozambique.

B. Governmental Approvals, Registrations, Filing Requirements

Please describe any necessary government approvals, registrations, or filing requirements that may apply to franchise transactions.

Other than the registration requirements referred to below—see Section III (Currency) and Section V (Trademarks)—no government approval, registration, or filing requirements apply specifically to franchise transactions.

C. Limits of Fees and Typical Term of Franchise Agreement

Please describe any limits upon the nature and extent of fees and the term of a typical franchise agreement.

As mentioned in Section I, since there is no specific regime governing the franchise agreement, parties are free to agree on the terms and conditions of a franchise agreement, subject to certain limits imposed by the Commercial Code and/or the Civil Code. The agreement must also always be in compliance with public policy principles of Mozambican law. Other than those caveats, there are no limits upon the nature and extent of fees or the term of a typical franchise agreement.

III. Currency

If all payments under a franchise agreement must be made in immediately available U.S. Dollars, please advise as to any restrictions, reporting requirements, or regulations concerning the exchange, repatriation, or remittance of U.S. Dollars.

According to Mozambican law, payments under a franchise agreement do not need to be made in immediately available U.S. Dollars.

Foreign exchange rules currently applicable in Mozambique are contained in (i) the *Foreign Exchange Law*, approved by *Law 11/2009, of March 11, 2009*; (ii) the *Foreign Exchange Regulations*, approved by *Decree 83/2010, of December 13, 2010*; and (iii) other ancillary regulations, including a number of instructions and orders of BoM, such as *BoM Order 6/GGBM/2005, of May 25, 2005, as amended*, which approved rules applicable to the import and export of goods and services.

BoM acts as the foreign exchange control authority and plays a decisive role in terms of the repatriation or payment of funds outside Mozambique. Any such transactions are subject to a prior authorization issued by BoM on a case-by-case basis. Essentially, under the current laws and regulations, any currency transfers between resident and non-resident entities are subject to different requirements depending on the nature of the underlying transaction.

Inflows of currency are subject to registration with BoM. Outflows (such as payments of the royalties and franchise fees to the franchisor) are subject to BoM's approval. The franchise agreement under which payments are being made is also subject to approval by the Ministry of Finance.

Payments made by Mozambican entities (i.e., the franchisee) to Mozambican bank accounts or other Mozambique resident entities (i.e., the franchisor) are free and not subject to any foreign exchange control.

IV. Taxes, Tariffs, and Duties

Please do not provide any in-depth comments on tax structuring. However, please provide your general comments on the typical amount of withholding tax that would apply and whether a "gross-up" provision contained in a franchise agreement would be enforceable in your country.

The Mozambican tax framework adopts a unitary income-tax system.

A. Applicable Rate

Services or fee payments (such as the payments made under a franchise agreement) made by resident entities to non-resident entities are subject to a 20% corporate income tax. This tax liability can be minimized if the entity receiving the payments is incorporated in a country with which Mozambique has a double taxation agreement. At the moment, South Africa, Portugal, Italy, the United Arab Emirates, Mauritius, Macau, India, Vietnam, and Botswana are the only countries that have a double taxation agreement with Mozambique.

B. Gross-up Clauses

Gross-up provisions are permitted—and even common—under Mozambican contractual practice and franchise agreements are not an exception.

V. Trademarks

Please advise us as to whether there are any special requirements for granting a valid trademark license, including the use of a registered user agreement or a short trademark license agreement and any required filing of such an agreement with the trademark authorities.

Intellectual property in Mozambique is regulated by the *Mozambican Industrial Property Code* (*Código de Propriedade Industrial de Mozambique*), which was approved by the *Council of Ministers' Decree 4/2006 of April 12, 2006*. Article 122 of that Code is the specific provision governing licensing agreements for trademarks. It establishes a very liberalized standard for entering into and enforcing licensing agreements. Under paragraph (1) of Article 122, owners of a trademark are entitled to enter into contracts to license use of that trademark to others. This same paragraph is unambiguous in its subsequent statement that such licensing will not deprive the owner of its rights of effective control over its products or services' specifications, their nature, or quality.

Under paragraph (2) of the Article, which deals with the enforceability of such agreements, the owner of the trademark may also grant the licensee powers to defend the trademark against breaches without depriving itself of any of its own rights in that respect.

Moreover, the enforcement of the licensing agreement vis-à-vis third parties is subject to notification of the agreement to the trademark office (*IPI—Instituto da Propriedade Industrial*), as specified in paragraph (3) of Article 122.

VI. Restrictions on Transfer

Please advise as to whether there are any restrictions on (1) a franchisor to restrict transfers by a master franchisee, any interest in a master franchisee, or the assets of the master franchisee or (2) the ability of a master franchisee to control and/or restrict transfers of a subfranchisee's rights under a master franchise agreement, interest in the subfranchisee, or the assets of the subfranchisee.

A. In Relation to Master Franchisee

As referred to in Section I.C., under Mozambican law there is no specific legal regime to govern the franchise agreement. The parties may agree to adopt any provision, which is not against the law. The restrictions on transfer referred to above do not violate the law, and, as such, may be included in a franchise agreement.

1. Assignment.

According to the Civil Code, neither party may assign its contractual position without the prior consent of the other party. While it is common for franchise agreements to condition the franchisee's right to assign its contractual position with the consent of the franchisor, it also applies automatically per direct operation of the law in case the agreement does not expressly provide for such a rule.

2. Change of Control.

It is permissible, under Mozambican law, to subject to the consent of the franchisor the right of the franchisee's shareholders (and the respective group members) to transfer their (direct and/or indirect) interests in the share capital of the franchisee.

3. Transfer of Assets.

A clause by virtue of which the franchisee becomes obliged upon termination of the franchise agreement to transfer to the franchisor (or to another entity designated by the franchisor) all the assets used in the franchise is permissible and common in franchise agreements. The parties are free to determine whether such provision shall be included in the agreement, and, if so, the mechanism to calculate the value of these assets.

B. In Relation to Subfranchisees.

4. Assignment.

As referred to in Section VI.A.1., according to the Civil Code, neither the master franchisee nor the subfranchisee may assign its contractual position without the prior consent of the other. Therefore, although not expressly provided for in the subfranchise agreement, a party may not assign its contractual position without the other's approval.

Moreover, the parties may also agree to subject the subfranchisee's right to assign its contractual position to the consent of the franchisor.

5. Change of Control.

As previously mentioned in Section VI.A.2., it is possible, under Mozambican law, to subject to the consent of the master franchisee the right of the subfranchisee's shareholders (and the respective group members) to transfer their interests in the share capital of the subfranchisee.

Also, the parties may further agree that the subfranchisee's shareholders (and their group companies) may only transfer their (direct and/or indirect) interests in the subfranchisee's share capital upon the master franchisee's approval.

6. Transfer of Assets.

As mentioned in Section VI.A.3., a clause by virtue of which the subfranchisee becomes obliged, upon termination of the subfranchise agreement, to transfer to the master franchisee (or to another entity designated by the master franchisee) all the assets used in the subfranchise agreement is permissible and also common in these types of agreements.

A provision may also be included in the agreement to obligate the subfranchisee to transfer to the franchisor the relevant assets upon termination of the subfranchise agreement.

It is entirely up to the parties whether such provisions are included in the agreement, and if so, the mechanism that is to be used to calculate the value of these assets.

VII. Termination

Please advise us as to any laws relating to termination in your country, such as agency laws, required indemnity provisions, notice or "good cause" requirements, or other laws affecting termination of a franchise agreement. Please describe.

As mentioned above in Section I.C., in the absence of a specific regime governing the franchise agreement, causes for termination of the agreement are those that are commonly accepted by law, such as (i) mutual agreement, (ii) unilateral termination, and (iii) the occurrence or nonoccurrence of any of the events agreed upon by the parties to constitute a cause for termination.

VIII. Governing Law, Jurisdiction, and Dispute Resolution

A. Choice of Law of Foreign Jurisdiction

Please confirm whether the choice of law of a foreign jurisdiction would likely to be upheld under the law of the country, except for certain matters such as trademarks, bankruptcy, and competition matters, which we assume would be governed by the law in your country.

Under the Civil Code, the parties may freely declare their transactions to be subject to a particular jurisdiction of their choice, including foreign jurisdictions. The party's choice of law, however, is not totally free. It must reflect a serious interest by the parties in having some connection with either any of the elements of the agreement or some connection with the chosen foreign jurisdiction.

Moreover, it is worth noting that under conflict of laws' principles, a choice of foreign law will not be permissible when it violates fundamental principles of Mozambican public policy, and the chosen law does not provide an alternative solution consistent with those principles. This means that the Mozambican court would apply the foreign law, but where the solution given by the foreign law is deemed to be offensive to Mozambique's public policy rules, the court would apply Mozambican law to the extent necessary to avoid such offence.

Also, where such agreements might be subject to any licenses or registration formalities (e.g., registration of trademark licensing agreements), the enforceability of the agreements shall be dependent on the compliance with any applicable formalities (see Section III).

B. International Arbitration Dispute Resolution

Please confirm that a court in your country would honor an election of international arbitration dispute resolution, and therefore refuse to hear any disputes arising under a franchise agreement.

The Mozambican legal framework governing arbitration is set forth in the *Arbitration, Conciliation and Mediation Law—Law 11/99, of July 8, 1999* (the "ACML"). The ACML is a fairly modern and sophisticated statute, which is primarily based on the Portuguese Arbitration Law.

The definition of international arbitration set out in the ACML follows the one adopted in the *1985 Model Law on International Commercial Arbitration of the United Nations Commission on International Trade Law* ("UNCITRAL"). International arbitration is defined as an arbitration in which international trade interests are at stake. The ACML then lists several instances where it deems that international trade interests are at stake. It includes circumstances where the parties to the arbitration are residents of different countries.

Under ACML, the parties are free to choose international arbitration rules (whether institutional or ad hoc rules) to govern the arbitration. Generally, the parties may choose a foreign country as the seat for arbitration proceedings.

Mozambican courts will uphold the judgment of a foreign court or a foreign arbitration award. However, the judgment would first have to undergo a review and confirmation process in the Mozambican courts. The procedure to have a foreign arbitral award recognized and enforced through the Mozambican courts is made in accordance with the *Convention on the Recognition and Enforcement of Foreign Arbitral Awards* (the "New York Convention")—to which Mozambique is a party.

The local courts' ability to challenge, to intervene, or accept an appeal from an arbitration/arbitral award varies depending on whether it is a (i) local arbitration/arbitral award or (ii) an international arbitration/arbitral award.

Local courts cannot challenge or intervene in a local arbitration / arbitral award. They may, however, accept an appeal for the annulment of the arbitral award in the following situations:

- one of the parties was under some incapacity;
- the agreement is not valid under the law to which the parties have subjected it or, if there is no such law indicated, under Mozambican law;
- a party against whom the award is invoked was not given proper notice of the appointment of the arbitrator or of the arbitration proceedings or was otherwise unable to present its case;
- the award does not fall within the terms of the submission to arbitration, or it contains decisions on matters beyond the

scope of the submission to arbitration, though the decisions on matters submitted to arbitration can be separated from those not so submitted, in which case only the latter category will be subject to annulment;

- the composition of the arbitral authority or the arbitral procedure was not in accordance with the agreement of the parties or was not in accordance with Mozambican law;

- the subject matter of the disagreement between the parties is not capable of settlement by arbitration under Mozambican law; or

- the recognition or enforcement of the award would be contrary to Mozambican public policy.

Local courts cannot challenge, intervene, or accept any appeal from international arbitration/arbitral awards. Moreover, as noted above, Mozambique is a party to the New York Convention, whereby the recognition and enforcement of the award may only be refused by the local courts in the situations listed in the convention and which are very similar to those described in subsections (a)–(g) above. However, as Mozambican courts are still fairly inexperienced when it comes to enforcement of foreign arbitral awards pursuant to the New York Convention, it is quite likely that unexpected problems will arise when one simply seeks to apply the terms and conditions set forth therein. Accordingly, obtaining recognition of a foreign arbitral award from the Mozambican courts may not be a straightforward exercise.

IX. Non-Competition Provisions

If the franchise agreement prohibits the master franchisee from engaging in certain competitive activities during the term of the agreement, and for a 12-month period after the termination or expiration of the agreement, please comment on the enforceability of non-competition covenants in your country.

Under Mozambican Commercial Code, the parties in a franchise agreement may freely agree on non-competition provisions, such as a prohibition on the franchisee of engaging in certain competitive activities during the term of the agreement and for a 12-month period after the termination or expiration of the agreement. Such provisions would be considered enforceable.

It is common to extend the prohibition of competition (i) to affiliates and related persons/entities of the franchisee and (ii) for a certain period after termination of the franchise agreement. However, as previously referenced in Section I.C., as a non-regulated agreement, the parties to a franchise agreement are free to agree on a non-competition provision, so long as its terms are always in compliance with general public policy principles of Mozambican law and are not deemed inconsistent with the anti-trust rules approved by Law 10/20/13, of April 11, 2013.

X. Language Requirements

Does the law in your country require that a franchise agreement be translated into the local language in order to be enforceable between the parties?

According to Article 459 of the Commercial Code, commercial agreements are valid irrespective of their language. However, if an agreement is to be filed with any public authority in a foreign language, a sworn translation in Portuguese shall be required.

XI. Other Significant Matters

Please advise as to whether there are any significant matters not addressed above of which a franchisor should be aware in connection with its entering into a franchise agreement in your country.

There are no other significant matters to be addressed.

Franchising in Nigeria

Theophilus Emuwa and Tiwalola Okeyinka

ǼLEX

Lagos, Nigeria

Nigeria

I. Introduction

A. Historical Background of Country

A series of constitutions after World War II granted Nigeria greater autonomy; independence came in 1960. Following nearly 16 years of military rule, a new constitution was adopted in 1999, and a peaceful transition to civilian government was completed. The government continues to face the daunting task of reforming a petroleum-based economy, whose revenues have been squandered through corruption and mismanagement, and institutionalizing democracy. In addition, Nigeria continues to experience longstanding ethnic and religious tensions. Although both the 2003 and 2007 presidential elections were marred by significant irregularities and violence, Nigeria is currently experiencing its longest period of civilian rule since independence. The general elections of April 2007 marked the first civilian-to-civilian transfer of power in the country's history.

B. Economy of the Country

Nigeria has undertaken several reforms over the past decade. Nigeria's former military rulers failed to diversify the economy away from its overdependence on the capital-intensive oil sector, which provides 95% of foreign exchange earnings and about 80% of budgetary revenues. Since 2008, the government has begun showing the political will to implement the market-oriented reforms urged by the IMF, such as to modernize the banking system, to curb inflation by blocking excessive wage demands, and to resolve regional disputes over the distribution of earnings from the oil industry. In 2003, the government began deregulating fuel prices, announced the privatization of the country's four oil refineries, and instituted the National Economic Empowerment Development Strategy, a domestically designed and run program modeled on the IMF's Poverty Reduction and Growth Facility for fiscal and monetary management. In November 2005, Abuja won Paris Club[319] approval for a debt-relief deal that eliminated US$18 billion of debt in exchange for US$12 billion in payments—a total package worth US$30 billion of Nigeria's total US$37 billion external debt. The deal subjects Nigeria to stringent IMF reviews. Based largely on increased oil exports and high global crude prices, GDP rose strongly in 2007–09.

GDP rose strongly in 2007–11 because of growth in non-oil sectors and robust global crude oil prices. President Goodluck Jonathan has established an economic team that includes experienced and reputable members and has announced plans to increase transparency, diversify economic growth, and improve fiscal management. Lack of infrastructure and slow implementation of reforms are key impediments to growth. The government is working toward developing stronger public-private partnerships for roads, agriculture, and power. Nigeria's financial sector was hurt by the global financial and economic crises, but the Central Bank governor has taken measures to restructure and strengthen the sector to include imposing mandatory higher minimum capital requirements.

C. Franchise Legal Overview

Currently, Nigeria's general commercial laws govern the rights and obligations of parties to a franchise agreement. Nigeria does not have franchise-specific legislation but it has enacted legislation governing the importation of intellectual property. Any agreement relating to the importation of intellectual property must be registered with Nigeria's National Office for Technology Acquisition and Promotion ("NOTAP"). NOTAP has a number of specifications that must be satisfied before it will register any agreement. According to trade publications, franchise opportunities in the country include, not only food

[319] A monthly meeting in Paris attended by creditors of 19 countries to discuss debt issues. Among other things, the Paris Club addresses the issue of coordinated debt relief for developing countries that cannot service their debt.

franchising but also retail, telecommunications, oil and gas, banking, and hospitality. To promote franchising activity in the country, the Nigerian International Franchise Association ("NIFA") assists franchisors and potential franchisees by providing services such as financial and marketing advice, consulting, franchise recruitment, and feasibility studies.

II. Regulatory Requirements

A. Pre-Sale Disclosure

Please describe any pre-sale franchise disclosure or similar requirements that may apply to franchise transactions.

No pre-sale franchise disclosure or similar requirements apply to franchise transactions under the laws of Nigeria.

B. Governmental Approvals, Registrations, Filing Requirements

Please describe any necessary government approvals, registrations, or filing requirements that may apply to franchise transactions.

NOTAP is charged with the responsibility of registering all agreements entered into for the transfer of foreign technology to Nigerian parties.

Section 4 of the *National Office for Technology Acquisition and Promotion Act*[320] ("NOTAP Act") states that such agreements are registrable if their purpose or intent is, in the opinion of the NOTAP, wholly or partially for or in connection with the following:

- use of trademarks;

[320] *Chapter N62 Laws of the Federation of Nigeria* ("LFN") 2004.

- use of patented inventions;
- supply of technical expertise in the form of technical assistance of any description whatsoever;
- supply of detailed engineering drawings;
- supply of machinery and plant; and
- provision of operating staff, managerial assistance, and the training of personnel.

A franchisor entering into a franchise agreement with a Nigerian party will have to register the agreement with NOTAP. To qualify for registration, the franchise agreement must comply with the specifications provided under Section 6 (2) of the NOTAP Act. The franchise agreement must:

- provide a transfer of technology not freely available in Nigeria;
- provide pricing and other valuable consideration commensurate with the technology acquired or to be acquired;
- not give the franchisor powers to regulate or intervene in the administration of any undertaking belonging to the franchisee;
- not oblige the franchisee to onerously or gratuitously assign to the franchisor or any designated persons, patents, trademarks, technical information, innovations, or improvements obtained by such franchisee with no assistance from the franchisor or such person;
- not impose limitations on technological research or development by the franchisee;

- not require the franchisee to acquire equipment, tools, parts, or raw materials exclusively from the franchisor or any other person or given source;
- not prohibit or restrict the exportation of the franchisee's products or services;
- not compel or oblige the franchisee to sell the products manufactured by it exclusively to the franchisor or any designated person or source;
- allow the franchisee to use complementary technologies;
- not compel the franchisee to use personnel designated by the franchisor either on a permanent basis or for any unconscionable period;
- not require the franchisee to appoint the franchisor as the exclusive sales agent;
- not exceed a period of ten years;
- not oblige the franchisee to introduce unnecessary design changes;
- not permit the franchisor to impose unnecessary and onerous obligations on the franchisee by means of quality controls or prescription of standards;
- not require the franchisee to pay in full for transferred technology that has not been exploited by the franchisee;
- not compel the franchisee to accept additional technology or other matter, such as consultancy services, international sub-contracting, turn-key projects, and similar package arrangements not required by the franchisee for or in connection with the principal purpose for which technology is to be or has been acquired by franchisee; or

- not oblige the franchisee to submit to foreign jurisdiction in any controversy arising from a decision concerning the interpretation or enforcement in Nigeria of any such contract or agreement or any provisions thereof.

NOTAP may register a franchise agreement notwithstanding the above specifications, if it is in the "national interest"[321] to do so.

Where the franchise would involve the use of the franchisor's trademark in the business in Nigeria, and it is intended that the franchise agreement be registered with NOTAP, the application for registration would have to be accompanied by evidence of the franchisor's right to those trademarks. A schedule of the trademarks and logo (where applicable) will suffice. *See also* Section III (Currency) of this chapter relating to bank approvals potentially required to authorize or effect transfers of payments due under a franchise agreement.

The documents required for filing a franchise agreement with NOTAP include:

- Duly completed NOTAP application form;
- List and proof of patent/trademark registration;
- Two (2) copies of NOTAP Questionnaire duly completed;
- Two (2) certified copies (by company secretary of the franchisee) of the franchise agreement to be registered;
- Certificate of incorporation of the franchisee;
- Memorandum and articles of association of the franchisee;
- Audited accounts for 3 years of the franchisee;

[321] Section 6 (3) NOTAP Act.

- List of expatriates and Nigerian understudy; and

- Comprehensive training schedule indicating number of personnel, place, duration, and the skill or knowledge to be acquired.

NOTAP may sometimes perform an inspection of an applicant's premises prior to granting approval of an agreement that has been submitted to it. Where NOTAP decides to do an inspection, approval may not be obtained until about a month after the inspection. Where NOTAP decides not to do a prior inspection, it typically takes about a month from the submission of the agreement to receive a response from NOTAP, possibly with approval.

C. Limits of Fees and Typical Term of Franchise Agreement

Please describe any limits upon the nature and extent of fees and the term of a typical franchise agreement.

1. Limits on Nature of Fees

a. Royalty Fees

The *Revised Guidelines on Acquisition of Foreign Technology* published by NOTAP in 2003 ("NOTAP Guidelines") stipulates that royalty fees in connection with trademark and know-how agreements, including franchise agreements, should not exceed 5% of the net sale value or profit before tax, where net sales value is not applicable. Net sales value is defined as the ex-factory sales price of the product, exclusive of excise duties and other taxes less the cost of the standard bought-out components and the landed cost of imported components, irrespective of the source of procurement, including freight, insurance, and custom duties. In practice, net sales value is interpreted to mean turnover.

However, in practice, NOTAP may not approve an agreement where royalty fees exceed 2.5% of the turnover of the franchisee. Also, NOTAP will not approve payment of trademark fees to be made in respect of any agreement where the trademark owner has more than 75% of the equity in the local company.

The NOTAP Guidelines state that where the Nigerian enterprise is acquiring the right to practice a process, the concept of know-how should be clearly expressed and defined in the contract. In this connection, the franchisor cannot charge a separate fee for concepts such as "technical information" or "technical services." It also provides that agreements that include provisions for payments for the use of foreign trademark will not be accepted for registration except if the trademark is internationally recognized and the product is meant for export.

b. Technical Services Fees

Fees for technical services must not be tied to sales or profit; instead they must be calculated on a per diem rate or man-hour, man-day, or man-month.

c. Management Fees

Management fees must not exceed 5% of profit before tax except for the management of hotels by international hotel chains, in which case a basic or lump sum fee not exceeding 5% of turnover plus an incentive fee not exceeding 12% of gross operating profit ("GOP") is currently applicable.

d. Consultancy Fees

Consultancy fees must not exceed 5% of the total project cost and must be limited to projects of very high technology content for which indigenous expertise is not available.

2. The term of a typical franchise agreement

Parties are at liberty to negotiate the term of their franchise agreement. NOTAP Guidelines provide that the term of a franchise agreement to be registered with NOTAP must not exceed ten years. In practice, NOTAP may not approve agreements with a duration exceeding three years. The NOTAP registration can be renewed for a further period.

III. Currency

If all payments under a franchise agreement must be made in immediately available U.S. Dollars, please advise as to any restrictions, reporting requirements, or regulations concerning the exchange, repatriation, or remittance of U.S. Dollars.

The certificate of registration issued by NOTAP will be required by the Central Bank of Nigeria to authorize or effect transfer of any payment due to the franchisor under the franchise agreement. Remittance of fees shall be made by an authorized dealer and is subject to submission and acceptance of the following basic documentation:

- a duly completed Form "A,"
- a certified copy of the franchise agreement registered by NOTAP,
- a certificate of registration issued by NOTAP,
- a demand note from the franchisor,
- evidence of payment of tax on the amount to be remitted,
- an audited account for the relevant period, and

- a certificate of satisfactory completion of the job issued by the Nigerian employer (applicable only to management fee and consultancy fees).

An authorized dealer is any bank licensed under the *Banks and Other Financial Institutions Act 1991*.[322] A completed Form "A" provides the particulars of the payee/applicant and the beneficiary, the purpose of the payment, and amount to be paid. It also contains a declaration by the applicant that the foreign currency will be used for the purpose stated in the form. See Appendix at the end of this chapter for example of Form "A."

IV. Taxes, Tariffs, and Duties

Please do not provide any in-depth comments on tax structuring. However, please provide your general comments on the typical amount of withholding tax that would apply and whether a "gross-up" provision contained in a franchise agreement would be enforceable in your country.

A. Applicable Rate

The applicable withholding tax rate for royalty payments made under a franchise agreement will be 10%. This tax exposure can be minimized if the party receiving the payments is incorporated in a country with which Nigeria has a double taxation agreement. Currently, Nigeria has signed and adopted double taxation agreements with the United Kingdom, France, Belgium, Pakistan, Romania, Canada, Czech Republic, China, Slovak Republic, The Netherlands, South Africa, and Italy. Nigeria has also negotiated and signed double taxation agreements with seven other countries but the agreements have not been ratified/ adopted. The countries are Sweden, South Korea, Spain, Russia, Mauritius, Denmark, and Algeria.

---

[322] Chapter B3 LFN 2004.

B. Gross-up Clauses

Paragraph 2 of the *Companies Income Tax (Rates, Etc., of Tax Deducted at Source (Withholding Tax)) Regulations* made pursuant to the *Companies Income Tax Act*,[323] states that "a deduction made from a payment shall not be regarded as an additional cost of the contract to be included in the contract price but as tax due on the payment." A gross-up clause would be in violation of this regulation only if it provides that the person making payment under a contract would be obliged to pay any withholding tax or other statutory deductions in addition to the contract price. Such a clause would be unenforceable. However, a gross-up clause that is drafted to state that the recipient would receive the amount it would have received prior to any deduction would be acceptable.

V. Trademarks

Please advise us as to whether there are any special requirements for granting a valid trademark license, including the use of a registered user agreement or a short trademark license agreement and any required filing of such an agreement with the trademark authorities.

Section 33 of the *Trade Mark Act*[324] requires that a trademark license agreement or registered user agreement must be registered with the Nigerian Trademark Registry. Registration as a registered user confers the same rights as those of the proprietor of the trademark(s) except the right to assign or transfer. Also, subject to the terms of the agreement between the proprietor and the registered user, a registered user of a trademark is entitled to require that the proprietor institute proceedings to prevent infringement of the trademark(s) in respect of which a registered user status has been granted or to

[323] Chapter C21 LFN 2004.

[324] Chapter T13 LFN 2004.

institute an action in his name if the proprietor refuses to take any action.

The Registrar of Trademarks is vested with the power to refuse the registration of a license agreement where it appears to the Registrar that the grant of registration will tend to facilitate trafficking in the trademark.

It will typically take about 4–6 weeks from filing to obtain registration for a license agreement.

VI. Restrictions on Transfer

Please advise as to whether there are any restrictions on (1) a franchisor to restrict transfers by a master franchisee, any interest in a master franchisee, or the assets of the master franchisee or (2) the ability of a master franchisee to control and/or restrict transfers of a subfranchisee's rights under a master franchise agreement, interest in the subfranchisee, or the assets of the subfranchisee.

No. There are no restrictions on a franchisor to restrict transfers by a master franchisee, any interest in a master franchisee, or the assets of the master franchisee, or the ability of the master franchisee to control and/or restrict transfers of a subfranchisee's rights under a master franchise agreement, interest in the subfranchisee, or assets of the subfranchisee. It is typical for agreements to make provisions to the effect that the franchise agreement will terminate in the event of a material change in the structure or business of the company.

VII. Termination

Please advise us as to any laws relating to termination in your country, such as agency laws, required indemnity provisions, notice or "good cause" requirements, or other laws affecting termination of a franchise agreement. Please describe.

There are no laws regulating termination of franchise agreements in Nigeria. Most agency relationships in Nigeria are based on an express or implied agreement between the parties.[325] Parties have a right to terminate an agreement or deem an agreement to have been terminated once any of the grounds for termination stated in the agreement occurs.

An agency relationship may be terminated by mutual agreement between the principal and the agent or on the death, bankruptcy, and/or insanity of either party. An agency relationship will also be terminated if its continuation becomes impossible, e.g., on grounds of frustration or a supervening impossibility.

If an agreement specifies a period of notice, the notice of termination must be for that period, but if no period is specified, a reasonable notice must be given. A principal who gives less notice than is reasonable may nevertheless succeed in terminating the relationship, but it will be deemed to have committed a breach of contract in doing so.

VIII. Governing Law, Jurisdiction, and Dispute Resolution

A. Choice of Law of Foreign Jurisdiction

Please confirm whether the choice of law of a foreign jurisdiction would likely to be upheld under the law of the country, except for certain matters such as trademarks, bankruptcy, and competition matters, which we assume would be governed by the law in your country.

Under Nigerian law, in the absence of fraud or misrepresentation, parties are bound by the terms of their contract.[326] Contracting parties also have the freedom to choose

[325] *Niger Progress Ltd v. North East Line Corporation* (1989) 3 N.W.L.R. (PT.107) 68.

[326] *See Omoniyi v. Alabi* [2004] 6 NWLR (Pt. 870) 551.

the law that would regulate their transaction and the courts would generally uphold foreign choice of law clauses as long as these do not violate the provision of any Nigerian law.

However, where the agreement is to be registered with NOTAP, by virtue of Section 6 (2) of the NOTAP Act, NOTAP may refuse to register any agreement which compels the franchisee to submit to foreign jurisdiction in any controversy arising for decision concerning the interpretation or enforcement in Nigeria of any such contract or agreement or any provisions thereof.

B. International Arbitration Dispute Resolution

Please confirm that a court in your country would honor an election of international arbitration dispute resolution, and therefore refuse to hear any disputes arising under a franchise agreement.

Once an agreement has been approved by NOTAP, a Nigerian court will honor an election of international arbitration dispute resolution.

Nigeria gives effect to some provisions of the *Convention on the Recognition and Enforcement of Foreign Arbitral Awards* (the "New York Convention")—to which it is a signatory.

IX. Non-Competition Provisions

If the franchise agreement prohibits the master franchisee from engaging in certain competitive activities during the term of the agreement, and for a 12-month period after the termination or expiration of the agreement, please comment on the enforceability of non-competition covenants in your country.

Non-competition provisions that are unreasonable as regards the person restrained in terms of the duration and geographical area covered are generally unenforceable in Nigeria. With respect to franchise agreements, and as specified in Section II.B., NOTAP will not register any agreement that would:

- require the franchisee to acquire equipment, tools, parts, or raw materials exclusively from the franchisor or any other person or given source;
- prohibit or restrict the exportation of the franchisee's products or services;
- compel or oblige the franchisee to sell the products manufactured by it exclusively to the franchisor or any designated person or source;
- prevent the franchisee from using complementary technologies;
- compel the franchisee to use personnel designated by the franchisor either on a permanent basis or for any unconscionable period; or
- require the franchisee to appoint the franchisor as its exclusive sales agent.

X. Language Requirements

Does the law in your country require that a franchise agreement be translated into the local language in order to be enforceable between the parties?

No. There is no law requiring a franchise agreement to be translated into a local language to be enforceable between the parties. However, agreements required or intended to be registered with NOTAP or any other regulatory body must be in the English language or must be accompanied by its English interpretation notarized in the country of origin.

XI. Other Significant Matters

Please advise as to whether there are any significant matters not addressed above of which a franchisor should be aware in connection with its entering into a franchise agreement in your country.

Policy arguments notwithstanding, many franchisors may object to any or all of the NOTAP specifications and may want to consider alternatives. One such alternative is to structure contracts around objectionable provisions of the NOTAP Act. For example, although NOTAP might take the position that the know-how and intellectual property rights being licensed by a franchisor are not valuable enough to Nigeria to justify a license fee at the upper end of the 5% range, in order to avoid such agreements being refused, applicants have in the past broken up fees into smaller and separate fees, e.g., a royalty fee for know-how, another fee for technical assistance, and a fee for a trademark license. However, in recent times such applications have not succeeded.

A more complete solution may be available to franchisors negotiating with Nigerian franchisees that have assets and/or accounts outside of Nigeria. In such cases, contractual provisions may be drafted that require the franchisee to remit royalties to the franchisor via offshore accounts, thereby obviating the need to go through the local Nigerian banking systems and, in turn, making it unnecessary to register agreements with NOTAP altogether.

Local Franchise Association

Please reference the existence of any franchise association in your country and its principal contact.

The local franchise association in Nigeria is the Nigerian International Franchise Association ("NIFA"). There is no legal requirement that a franchisor become a member. The website address of NIFA is www.nigerianfranchise.org and e-mails can also be sent to nifa@nigerianfranchise.org or info@nigerianfranchise.org.

Franchise Specific Legislation in Nigeria

Please provide any insight as to any proposed franchise specific legislation that may be under consideration in your jurisdiction.

There are no proposed franchise specific legislations under consideration in Nigeria.

Franchise Brands in Nigeria

Please provide a sample of the franchised brands that operate in your country.

Some of the franchise brands in Nigeria include:

a. Fast food/restaurant

- Dominos
- Steers
- Cold Stone Creamery
- Johnny Rockets
- Ocean Basket
- Debonairs
- Kentucky Fried Chicken
- Butterfields
- Barcelos
- Mugg & Bean
- Creamy Inn Ice Cream
- Chicken Inn
- Southern Fried Chicken

b. Clothing and accessories

- Woolworths
- Mango
- Truworths
- Etam

- Zara outlet
- Mr. Price
- T.M. Lewin
- Nike
- Adidas
- Levi's
- United Colours by Benetton
- Wrangler

c. Beauty

- Black Up cosmetics
- MUD Cosmetics

d. Hotels

- Protea Hotels
- Hilton Hotels
- Meridien Hotels
- Southern Sun
- Best Western Hotel
- Intercontinental Hotels
- Radisson Blu
- Sheraton Hotels
- Hawthorn Suites by Wyndham
- Sun International

e. Supermarkets

- Shoprite
- Game

f. Car Rental services

- Hertz
- Avis

Appendix: Nigeria – Form A

FEDERAL REPUBLIC OF NIGERIA
FOREIGN EXCHANGE (MONITORING/MISCELLANEOUS PROVISIONS) DECREE 1995

FORM A

VALID FOR FOREX? (Y/N) [ ]

YEAR [| | |]

ORIGINAL APPLICATION NUMBER AA 00056

(FOR INVISIBLE TRADE TRANSACTIONS)
(TO BE COMPLETED IN DUPLICATE)

Authorized Dealer's Code [| | |]

*Please fill in appropriate information in the blank spaces provided
*Use capital letters throughout this form

1. ______________________________
Name and address of Applicant's Banker (Authorized Dealer)

2. PARTICULARS OF APPLICANT
APPLICANT'S NAME: ______________________________
(Surname First, where applicable)
ADDRESS: ______________________________
(P.O. Box is not acceptable)
____
TOWN: ____________ STATE: ____________ PHONE/FAX: ____________
PASSPORT/REGISTRATION/CERTIFICATE OF INCORPORATION NUMBER ____________
*AIR TICKET NUMBER: ____________ AIRLINE: ____________
*ROUTE: ______________________________
*Complete only where applicable

3. PARTICULARS OF BENEFICIARY
BENEFICIARY'S NAME: ______________________________
ADDRESS: ______________________________
(P.O. Box is not acceptable)
____
TOWN: ____________ STATE: ____________ PHONE/FAX: ____________
COUNTRY: ____________ CODE: ____________
PASSPORT/REGISTRATION/CERTIFICATE OF INCORPORATION NUMBER ____________

4. PURPOSE OF PAYMENT
____
Sectorial Purpose Code: ______________________________

5. ______________________________
AMOUNT APPLIED FOR IN FOREIGN CURRENCY (IN WORDS)
AMOUNT: [ ] Currency Code: ____________
Exchange Rate: ______________________________
Payment Mode: ____________ Code: ____________

7. APPLICANT'S DECLARATION
I/We declare that the above statements are true and that the foreign currency will be used solely for the purpose stated in accordance with the approved guidelines.
** Any false declaration will make me/us liable for prosecution

____
Stamp, Signature & Date

____
Full Name:

AUTHORISED DEALER'S ENDORSEMENT

____
Stamp, Signature & Date

Full Name: ____________

OFFICIAL USE ONLY

Amount Approved: [ ] Currency Code: ____________

____
Approving Officer's Signature & Date
Full Name: ____________
Status: ____________

Franchising in Rwanda

Désiré Kamanzi

ENSafrica | Rwanda

Kigali, Rwanda

Rwanda

I. Introduction

A. Historical Background of Country

Rwanda held its first local elections in 1999 and its first post-genocide presidential and legislative elections in 2003. In 2009, Rwanda staged a joint military operation with the Congolese Army in the Democratic Republic of the Congo to rout out the Hutu extremist insurgency there and Kigali and Kinshasa restored diplomatic relations. Rwanda also joined the Commonwealth of Nations in late 2009. Commonly known as the Commonwealth, it is an intergovernmental organization of 53 member states that were mostly territories of the former British Empire. In January 2013, Rwanda assumed a nonpermanent seat on the UN Security Council for the 2013–14 term.

B. Economy of the Country

Rwanda is a rural country with about 90% of the population engaged in (mainly subsistence) agriculture and some mineral and agro-processing. Tourism, minerals, coffee, and tea are Rwanda's main sources of foreign exchange. Minerals exports declined 40% in 2009–10 due to the global economic downturn. However, Rwanda has made substantial progress in stabilizing and rehabilitating its economy to pre-1994 levels. GDP has rebounded with an average annual growth of 7%–8% since 2003 and inflation has been reduced to single digits. Rwanda continues to receive substantial aid money and obtained IMF-World Bank Heavily Indebted Poor Country (HIPC) initiative debt relief in 2005–06. In recognition of Rwanda's successful management of its macro economy, in 2010, the IMF graduated Rwanda to a Policy Support Instrument (PSI). Rwanda also received a Millennium Challenge Threshold Program in 2008.

Africa's most densely populated country is trying to overcome the limitations of its small, landlocked economy by leveraging regional trade. Rwanda joined the East African Community and is aligning its budget, trade, and immigration policies with its regional partners. The government has embraced an expansionary fiscal policy to reduce poverty by improving education, infrastructure, and foreign and domestic investment and pursuing market-oriented reforms. The Rwandan government is seeking to become a regional leader in information and communication technologies.

In 2010, Rwanda neared completion of the first modern Special Economic Zone (SEZ) in Kigali. The SEZ seeks to attract investment in all sectors, but specifically in agribusiness, information and communications technologies, trade and logistics, mining, and construction. The global downturn hurt export demand and tourism, but economic growth has recovered, driven in large part by the services sector, but inflation has grown. On the back of this growth, the government is gradually ending its fiscal stimulus policy while protecting aid to the poor.

C. Franchise Legal Overview

In Rwanda, there is no specific law that regulates franchise agreements and/or transactions. Nevertheless, the country has a strong willingness to unlock the opportunities in the franchising business area for Rwandans to exploit them.

Rwanda Development Board (RDB) and the Private Sector Federation (PSF) have set up a franchise association in the country, a move aimed at expanding businesses. The RDB and PSF seek to help entrepreneurs develop capacity to grow strong brands that can attract buyers.

II. Regulatory Requirements

A. Pre-Sale Disclosure

Please describe any pre-sale franchise disclosure or similar requirements that may apply to franchise transactions.

No pre-sale franchise disclosure or similar requirements apply to franchise transactions under the laws of Rwanda.

B. Governmental Approvals, Registrations, Filing Requirements

Please describe any necessary government approvals, registrations, or filing requirements that may apply to franchise transactions.

Rwanda law is not prescriptive in regard to what formalities are required for a franchise transaction.

Notwithstanding the above, a Rwandan franchisor or franchisee will be subject to the regular registration procedures and filing requirements required for performing business activities in Rwanda, such as, inter alia, business registration with the Office of the Registrar General.

C. Limits of Fees and Typical Term of Franchise Agreement

Please describe any limits upon the nature and extent of fees and the term of a typical franchise agreement.

In the absence of a specific legal framework governing franchise agreements, the parties are free to agree on the terms and conditions of a franchise agreement and to carry out their activities in circumstances and in a manner that does not contravene the existing laws of Rwanda.

III. Currency

If all payments under a franchise agreement must be made in immediately available U.S. Dollars, please advise as to any restrictions, reporting requirements, or regulations concerning the exchange, repatriation, or remittance of U.S. Dollars.

There are no specific restrictions on payments made available in U.S. Dollars in Rwanda. However, these payments should not offend the Rwandan law on *Anti-Money Laundering and Combating the Financing of Terrorism.*

IV. Taxes, Tariffs, and Duties

Please do not provide any in-depth comments on tax structuring. However, please provide your general comments on the typical amount of withholding tax that would apply and whether a "gross-up" provision contained in a franchise agreement would be enforceable in your country.

A. Applicable Rate

A withholding tax of 15% is levied on the following payments made by resident individuals or resident entities including tax exempt entities:

1. dividends;
2. interests;
3. royalties;
4. service fees including management and technical service fees;
5. performance payments made to an artist, a musician, or an athlete irrespective of whether paid directly or through an entity that is not resident in Rwanda; and
6. lottery and other gambling proceeds.

The withholding agent is required to file a tax declaration and remit the tax withheld to the tax administration within 15 days after the tax is withheld.

According to Article 9 of the *Income Tax Act*,[327] a withholding tax of 5% of the value of goods imported for commercial use is

[327] *Law n°16/2005 of 18/08/2005 on Direct Taxes on Income* as amended to date.

payable at the customs on the CIF (Cost, Insurance and Freight) value before goods are released by customs.

A withholding tax of 3% on the sum invoices (excluding VAT) is retained by public institutions for supply of goods and services made to them based on public tenders.

B. Gross-up Clauses

Gross-up provisions may be permissible as long as parties to a lawful agreement have mutual assent, full capacity to contract, and the agreement was made in the absence of any duress or undue influence.

V. Trademarks

Please advise us as to whether there are any special requirements for granting a valid trademark license, including the use of a registered user agreement or a short trademark license agreement and any required filing of such an agreement with the trademark authorities.

Intellectual property in Rwanda is regulated by *Law n° 31/2009 of 26/06/2009 on the Protection of Intellectual Property* ("IP Law").

Article 155 of the IP Law is the specific provision governing licensing agreements for trademarks. It stipulates that "[a]ny license contract relating to a registered mark or for which registration is requested shall provide that the licensor exercises effective control over the quality of the goods or services of the licensee, for which the mark is used. If the license contract does not provide for such quality control or the quality control is not actually exercised within the prescribed period and in the requisite manner, the license contract shall not be valid and may not be implemented."

The article also provides that to be enforceable against third parties, license agreements for registered marks must be recorded into the register of marks.

VI. Restrictions on Transfer

Please advise as to whether there are any restrictions on (1) a franchisor to restrict transfers by a master franchisee, any interest in a master franchisee, or the assets of the master franchisee or (2) the ability of a master franchisee to control and/or restrict transfers of a subfranchisee's rights under a master franchise agreement, interest in the subfranchisee, or the assets of the subfranchisee.

Rwandan Law does not specifically prescribe any specific restrictions on the franchisor's ability to restrict:

- transfers by a master franchisee,
- any interest in a master franchisee, or
- the assets of the master franchisee.

Nor do any restrictions exist relating to:

- the master franchisee's ability to control and/or restrict a subfranchisee,
- transfers of a subfranchisee's rights under a master franchise agreement,
- any interest in the subfranchisee, or
- the assets of the subfranchisee.

VII. Termination

Please advise us as to any laws relating to termination in your country, such as agency laws, required indemnity provisions, notice or "good cause" requirements, or other laws affecting termination of a franchise agreement. Please describe.

There are no laws regulating termination of franchise agreements in Rwanda.

Normally, in Rwanda, termination will arise upon the mutual agreement or by breach of performance of material contractual obligation by either of the parties.

Total breach of the contract gives right to damages based on the non-performed obligations.[328] Partial breach of the contract gives right to damages based on only part of remaining obligations to perform.[329]

VIII. Governing Law, Jurisdiction, and Dispute Resolution

A. Choice of Law of Foreign Jurisdiction

Please confirm whether the choice of law of a foreign jurisdiction would likely to be upheld under the law of the country, except for certain matters such as trademarks, bankruptcy, and competition matters, which we assume would be governed by the law in your country.

Under Rwanda contract law,[330] the parties may freely declare their transactions to be subject to a particular jurisdiction of their choice, including foreign jurisdictions. The party's choice of law, however, must reflect a serious interest of the parties, have some connection with any of the elements of the agreement, or have some connection with the chosen foreign jurisdiction.

---

328 Article 81 of the *Law n° 45/2011 of 25/11/2011 Governing Contracts.*

329 *Id.*

330 *Law n°45/2011 of 25/11/2011 governing Contracts.*

Under conflict of laws principles, a choice of foreign law will not be permissible when it would violate fundamental principles of Rwanda public policy and such foreign law is not capable of providing an alternative solution consistent with those principles.

B. International Arbitration Dispute Resolution

Please confirm that a court in your country would honor an election of international arbitration dispute resolution, and therefore refuse to hear any disputes arising under a franchise agreement.

Rwanda courts will generally give effect to the parties' right to freedom of contract and to the legal system under which they choose to contract.

It is also noteworthy that Rwanda is a signatory of the *Convention on the Recognition and Enforcement of Foreign Arbitral Awards*[331] (the "New York Convention"). This means that Rwanda recognizes and enforces foreign arbitral awards.

The law in Rwanda regulating and governing arbitration is set out in the *Law n° 05/2010 of 10/01/2010* establishing the Kigali International Arbitration Center and determining its organization, functioning, and competence. Upon a dispute arising, parties may choose their arbitrators or mediators in accordance with this law.

[331] The *United Nations Commission on International Trade Law* (UNCITRAL) announced on November 3, 2008 that Rwanda became the 143rd country to accede to the *Convention on the Recognition and Enforcement of Foreign Arbitral Awards*. The convention entered into force in Rwanda on January 29, 2009. Under the treaty, courts of the States Parties are required "to enforce arbitration agreements and to recognize and enforce arbitral awards made in other States."

IX. Non-Competition Provisions

If the franchise agreement prohibits the master franchisee from engaging in certain competitive activities during the term of the agreement, and for a 12-month period after the termination or expiration of the agreement, please comment on the enforceability of non-competition covenants in your country.

Since there is no specific legal regime governing franchise agreements in Rwanda, the parties themselves may agree on non-competition provisions. However, such provisions shall not be against public policy of Rwanda law and should also not hinder others from engaging in competing in market forces.

X. Language Requirements

Does the law in your country require that a franchise agreement be translated into the local language in order to be enforceable between the parties?

Rwanda legislation does not require that a franchise agreement be translated into local language in order to be enforceable between the parties. Please note however that Rwanda has three official languages: Kinyarwanda, French and English.

XI. Other Significant Matters

Please advise as to whether there are any significant matters not addressed above of which a franchisor should be aware in connection with its entering into a franchise agreement in your country.

There are no other significant matters to address.

Franchising in South Africa

Taswell Papier

ENSafrica

Cape Town, South Africa

South Africa

I. Introduction

A. Historical Background of Country

Dutch traders landed at the southern tip of modern day South Africa in 1652 and established a stopover point on the spice route between the Netherlands and the Far East, founding the city of Cape Town. After the British seized the Cape of Good Hope area in 1806, many of the Dutch settlers (the "Boers") trekked north to found their own republics. The discovery of diamonds (1867) and gold (1886) spurred wealth and immigration and intensified the subjugation of the native inhabitants.

The Boers resisted British encroachments but were defeated in the Boer War (1899–1902); however, the British and the Afrikaners, as the Boers became known, ruled together from 1910 under the Union of South Africa, which became a republic in 1961 after a whites-only referendum. In 1948, the National Party was voted into power and instituted a policy of apartheid—the separate development of the races—which favored the white minority at the expense of the black majority.

The African National Congress ("ANC") led the opposition to apartheid and many top ANC leaders, such as Nelson Mandela, spent decades in South Africa's prisons. Internal protests and insurgency, as well as boycotts by some Western nations and institutions, led to the regime's eventual willingness to negotiate a peaceful transition to majority rule. The first multi-racial elections in 1994 brought an end to apartheid and ushered in majority rule under an ANC-led government.

South Africa since then has struggled to address apartheid-era imbalances in proper housing, education, and health care. ANC infighting, which has grown in recent years, came to a head in September 2008 when President Thabo Mbeki resigned, and Kgalema Motlanthe, the party's General-Secretary, succeeded him as interim president. Jacob Zuma became president after the ANC won general elections in April 2009. In January 2011,

South Africa

South Africa assumed a non-permanent seat on the UN Security Council for the 2011–12 term.

B. Economy of the Country

South Africa is a middle-income, emerging market with an abundant supply of natural resources; well-developed financial, legal, communications, energy, and transport sectors; a stock exchange that is the 18th largest in the world; and modern infrastructure supporting a relatively efficient distribution of goods to major urban centers throughout the region. At the end of 2007, South Africa began to experience an electricity crisis. State power supplier Eskom encountered problems with aged plants, necessitating "load-shedding" cuts to residents and businesses in the major cities.

Growth was robust from 2004 to 2007 as South Africa reaped the benefits of macroeconomic stability and a global commodities boom, but began to slow in the second half of 2007 due to the electricity crisis and the subsequent global financial crisis' impact on commodity prices and demand. GDP fell nearly 2% in 2009.

Unemployment remains high and outdated infrastructure has constrained growth. Daunting economic problems remain from the apartheid era—especially poverty, lack of economic empowerment among disadvantaged groups, and a shortage of public transportation. South Africa's former economic policy was fiscally conservative, focusing on controlling inflation, and attaining a budget surplus. The current government largely follows the same prudent policies, but must contend with the impact of the global crisis and is facing growing pressure from special interest groups to use state-owned enterprises to deliver basic services to low-income areas and to increase job growth. More than a quarter of South Africa's population currently receives social grants.

South Africa

C. Franchise Legal Overview

In recent times, "*South Africa has [had] one of the fastest-growing franchise markets in the world.*"[332] This is primarily due to the potential of franchising as a powerful tool to stimulate the growth of the small to medium enterprise sector ("SMEs") of the South African economy, thus increasing employment, ensuring sustainable economic growth and, importantly, facilitating broader access to the economy. This becomes particularly evident "*when comparing franchise outlets with independent businesses (...) In South Africa, research has indicated that failure rates of franchisees are estimated to be five times lower than those of independent SMEs.*"[333]

No legislation previously existed to control the franchise industry and, as a result, the courts grappled with the issue of the classification and treatment of the franchise relationship in terms of the common law of South Africa. Although courts have in the past equated the franchise relationship to that of a fiduciary relationship, the concept of a fiduciary relationship conflicts with the reciprocal nature of a franchise agreement, in that "*a fiduciary is someone who must act primarily for the other's benefit and not for his own benefit. The principal is entitled to receive 'single-minded loyalty' from his fiduciary...*"[334] The Competition Tribunal, for example, has found that the franchise relationship is inconsistent with traditional concepts of agency,[335] due to, *inter alia*, the investment of the franchisee's own capital, its payment of its own operating expenses, and the intended enjoyment of net profits. The law of contract is not always appropriate either, due to the potential for the abuse of

---

332 Woker T, *The Franchise Relationship and the Problem of Encroachment: Silent Pond Investments CC v. Woolworths (Pty) Ltd*, (2008) 20 SA Merc LJ 402.

333 Wadula P, *The Franchising Way for SMEs, Enterprise* (May 2006).

334 Woker, *supra* note 330, at 406.

335 *Cancun Trading & Others v. Seven-Eleven Corporation SA (Pty) Ltd* [1999–2000] CPLR 173 (CT).

bargaining power by the generally economically stronger franchisor. The relationship does not fit easily with the concept of an employment relationship either.

The South African Legislature, in remedying this situation, elected to include franchise-specific provisions throughout the *Consumer Protection Act 68 of 2008* (the "CPA"), which is now the primary legislation regulating franchise agreements. It is important to note that, in terms of the CPA, a franchisee is also classed as a "consumer," and thus enjoys many of the protections afforded to the average consumer, for example, the right to fair and honest dealing and the right to select suppliers.

II. Regulatory Requirements

A. Pre-Sale Disclosure

Please describe any pre-sale franchise disclosure or similar requirements that may apply to franchise transactions.

Providing franchisees with the right to disclosure was a driving force behind the inclusion of franchisees in the CPA. To this end, the CPA required regulations to be promulgated (the "CPA Regulations") by the Department of Trade and Industry ("DTI") requiring franchisors to disclose certain information to prospective franchisees.

The Minister of the DTI issued the CPA Regulations, which came into force on April 1, 2011. Regulation 3 specifically sets out the requirements pertaining to the disclosure documents that a franchisor must provide to a prospective franchisee at least fourteen days prior to executing the franchise agreement. The regulations seem to predominantly concern the financial health of the franchise business as a whole. Regulation 3 of the CPA Regulations is annexed hereto as Appendix at the end of this chapter.

It must be noted that in addition to the pre-sale disclosure requirements in Regulation 3 of the CPA Regulations, the CPA also provides for a general right to disclosure and information that impose ongoing duties.[336]

B. Governmental Approvals, Registrations, Filing Requirements

Please describe any necessary government approvals, registrations, or filing requirements that may apply to franchise transactions.

While there are no government approvals or filing registration requirements specific to the context of franchising, South Africa's exchange control rules can have application to franchising. The present South African exchange control measures are set out in the *Exchange Control Regulations* made in terms of section 9 of the *Currency and Exchanges Act, 9 of 1933* (the "Exchange Control Regulations").

The South African Reserve Bank (the "SARB") has a wide discretion with respect to exchange control measures and this discretion is exercised on a case-by-case basis.

In terms of Regulation 3(1)(c) of the *Exchange Control Regulations*, (without approval granted by the SARB or a person authorized by the SARB, i.e., an "Authorized Dealer"), no person is permitted to make any payment to, or in favor or on behalf of, a person resident outside South Africa, or place any sum to the credit of such person.

Typically, in a franchise agreement, the franchisee pays the franchisor a royalty for the use of the brand name and operating system required to operate the business.

In terms of the aforementioned Regulation 3(1)(c), the payment of royalties under a franchise agreement by a South African franchisee to a non-resident franchisor requires exchange control approval from the SARB. This means that a formal application

[336] *See* Part D of Chapter 2 of the CPA.

requesting approval of the franchise agreement should be made to the SARB.

Where the franchise agreement includes the manufacturing of products within South Africa, the SARB refers the application to the DTI for consideration.

The SARB has appointed the DTI as a consultant to screen license agreements on its behalf and to advise it whether to approve payment of royalties. When the franchise agreement involves the local manufacture of products or the provision of certain services, the DTI acts as an adviser to the SARB. Where no local manufacturing is involved, the SARB does not consult the DTI and considers such agreements on its own. However, all agreements that contain any clauses that stipulate down payments, minimum payments, and once-off payments will be considered for recommendation to the SARB by the DTI.

The DTI applies a set of procedures that it has developed over time and that are set out in the guidelines to be applied by the DTI when considering the recommendation of license agreements to the SARB (the "Guidelines"). However, these Guidelines are also applied by the SARB in approving agreements where no local manufacturing is involved. *See also* Section V (Trademarks) of this chapter relating to nonmandatory recordal of licensees under the Trade Marks Act 194 of 1993.

C. Limits of Fees and Typical Term of Franchise Agreement

Please describe any limits upon the nature and extent of fees and the term of a typical franchise agreement.

In terms of the *Exchange Control Manual of the SARB* as well as the Guidelines, generally the DTI and the SARB would approve the payment of royalties of between 4% and 6%, assuming such royalties are calculated as a percentage of the manufacturing cost or net selling price excluding any taxes such as value-added tax.

In essence, the Guidelines distinguish between two categories of goods for the purposes of determining an acceptable royalty fee. In this regard, the DTI considers the following royalty percentages to be acceptable:

Category	Royalty percentage
Consumer goods/know-how	0% to 4%
Intermediate and final capital goods/ know-how	0% to 6%

The Guidelines also deal specifically with agreements other than manufacturing agreements, and state that the royalty should be expressed as a percentage of the net income value arising from the application of the know-how, less the in-house cost of purchases directly or indirectly from the franchisor, related to the know-how, as well as value-added tax. In the case of consumer goods, the norms extend to a range of approximately 0% to 4%.

Fees paid for technology should be based on actual performance (i.e., on the sales actually achieved) and minimum payments or annual payments are, as a rule, not acceptable. Down payments/ up-front payments other than nominal amounts will be considered only if actual costs of transferring technology (tangible items) are involved. The applications must clearly quantify and substantiate such costs.

Payments for trademarks will be considered if such trademarks are linked to the furnishing of technology. Payment for the use of a trademark should not exceed 1.5% of the applicable denominator determined with reference to the Guidelines and the total royalty payment (i.e., for the use of the trademark and the provision of technology) should not exceed the maximum percentages as stated above.

The Guidelines specifically provide that exchange control approval will normally be granted for an initial period of up to five years, after which application may be made for an extension should the agreement itself be for a longer period. Extensions may be granted for periods of up to five years.

III. Currency

If all payments under a franchise agreement must be made in immediately available U.S. Dollars, please advise as to any restrictions, reporting requirements, or regulations concerning the exchange, repatriation, or remittance of U.S. Dollars.

Any payments by a franchisee who is a resident of South Africa will be subject to exchange control requirements imposed by the SARB. A South African franchisee will not be permitted to make payments under a franchise agreement offshore (whether these are structured as franchise fees, royalties, or any other type of payment) without prior approval from the SARB or an Authorized Dealer in foreign exchange (i.e., at most commercial banks) in certain circumstances. The SARB or Authorized Dealer will consider the terms of such payment and approval will normally be for a specified period of time and will need to be renewed when appropriate. If there is any substantive amendment of the terms of a franchise agreement in relation to such payment, the parties may need to seek approval from the SARB or Authorized Dealer for the amended structure of the payments.

The SARB or Authorized Dealer in adjudicating the approval of the payments under a franchise agreement would consider the amounts of such payment in relation to the counter-consideration received by the franchisee. Authorized Dealers are permitted to approve payments for franchise agreements where the term does not exceed five years. In all other instances approval from the SARB is required. Therefore, a period of five years, with provision for the parties to renew the agreement, would be considered acceptable.

As per the Guidelines, royalties should preferably be based on the price in South African Rand and should not be linked to a foreign currency or price index.

South Africa

IV. Taxes, Tariffs, and Duties

Please do not provide any in-depth comments on tax structuring. However, please provide your general comments on the typical amount of withholding tax that would apply and whether a "gross-up" provision contained in a franchise agreement would be enforceable in your country.

A. General taxation principles

In terms of the *South African Income Tax Act 58 of 1962* (the "Income Tax Act"), South Africa taxes residents on their worldwide income and non-residents on South African sourced and deemed sourced income, subject however to relief afforded by a double taxation agreement ("DTA") where applicable. On the assumption that the franchisor is not a resident of South Africa, the franchisor will be taxed in South Africa on South African sourced and deemed sourced income only, subject to DTA relief.

South Africa has double taxation agreements with numerous African countries, as well as several other countries throughout the world including the United States.[337]

South Africa's residence test looks to incorporation as well as "effective management" of the company.

---

[337] The African countries are: Algeria, Botswana, Democratic Republic of Congo, Egypt, Ethiopia, Ghana, Lesotho, Malawi, Mauritius, Mozambique, Namibia, Nigeria, Rwanda, Seychelles, Sierra Leone, Swaziland, Tanzania, Tunisia, Uganda, Zambia, and Zimbabwe. Countries in the rest of the world are: Australia, Austria, Belarus, Belgium, Brazil, Bulgaria, Canada, China, Croatia, Cyprus, Czech Republic, Denmark, Finland, France, Germany, Greece, Hungary, India, Indonesia, Iran, Ireland, Israel, Italy, Japan, Korea, Kuwait, Luxembourg, Malaysia, Malta, Mexico, Netherlands, New Zealand, Norway, Oman, Pakistan, Poland, Portugal, Romania, Russian Federation, Saudi Arabia, Singapore, Slovak Republic, Spain, Sweden, Switzerland, Taiwan, Thailand, Turkey, Ukraine, United Kingdom, and United States.

The concept of the “source” of income is not defined in the Income Tax Act and has developed over the years with reference to case law. The Income Tax Act furthermore contains various “deeming” provisions, which deem certain forms of income to be sourced in South Africa.

B. South African taxation treatment of royalty income received by a non-resident

For South African tax purposes, royalty income received by a non-resident in respect of the following is statutorily deemed to have accrued from a source within South Africa:

- if the royalty (being an amount that is received or accrued in respect of the use, right of use, or permission to use any intellectual property, namely any patent, trademark, design, or copyright or any model, plan, pattern, formula, or process or any other property or right of a similar nature) is attributable to an amount incurred by a person that is resident; or

- is received or accrued in respect of the imparting of, or undertaking to impart, any scientific, technical, industrial, or commercial knowledge or information for use in South Africa, or attributable to an amount incurred by a person that is resident.

Such deemed South African sourced royalty income is taxed in the hands of the non-resident receiving it by a final withholding tax calculated at a rate of 15% of the gross royalty received or accrued. If the royalty income is subject to the withholding tax, it is exempt from normal tax.

However, where such royalty income is effectively connected with a permanent establishment of the non-resident receiving it in South Africa, the royalty income is subject to normal tax and the withholding tax regime does not apply. *See* subsection D.

C. Reduction of the withholding tax by a DTA

Certain DTAs limit South Africa's right to tax the royalty income. Depending on the jurisdiction in which the non- resident franchisor by whom the royalty income is received or to whom the royalty income has accrued is a tax resident, relief from the withholding tax by way of a reduced withholding tax rate or 0% withholding tax may be available in terms of a DTA.

The definition of "royalties" in most DTA's would be narrower than the application of South Africa's domestic law definition. However, even if service fees that may be contemplated in the franchise agreement do not fall within the ambit of "royalties" as defined in the DTA, such service fees should fall within the general "business profits" clause of the DTA, which provides for relief from South African tax, except insofar as such profits are attributable to a permanent establishment in South Africa.

D. Royalty income effectively connected with a permanent establishment in South Africa

As indicated above, where the deemed South African sourced royalty income is effectively connected with a "permanent establishment" of the non-resident receiving it in South Africa, the royalty income is subject to normal tax and the withholding tax regime does not apply.

The normal tax rate applicable would not exceed 40% in the case of an individual or 28% in the case of a company and the normal tax would be calculated on taxable income, which would be determined as the sum of the royalty income received or accrued less any permissible deductible expenditure incurred in the production of such royalty income.

To determine whether the South African sourced royalty income will be subject to a withholding tax or normal tax the following should be considered:

- the determination of whether the non-resident has a "permanent establishment" in South Africa; and

- once it is determined that the non-resident has a "permanent establishment" in South Africa, the determination of whether the royalty income is effectively connected with such "permanent establishment."

A "permanent establishment" is defined in the Income Tax Act with reference to the definition used in Article 5 of the *Model Tax Convention on Income and Capital of the Organisation for Economic Cooperation and Development* ("OECD"). Here it is defined as a fixed place of business through which the business of an enterprise is wholly or partly carried on. Generally, the business need not be of a productive nature, but it must serve the enterprise's overall purpose and it must be an activity. However, generally, activities that are of a preparatory or auxiliary character (i.e., not an essential part of the entity's commercial activity) are deemed not to create a permanent establishment.

The royalty income would be effectively connected with the permanent establishment in South Africa if such royalty income is attributable to such permanent establishment.

E. Enforceability of a "gross-up" provision contained in a franchise agreement

Provided that any gross-up provisions contained in a franchise agreement do not contravene the exchange control rules, as discussed above, they are enforceable under South African law.

V. Trademarks

Please advise us as to whether there are any special requirements for granting a valid trademark license, including the use of a registered user agreement or a short trademark license agreement and any required filing of such an agreement with the trademark authorities.

There are no specific requirements for a trademark license to be valid in South Africa. The *Trade Marks Act 194 of 1993* makes provision for the recordal of licensees as registered users; however, such recordal is not mandatory. It should be noted that where a license involves the payment of royalties to a non-resident, exchange control approval is required, as noted above.

VI. Restrictions on Transfer

Please advise as to whether there are any restrictions on (1) a franchisor to restrict transfers by a master franchisee, any interest in a master franchisee, or the assets of the master franchisee, or (2) the ability of a master franchisee to control and/or restrict transfers of a subfranchisee's rights under a master franchise agreement, interest in the subfranchisee, or the assets of the subfranchisee.

Under South African law it is entirely permissible for an agreement to stipulate that certain restrictions on transfer, as well as pre-emptive rights in favor of the franchisor, will be applicable in instances where the master franchisee intends to dispose of the business, the assets of the franchising entity (normally owned by the franchisor), or its controlling interest in the franchise entity. A franchise agreement may also provide for so-called "step-in" rights in favor of the franchisor where there are concerns relating to the prudent management of the franchise entity and franchisee.

It should, however, be noted that the enforceability of such rights may be complicated by the business rescue provisions contained in the *Companies Act 71 of 2008* (the "Companies Act"), which legislation came into force on May 1, 2011. Section 136(2) of the Companies Act permits a 'business rescue practitioner' (being the person appointed to oversee the business rescue proceedings) to, for the duration of the business rescue proceedings:

- entirely, partially, or conditionally suspend, for the duration of the business rescue proceedings, any obligation of the company that—
    - arises under an agreement to which the company was a party at commencement of business rescue proceedings; and
    - would otherwise become due during those proceedings; or
- apply urgently to court to entirely, partially, or conditionally cancel, on any terms that are just and reasonable in the circumstances, any obligation of the company contemplated in the above paragraph (a).

This essentially means that the business rescue practitioner can elect whether to abide by such step-in rights or pre-emptive provisions, leaving any party to an agreement that was suspended or cancelled with a right to claim only damages in terms of section 136(3). These provisions are akin to Chapter 11 proceedings in the USA, although not exactly the same.

VII. Termination

Please advise us as to any laws relating to termination in your country, such as agency laws, required indemnity provisions, notice or "good cause" requirements, or other laws affecting termination of a franchise agreement. Please describe.

Pursuant to Regulation 2(3)(v) of the CPA Regulations, a franchise agreement must stipulate the basis upon which either is entitled to terminate the agreement between them. This will include any ancillary agreements, such as licensing or agency agreements. Generally, agreements provide for termination on notice (which is not necessarily within a reasonable time—provided the parties have agreed, this could be as little as 24 hours), upon breach of the agreement, default, or insolvency. With particular reference to termination in the event of insolvency, the business rescue provisions of the Companies Act discussed above should be borne in mind, as these may complicate the ability of parties to terminate their agreements on this basis.

Indemnity provisions are permissible and enforceable in South Africa, subject to the provisions of the CPA.

VIII. Governing Law, Jurisdiction, and Dispute Resolution

A. Choice of Law of Foreign Jurisdiction

Please confirm whether the choice of law of a foreign jurisdiction would likely to be upheld under the law of the country, except for certain matters such as trademarks, bankruptcy, and competition matters, which we assume would be governed by the law in your country.

As per the Guidelines, every effort should be made to ensure that agreements are construed and interpreted under the laws and jurisdiction of South Africa. However, where parties have elected to conclude their agreements with reference to the laws of another jurisdiction, the courts will generally hold them to this, subject to the comments below.

B. International Arbitration Dispute Resolution

Please confirm that a court in your country would honor an election of international arbitration dispute resolution, and therefore refuse to hear any disputes arising under a franchise agreement.

As stated above, the South African courts will generally give effect to the parties' right to freedom of contract and to the legal system under which they choose to contract. However, this will not necessarily be the case at all times. Where, for example, public policy considerations are at play or where gross irregularity has occurred in the conclusion of the agreement or an arbitral award, the courts may elect to apply the principles of South African law. As such, it cannot be said with certainty that a court in South Africa would refuse to hear a dispute relating to a franchise agreement concluded under the laws of another jurisdiction.

The common law position in *Jones v. Krok,*[338] the Appellate Division (now the Supreme Court of Appeal), held that:

> *"...the present position in South Africa is that a foreign judgment is not directly enforceable, but constitutes a cause of action and will be enforced by our Courts provided (i) that the court which pronounced the judgment had jurisdiction to entertain the case according to the principles recognised by our law with reference to the jurisdiction of foreign courts; (ii) that the judgment is final and conclusive in its effect and has not become superannuated; (iii) that the recognition and enforcement of the judgment by our courts would not be contrary to public policy; (iv) that the judgment was not obtained by fraudulent means; (v) that the judgment does not involve the enforcement of a penal or revenue law of the foreign state; and (vi) that enforcement of the judgment is not precluded by the provisions of the Protection of Business Act 99 of 1978, as amended."*

Foreign judgments may be enforced at common law by an action for provisional sentence or summary judgment (if the judgment sounds in money) or a declaratory order. The practice, as pointed out by the Supreme Court of Appeal, has evolved on the basis that the judgment is prima facie proof that the judgment debtor is indebted in the amount of the judgment.

---

[338] [1995] 2 ALL SA 30 (A) at 34-35.

South Africa

In order for a South African court to recognize that the foreign court in question exercised competent jurisdiction over the defendant, regard will be had to the principles of South African law in this respect. Accordingly, jurisdiction will be found where:

- at the time of the commencement of the action the defendant is physically present within the state to which the court belongs; or

- at the time of the commencement of the action the defendant, although not physically present within such state, is either (i) domiciled, or (ii) resident within such state; or

- the defendant has submitted to the jurisdiction of the court.

With specific relevance to a typical franchise agreement, which will contain a submission to jurisdiction clause, submission to the jurisdiction of the forum is recognized as a basis for the competence of a foreign court for the purposes of enforcing a foreign judgment. Generally speaking, two categories of submission are recognized: namely, submission by unilateral conduct or acquiescence and submission by agreement, and the key factor in proving the existence of either form of submission to a certain jurisdiction will be the intention of the parties.

South Africa is a signatory to the *Convention on the Recognition and Enforcement of Foreign Arbitral Awards* (the "New York Convention").

1. The Protection of Businesses Act 99 of 1978 (the "PBA")

Section 1(a) of the PBA provides that "*no judgment, order, direction, arbitration award, interrogatory, commission rogatoire, letters of request or any other request delivered, given or issued or emanating from outside the Republic in connection with any civil proceedings and arising from any act or transaction contemplated in subsection (3)*" shall be enforceable without the permission of the Minister of Economic Affairs.

Section 1(3) provides that "*an act or transaction shall be an act or transaction which took place at any time, whether before or after the commencement of the Act, and is connected with the mining, production, importation, exportation, refinement, possession, use or sale of or ownership to any material, of whatever nature, whether within, outside, into or from the Republic.*"

Accordingly, in order for the PBA to be applicable, the underlying transaction giving rise to the judgment debt must fall within the ambit of the definition of an "act or transaction." It is likely that a franchise agreement would fall into such classification, and would thus not be precluded from the application of the common law principles above. However, this can only be conclusively determined with reference to the facts of each case.

2. *The Enforcement of Foreign Civil Judgments Act 32 of 1998* (the "Foreign Judgments Act")

The Foreign Judgments Act provides for the recognition of civil judgments given in foreign jurisdictions and the enforcement thereof by the South African courts.

The applicability of the Foreign Judgments Act relies, however, on such foreign judgments falling within certain key definitions, namely:

- "judgments," which are defined as "*any final judgment or order for the payment of money[...]in any civil proceedings which is enforceable by execution in the country in which it was given or made...*" The Foreign Judgments Act excludes, for its purposes, judgments, on appeal from courts not falling within the definition of "court" in terms of the Foreign Judgments Act and judgments dealing with certain types of matters, such as the payment of taxes or fines, or matters dealing with maintenance claims; and

- "courts," which are defined as "*in relation to a designated country, means the Supreme or High Court or any magistrate's court (including a regional court) of that country...*" It is thus not clear whether the Foreign Judgments Act also excludes judgments of special courts, for example, tax or labor courts. Such courts are not necessarily ingrained within the hierarchy of a country's courts, and thus may not fall within the definition of a "court," as contemplated in the Foreign Judgments Act. Whether a judgment is considered in South African law as that of a "court" for the purposes of the Foreign Judgments Act should be judged on an individual basis, having regard to the relevant country's hierarchy of courts.

Under Section 2(1) of the Act, the legislation applies to any countries designated for the purposes of the Foreign Judgments Act. Currently, only Namibia and Zimbabwe are designated countries.

The Foreign Judgments Act also provides for the setting aside of a foreign judgment upon application by the judgment debtor, but sets out specific grounds for such application, including:

- where the judgment was registered in contravention of the Foreign Judgments Act;
- where the enforcement of the judgment would be contrary to public policy considerations in South Africa;
- where the judgment was lodged in South Africa by a person other than the judgment creditor; and

- where the judgment may not in terms of law be enforced in South Africa.

Section 8 of the Foreign Judgments Act provides that where a notice is issued to the judgment debtor informing them of the registration of the judgment in South Africa, the notice shall also act as an interdict against the judgment debtor, and against any other persons having knowledge of such notice, such that neither the judgment debtor or any other such informed party may "*remove or dispose of any assets of the judgment debtor if such removal or disposal would prejudice the execution of the judgment.*"

3. *The Recognition and Enforcement of Foreign Arbitral Awards Act 40 of 1977* (the "Arbitral Awards Act")

The Arbitral Awards Act serves to ensure the enforceability of foreign arbitral awards in South Africa. For the purposes of the Arbitral Awards Act, a foreign arbitral award includes any arbitral award made outside of South Africa. As such, the Arbitral Awards Act has wider applicability for franchisors, at the very least in a geographical context, than the Foreign Judgments Act.

Section 2(1) of the Arbitral Awards Act provides that any foreign arbitral award may be made an order of court, subject to the grounds of refusal set out in Section 4 of the Arbitral Awards Act, and to the fulfillment of the procedural requirements for the award to be made an order of court. A court may refuse the application on grounds stipulated in Section 4, which include:

- where the court finds that the referral of the dispute to arbitration was unlawful or impermissible in terms of South African law;

- where the parties to the agreement had no capacity to contract in terms of the law of the chosen jurisdiction;

- where the agreement upon which the award is given is invalid in terms of the law of the chosen jurisdiction; or
- where enforcement of the award would be contrary to public policy.

IX. Non-Competition Provisions

If the franchise agreement prohibits the master franchisee from engaging in certain competitive activities during the term of the agreement, and for a 12-month period after the termination or expiration of the agreement, please comment on the enforceability of non-competition covenants in your country.

Restraint of trade (i.e., non-compete) protections are often included in employment contracts, but are also used in the franchising context, and are in principle valid. However, when the franchisor seeks to enforce restraint provisions, the courts retain discretion as to whether to enforce the restraint in question, and will not enforce the restraint in a particular case where it is considered that this would be contrary to the public interest or unreasonable. The courts will consider the merits of the enforceability of each restraint on a case-by-case basis, and the reasonableness of the restraint is assessed with reference to a number of factors.

The decision on whether to uphold a restraint of trade concerns an analysis of the broad interests of the public and the interests of the contracting parties themselves. With regard to the interests of the public, the tension lies between two competing interests, being that agreements solemnly entered into should be upheld and enforced, and, on the other hand, that persons should generally be free to engage in economic activity, and should not be rendered unproductive.

Reasonableness as between the parties themselves depends on many factors, the most important of which are:

- whether the franchisor has a "proprietary" interest that may legitimately be protected by means of a restraint agreement,
- the geographical area of the restraint,
- the duration of the restraint, and
- whether adequate consideration has been given for the restraint.

Less important, but not entirely irrelevant, are:

- a concession by the franchisee that the restraint is reasonable, normally implied where the franchisee has signed a franchise agreement containing a clause to this effect; and
- an inequality of bargaining power.

In trying to balance all these various factors, the court should address four questions:

- Does the franchisor have an interest deserving of protection upon termination of the franchise contract?
- If so, is such interest being prejudiced by the franchisee?
- If so, how does the franchisor's interest weigh against the franchisee's interest in not being rendered economically unproductive for a period of time?
- Is there some broader aspect of public policy, unrelated to the personal interests of the individuals concerned that demands that the restraint should or should not be enforced?

The restraint should go no further than is necessary to protect the proprietary interests of the franchisor. Where it goes too far, the court may order partial enforcement (e.g., for a lesser period or within a more circumscribed territory), if necessary, by severing objectionable parts of the restraint from the agreement.

Courts have re-iterated in several judgments that the creation of a fixed principle applicable to all contracts in restraint of trade, regardless of the true nature of the transaction giving rise thereto, would not promote the objectives of the Constitution of South Africa, and have concluded that the reasonableness of the restraint is therefore always a question that must be objectively determined with reference to the particular facts of each case.[339]

An example of our courts upholding a restraint of trade as reasonable is in the case of *Basson v. Chilwan and Others*,[340] where the Supreme Court of Appeal enforced a restraint against a business partner who, although contributing virtually nothing towards the business venture financially speaking, held certain knowledge and skills that were deemed essential to the success of the business, and the partners, unwilling to let him leave the business and become a competitor in the market, sought to restrict this by a restraint of trade provision.

Further, an example of our courts dismissing a restraint of trade as unreasonable is in the case of *Coetzee v. Comitis and Others*,[341] where the Constitutional Court, in a rather interesting case, held that the National Soccer League's rules demanding that a player must await a clearance certificate prior to him being able to sign with another club constituted a restraint of trade, and that this restraint infringed upon the player's freedom of movement, his right to choose a profession or occupation freely, and his right to dignity. As a result the court held that the compensation regime of the league constituted a restraint of trade that was unreasonable, that public policy required it to be

---

339 *Knox D'Arcy Limited and Another v. Shaw and Another* 1995 (12) BCLR 1702 (W) at 1710.

340 [1993] 2 All SA 373 (A).

341 2001 (4) BCLR 323 (C).

declared unlawful, and subsequently declared it to be inconsistent with the provisions of the Constitution of South Africa, and therefore invalid.

Examples of protectable interests include trade secrets and other confidential information; know-how; customer lists and connections; and goodwill, while a business' interest in eliminating the competition and investment of time and money in training a franchisee are not considered protectable interests in South African law. Whether the latter can be extended to include time and money spent training and nurturing a franchisee with regard to, inter alia, the franchisor's business model and systems remains unclear.

The reasonableness of the restraint is judged as at the time when the court is asked to rule on the matter, not the time of entry into the agreement. A franchisor's trade secrets and confidential information enjoy protection from the misuse thereof by a franchisee under the common law but most franchisors in any event include specific contractual protections in this regard in their written franchise contracts.

X. Language Requirements

Does the law in your country require that a franchise agreement be translated into the local language in order to be enforceable between the parties?

South African law does not stipulate that a franchise agreement should be in a particular language. However, the provisions of Section 7(1) of the CPA, which states that the franchise agreement must be in writing and in plain and understandable language, should be borne in mind.

XI. Other Significant Matters

Please advise as to whether there are any significant matters not addressed above of which a franchisor should be aware in connection with its entering into a franchise agreement in your country.

Certain franchise agreements include an advertising fee, being a contribution the franchisee may be required to make to the network's advertising fund, a fund usually administered by the franchisor and used to fund national advertising and marketing programs. It is either a percentage of sales, typically ranging from 0.5% to 3%, or a fixed monthly fee and is charged over and above the royalty. It should be noted that if the advertising fee together with the royalty fee exceed the maximum percentages as indicated in Section II.C. above, the franchise agreement may be declined by the SARB or the DTI.

Appendix: South Africa – Regulation 3 under the Consumer Protection Act 68 of 2008

3. Disclosure document for prospective franchisee.

(1) Every franchisor must provide a prospective franchisee with a disclosure document, dated and signed by an authorised officer of the franchisor, at least 14 days prior to the signing of a franchise agreement, which as a minimum must contain:

(a) the number of individual outlets franchised by the franchisor;

(b) the growth of the franchisor's turnover, net profit, and the number of individual outlets, if any, franchised by the franchisor for the financial year prior to the date on which the prospective franchisee receives a copy of the disclosure document;

(c) a statement confirming that there have been no significant or material changes in the company's or franchisor's financial position since the date of the last accounting officer, or auditor's certificate or certificate by a similar reviewer of the company or franchisor, that the company or franchisor has reasonable grounds to believe that it will be able to pay its debts as and when they fall due;

(d) written projections in respect of levels of potential sales, income, gross, or net profits or other financial projections for the franchised business or franchises of a similar nature with particulars of the

assumptions upon which these representations are made.

(2) Each page of the disclosure document contemplated in subregulation (1) above must be qualified in respect of the assumptions contained therein.

(3) The disclosure document contemplated in subregulation (1) above must be accompanied by a certificate on an official letterhead from a person eligible in law to be registered as the accounting officer of a close corporation, or the auditor of a company, as the case may be, certifying that:

(a) the business of the franchisor is a going concern;

(b) to the best of his or her knowledge the franchisor is able to meet its current and contingent liabilities;

(c) the franchisor is capable of meeting all of its financial commitments in the ordinary course of business as they fall due; and

(d) the franchisor's audited annual financial statements for the most recently expired financial year have been drawn up:

(i) in accordance with South African generally accepted accounting standards;

(ii) except to the extent stated therein, on the basis of accounting policies consistent with prior years;

(iii) in accordance with the provisions of the Companies Act (No. 61 of 1973 or any legislation which replaces this Act), and all other applicable laws; and

(iv) fairly reflecting the financial position, affairs, operations, and results of the franchisor as at that date and for the period to which they relate.

(4) The disclosure document contemplated in subregulation (1) above must be accompanied by:

(a) a list of current franchisees, if any, and of outlets owned by the franchisor, stating, in respect of any franchisee:

(i) the name under which it carries on business;

(ii) the name of its representative;

(iii) its physical address; and

(iv) its e-mail and office telephone number, together with a clear statement that the prospective franchisee is entitled to contact any of the franchisees listed, or alternatively to visit any outlets operated by a current franchisee to assess the information disclosed by the franchisor and the franchise opportunity offered by it;

(b) an organogram depicting the support system in place for franchisee.

Franchising in Tunisia

Yessine Ferah

FERAH & Associates Law Firm

Tunis, Tunisia

Tunisia

I. Introduction

A. Historical Background of Country

Tunisia became an independent state in 1956. The country's first president, Habib Bourguiba, established a strict one-party state. He dominated the country for 31 years, repressing Islamic fundamentalism and establishing rights for women. In November 1987, Bourguiba was removed from office and replaced by Zine el Abidine Ben Ali in a coup. Street protests that began in Tunis in December 2010 over high unemployment, corruption, widespread poverty, and high food prices escalated in January 2011, culminating in rioting that led to hundreds of deaths. On January 14, 2011, the same day Ben Ali dismissed the government, he fled the country, and by late January 2011, Prime Minister Mohamed Ghannouchi announced the formation of a "national unity government" with the head of the Chamber of Deputies, Fouad M'Bazaa, as the interim president. Elections for the new Constituent Assembly were held in late October 2011, and in December, it elected human rights activist Moncef Marzouki as interim president. The Consistent Assembly adopted a new constitution on January 26, 2014. The Independent High Committee for the Elections anticipated that the presidential and parliamentary elections would be held before the end of 2014.

B. Economy of Country

Tunisia has a diverse, market-oriented economy, with important agricultural, mining, tourism, and manufacturing sectors but it faces an array of challenges. Following an ill-fated experiment with socialist economic policies in the 1960s, Tunisia successfully focused on bolstering exports, foreign investment, and tourism. Key exports now include textiles and apparel, food products, petroleum products, chemicals, and phosphates, with about 80% going to the European Union. Tunisia achieved four decades of 4-5% annual GDP growth. The overthrow of the government in January 2011 sent Tunisia's economy into a tailspin. The country's new government faces immediate challenges stabilizing the economy. It must reassure businesses and investors, bring budget and current account deficits under control, shore up the country's financial system, bring down high unemployment, and reduce economic disparities between the more developed coastal region and the impoverished interior.

C. Franchise Legal Overview

Before August 12, 2009, a franchise agreement in Tunisia was considered a sui generis contract governed primarily by the general legal regime applicable to contracted obligations under the *Tunisian Civil Code* (*Code des Obligations et des Contrats*).

Currently, *Law n° 2009-69*, dated August 12, 2009 (the "2009 Law"), regulates franchise agreements. The 2009 Law defines franchise agreements and stipulates the principal requirements to be fulfilled in a franchise relationship.

Article 14 of the 2009 Law defines the franchise agreement as "a contract through which the trademark owner grants the right of its use to a natural person or to a legal entity called franchisee, to distribute the products or provide services in return for consideration." Article 14 also provides that a "franchise network" consists of independent shops operating under the same trademark and pursuant to unified business methods, premises planning, management methods, marketing and sources of supply.

Article 15 of the 2009 Law and *Decree n° 2010-1501* (the "Decree"), which was enacted on June 21, 2010, provides compulsory terms and conditions of a franchise agreement. It also lists the basic information that must be included in a pre-sale disclosure document that must be provided to the franchisee at least twenty (20) days before signing the franchise agreement.

Article 6 of Tunisia's competition law ("Competition Law") provides that a franchise agreement is not deemed anticompetitive, if the parties justify that the franchise agreement is necessary to guarantee technical or economic progress and if the agreement provides users with a fair share of benefits. Such franchise agreements, however, remain subject to the authorization of the Trade Minister of Tunisia, pursuant to the advice of the Competition Council of Tunisia.[342] On July 28, 2010, the Trade Minister of Tunisia enacted an order (the "Trade Minister Order") relating to the automatic authorization of some franchise agreements in specific industry sectors.

II. Regulatory Requirements

A. Pre-Sale Disclosure

Please describe any pre-sale franchise disclosure or similar requirements that may apply to franchise transactions.

Article 15 of the 2009 Law and the Decree require that the franchisor provide to the franchisee the franchise agreement and a disclosure document containing certain information relating to the franchisor and its activity at least twenty (20) days before signing the franchise agreement.

Article 3 of the Decree provides that the disclosure document must include:

- the legal form of the franchisor's enterprise and the nature of its activity;
- the identity and address of the franchisor, if the franchisor is a natural person;
- the identity of the legal representative, the head office address, the list of managers/directors and franchisor's amount of capital, if the franchisor is a legal entity;
- a presentation of the history of the franchisor's enterprise;

[342] The Competition Law was adopted by the *Law n° 91-64* dated 29 July 1991. It has been amended in 1993, 1995, 1999, 2003 and 2005.

- information related to the franchisor's registration number in the trade register (or any equivalent registration number);
- proof of ownership of the trademark or the corporate name;
- information relating to the registration of the trademark with the national register of trademarks;
- information about the franchise network;
- the list of franchisees in Tunisia, their addresses, dates on which they joined the franchise network and a list of former franchisees;
- information about the franchisor's activity sector and the opportunities in Tunisia and other areas where the mark is represented;
- the nature and the amount of expenses and investment specific to the trademark or the corporate name; and
- the financial statements of the franchisor.

B. Governmental Approvals, Registrations, Filing Requirements

Please describe any necessary government approvals, registrations, or filing requirements that may apply to franchise transactions.

1. Authorization of the Trade Minister

Certain franchise agreements, depending on the industry in which they operate, may require the authorization of the Trade Minister of Tunisia prior to their execution. The relevant legislation in this area is Article 5 and Article 6 of the Competition Law, the Decree and the Trade Minister Order.

a. Article 5 of the Competition Law

Article 5 of the Competition Law prohibits joint operations, collusion and express or tacit agreements that have an anti-competitive objective or effect and which:

- obstruct price setting by the rule of supply and demand;
- limit access to the market by other enterprises or limit the free exercise of competition in that market;
- either limit or control production, commercialization, investments, or technical progress; or
- divide markets or sources of supply.

Article 5 of the Competition Law also prohibits:

- abuse of a dominant position in the domestic market or a substantial part of that market, or abuse of a state of economic dependency of customers or suppliers who do not have any alternative solutions for commercialization, supply or provision of service. Abuse of a state of economic dependency may consist notably of the refusal to sell or to purchase tied goods or services, the imposition of de minimus prices for resale, discriminatory conditions, or the termination of commercial relationships without objective cause or because the other party refused to accept exorbitant commercial conditions;
- any offer or application of prices so abusively low that they threaten the balance of economic activity and honest competition on the market; and

- any engagement, convention or contractual clause relating to the practices prohibited under the terms of this Section.

b. Article 6 of the Competition Law

Article 6 of the Competition Law provides that certain agreements and practices are not considered anticompetitive if they guarantee technical or economic progress and provide users with a fair share of benefits. Such agreements and practices are subject to the authorization of the Trade Minister, after consultation with the Competition Council of Tunisia.

c. Application of Articles 5 and 6 of the Competition Law

It follows from a combined reading of the provisions of the Decree and Articles 5 and 6 of the Competition Law that all franchise agreement are in principle prohibited by Article 5 of the Competition Law; however, franchise agreements may be authorized by the Trade Minister, if they fulfill the conditions of Article 6 of the Competition Law.

d. Trade Minister Order

Notwithstanding Articles 5 and 6 of the Competition Law, franchise agreements in certain activity sectors determined by order of the Trade Minister will be automatically authorized and do not require any further approval of the Trade Minister.[343] These sectors are set by the Trade Minister Order and are referenced below. For national brands, all sectors are

---

[343] This interpretation is confirmed by provisions of the Trade Minister Order which provide that, pursuant to Article 6 of the Competition Law, franchise agreements in the sectors noted in the table appended to the order, are granted an automatic authorization from the general prohibition of agreements and practices referred to in the Competition Law.

automatically authorized. For foreign brands, only the following sectors are automatically authorized:

Distribution Sectors	**Tourism Sectors**
➢ Perfumery, beauty products and cosmetics	➢ Car rental
➢ Clothing	➢ Areas of leisure
➢ Footwear	➢ Management of hotels
➢ Leather goods	➢ **Training Sectors**
➢ Sports articles and shoes	➢ Professional training
➢ Diet products	
➢ Watches	➢ **Other economic sectors**
➢ Giftware items	➢ Rescue services
➢ Eyewear	➢ Beauty, hairdressing, and personal hygiene salons
➢ Household electrical appliances	➢ Repair and maintenance services (cars, electronics)
➢ Furniture	➢ Services supporting efforts to quit smoking
➢ Indoor plants and flowers	➢ Care services in hotels
➢ Sanitary items and hardware	➢ Thalassotherapy
➢ Electronics and computer hardware	
➢ Bookstores	
➢ Capital goods for various sectors	

e. Potential Conflicts Under Tunisian Law

The automatic authorization of certain franchise agreements specified in the Decree and the Trade Minister Order, without verifying the fulfillment of the conditions of Article 6 of the Competition Law, squarely puts the Decree and the Trade Minister Order in conflict with the Competition Law. *Consequently, it is not prudent to assume that a franchise agreement will be granted automatic and general authorization without appealing to the Trade Minister for approval.*[344]

f. Obtaining Trade Minister Authorization

In the event a franchisor is required to obtain authorization, there are specific documents that must be submitted to the Trade Minister including:

- an application in the form of a cover letter;
- a copy of the draft franchise agreement; and

---

[344] A reading of the provisions of the 2009 Law, the Decree, the Trade Minister Order and the Competition Law suggest there is some potential conflict in Tunisian law that raises a number of important considerations.

The Decree suggests that certain franchise agreements in certain economic sectors, will be automatically authorized by the Trade Minister; however, Article 15 of the 2009 Law provides that the Decree shall only set forth the compulsory minimum terms of the franchise agreement and the required disclosures.

The 2009 Law regulates franchise agreements and places no restrictions on such agreements. In some cases, however, the Decree and Trade Minister Order limit the circumstances under which franchise agreements become effective. Consequently, the Decree and the Trade Minister Order may conflict with the 2009 Law and/or Article 6 of the Competition Law.

Further, the 2009 Law, the Decree and the Trade Minister Order do not address potential conflicts with the Competition Law. Specifically, the 2009 Law regulates franchise agreements without addressing potential conflicts with the general prohibitions against "anticompetitive practices, agreements and activities" of the Competition Law. Also, the "automatic authorization" granted by the Decree potentially conflicts with the general prohibitions against "anticompetitive practices, agreements and activities" of the Competition Law.

- a technical and economic study showing that the franchise agreement is not anti-competitive, is necessary to guarantee technical or economic progress, and that it provides users with a fair share of benefits.

Again, it is important to note that this is an evolving area of Tunisian law and the interplay between the 2009 Law, the Decree, the Trade Minster Order and the Competition Law have yet to be determined. It is prudent to consult with local counsel in Tunisia to determine the applicability of the foregoing laws to specific circumstances and whether Trade Minister authorization will be required.

2. The Central Bank of Tunisia's Prior Authorization

In principle, based on the Exchange Control Regulations in Tunisia (the "Regulations"), payments made by a resident to a party outside of Tunisia pursuant to an agreement are subject to the prior authorization of the Central Bank of Tunisia (the "CBT"). This means that, in principle, such agreement is itself subject to CBT's prior authorization.

The issue of whether payments made under a franchise agreement and whether such agreement is therefore subject to the authorization of the CBT is not clear under the Regulations.

Under the Regulations, there are two kinds of operations:

- "Current operations" where payments outside of Tunisia can be made freely without authorization (but following a specific procedure); and

- Other or "non-current operations" where payments outside of Tunisia require the prior authorization of the CBT.

Pursuant to the Regulations, current operations include payments made outside Tunisia in consideration of "...intellectual property rights like…the use of the trade name and the brand name." It is unclear whether the CBT will consider payments made under a franchise agreement as a current operation because payments under such an agreement must be related to "production" of goods as opposed to the use of a trademark.

Based on the foregoing, it is prudent for the parties to (i) seek confirmation that the payments to be made under their franchise agreement are current operations and (ii) seek authorization in case the CBT does not consider them as such.

There are no specific documents to be submitted to the CBT, but usually the application is made in the form of a cover letter with a draft of the franchise agreement appended. The CBT will examine the file and may request, if necessary, additional documents or information. In principle, the CBT gives its provisional approval on the draft franchise agreement, and once executed by the parties, the CBT gives its final authorization. Accordingly, the franchise agreement is, in principle, submitted again to the CBT once signed by the parties. The CBT will inform the parties about its final authorization.

The timeline for obtaining CBT authorization is approximately two months, but this timeline could be affected by several factors including the number of cases pending before the CBT. The CBT has the ability to reject the filing or modify its terms. Please note that there are no specific standards used to approve an agreement but the approval depends on the sector, the circumstances, the parties concerned, etc.

3. Registration before the Tax Office

A franchise agreement is not required to be registered with the Tax Office of Tunisia. However, registration, even though not mandatory, ensures enforceability against third parties.

C. Limits of Fees and Typical Term of Franchise Agreement

Please describe any limits upon the nature and extent of fees and the term of a typical franchise agreement.

There are no limits upon the nature and extent of fees and the term of a typical franchise agreement.

III. Currency

If all payments under a franchise agreement must be made in immediately available U.S. Dollars, please advise as to any restrictions, reporting requirements, or regulations concerning the exchange, repatriation, or remittance of U.S. Dollars.

Based on the Regulations, any payments, regardless of the currency, made by a resident franchisee to a party outside of Tunisia, pursuant to a franchise agreement, are likely subject to the authorization of the Central Bank of Tunisia. See Section II.B.2.

IV. Taxes, Tariffs and Duties

Please do not provide any in-depth comments on tax structuring. However, please provide your general comments on the typical amount of withholding tax that would apply and whether a "gross-up" provision contained in a franchise agreement would be enforceable in your country.

If the franchise agreement is registered with the Tax Office, as mentioned in Section II.B.1. above, a duty of 20 Tunisian dinars (approximately US$ 12.50) per page (including the pages of all the originals presented for registration) will be due.

Moreover, payments due under the franchise agreement are subject to:

- a value added tax ("VAT") of 18%; and

- A 15% withholding tax calculated on the amounts paid, including the VAT, whether the franchisor is established in or outside of Tunisia.

Tunisia has double taxation treaties with a number of jurisdictions, including the United States.[345]

Any "gross up" provisions contained in franchise agreements are enforceable in Tunisia.

V. Trademarks

Please advise us as to whether there are any special requirements for granting a valid trademark license, including the use of a registered user agreement or a short trademark license agreement and any required filing of such an agreement with the trademark authorities.

There are special requirements under Tunisian law for granting a trademark license. Such a license could be deemed to fall under the purview of Article 14 of the 2009 Law because this legislation defines the franchise agreement as a contract through which the trademark owner[346] grants the right to use the mark to a natural person or to a legal entity.

In Tunisia, trademark ownership is established through registration of the trademark with the National Institute for Standardization and Industrial Property (*Institut National de la*

---

[345] Tunisia has double taxation treaties with Algeria, Arab Maghreb Union, Austria, Belgium, Burkina Faso, Canada, China, Czech Republic, Denmark, Egypt, Ethiopia, France, Germany, Great Britain, Greece, Hungary, Indonesia, Iraq, Iran, Italy, Jordan, Korea, Kuwait, Lebanon, Libya, Luxembourg, Mali, Malta, Mauritania, Morocco, Netherlands, Norway, Pakistan, Poland, Portugal, Oman, Qatar, Romania, Senegal, South Africa, Spain, Sudan, Sweden, Switzerland, Syria, Turkey, U.A.E., United States and Yemen.

[346] Article 16 of the 2009 Law provides that the franchisor must be the owner of the trademark.

Normalisation et de la Propriété Industrielle). The trademark's registration number must be referenced in the franchise agreement and registered with the National Institute of Standardization and Industrial Property in order for franchisee's and franchisor's rights to be enforceable against third parties.

VI. Restrictions on Transfer

Please advise as to whether there are any restrictions (1) on a franchisor to restrict transfers by a master franchisee, any transfer of interest in a master franchisee, or the assets of the master franchisee or (2) the ability of a master franchisee to control and/or restrict transfers of a subfranchisee's rights under a master franchise agreement, interest in the subfranchisee, or the assets of the subfranchisee.

There are no restrictions:

- on a franchisor's ability to restrict transfers by a master franchisee, any transfer of interest in a master franchisee, or transfer of any assets of the master franchisee; or
- on the ability of a master franchisee to control and/or restrict transfers of a subfranchisee's rights under a master franchise agreement, any interest in the subfranchisee, or any assets of the subfranchisee.

VII. Termination

Please advise us as to any laws relating to termination in your country, such as agency laws, required indemnity provisions, notice or "good cause" requirements, or other laws affecting termination of a franchise agreement. Please describe.

A. Termination from the Competition Law Perspective

In some instances, the Tunisian Competition Council may consider the termination of a commercial relationship by the franchisor as anticompetitive. It may prevent the franchisor from terminating a franchise agreement, without an objective reason.

The illegal abuse of a party's state of economic dependency is one reason that may be cited as a cause of termination and such terminations are prohibited under the Competition Law. According to such law, it is considered an abuse of third parties' state of economic dependency to terminate an agreement without cause or to terminate because the other party refused to accept exorbitant commercial conditions. If such a violation of the law is found, the Competition Law (and thus the Tunisian Competition Council) may invalidate the franchise agreement irrespective of the choice of the law and the choice of dispute resolution agreed to between the parties. Moreover, the Competition Law may subject the franchisor to sanctions (e.g., fines).

From a Competition Law perspective, a state of economic dependency exists only if the franchisee is unable to conduct any business without the involvement of the franchisor due to some or all of the following:

- the brand notoriety of the franchisor;
- the market share of the franchisor;
- the franchisor's share of the turnover of the franchisee; or
- the absence of equivalent solutions (e.g. business alternatives) for the franchisee.

Where the franchisee has an exclusive arrangement with the franchisor, the state of economic dependency is more easily proved. However, even the question of the legality of exclusivity is not clear-cut under Tunisian law. Some jurists consider that all forms of exclusivity are forbidden in Tunisia, despite the fact that certain sectors continue to operate under exclusive arrangements.

B. Termination under the Insolvency Legal Regime

Under Tunisian law, if a franchisee is experiencing financial difficulties, it is sometimes determined that certain outstanding contracts (such as a franchise agreement) concluded with such an entity cannot be terminated. This is a matter of public policy and overrules all the provisions of the law applicable to the franchise agreement, and the dispute resolution agreed to between the parties.

C. Termination from a Civil Law Perspective

The Competition Law deals only with offenses against competition, and sanctions such offenses by various penalties (e.g., fines). If the Tunisian Competition Council determines that the franchisor abused the state of economic dependency of the franchisee, the franchisee may bring a civil lawsuit before the Tunisian civil courts to claim compensation for damages suffered. Such a lawsuit is based on the tort caused to the franchisee and may be brought before the Tunisian courts, notwithstanding the choice of the law and the choice of dispute resolution agreed between the parties.[347]

The courts may award compensation in favor of the franchisee. Such an award is intended to allow the franchisee to reorganize itself and to find other commercial opportunities.

[347] The *Tunisian Code of International Private Law* was adopted by Law *n° 98-97* dated November 27, 1998. Article 5, paragraph 1 of the Code provides that: "Tunisian courts are also competent to judge…the cases based on tort if the act which caused the damage or the damage itself occurred in Tunisia."

VIII. Governing Law, Jurisdiction, and Dispute Resolution

A. Choice of Law of Foreign Jurisdiction

Please confirm whether the choice of law of a foreign jurisdiction would likely to be upheld under the law of the country, except for certain matters such as trademarks, bankruptcy, and competition matters, which we assume would be governed by the law in your country.

Except the matters mentioned in Section VII above and certain other matters, such as exchange control issues, that would be governed by Tunisian law, the choice of law of a foreign jurisdiction in a franchise agreement would be upheld under the laws of Tunisia. Article 62 of the Tunisian Code of International Private law provides that the contract (e.g. a franchise agreement) is governed by the law chosen by the parties. If the parties have not chosen a governing law, and if the contract concerns a professional or commercial activity, the law to be taken into consideration is the law of the country where the party whose contractual obligation is being determined is domiciled or where that party has a principal office. Moreover, Article 69 of the Code provides that contracts related to intellectual property are governed by the law of the country of the person who transferred or relinquished the intellectual property rights unless a different governing law is chosen by the parties.

B. International Arbitration Dispute Resolution

Please confirm that a court in your country would honor an election of international arbitration dispute resolution, and therefore refuse to hear any disputes arising under a franchise agreement.

Except the matters mentioned in Section VII above and certain other matters, such as exchange control issues, that would be governed by Tunisian courts, a court in Tunisia would honor an election of an international arbitration dispute resolution and refuse to hear any dispute arising under a franchise agreement.

Based on Article 52 of the *Tunisian Arbitration Code*,[348] a Tunisian court that considers a matter subject to an arbitration agreement must refer the parties to arbitration, if one of the parties so requests. The request must be made no later than the day the party presents to the court its statement on the substance of the matter, unless it appears to the court that the arbitration agreement is void, ineffective or cannot be enforced. Article 53 of the same code provides that when such a lawsuit is brought before a court, and the matter was not yet referred to the arbitration court, the court must declare itself incompetent, unless it appears that the arbitration agreement is clearly void.

An arbitration agreement may be considered clearly void when for example it was the result of outright fraud (i.e., forgery of a signature); if one of the parties to the agreement did not have the capacity or the power to sign the agreement or when the arbitration agreement was signed under duress.

The court cannot declare its incompetence automatically if none of the parties put forward the arbitration agreement.

It is important to note that Article 54 of the *Tunisian Arbitration Code* provides that a party may request a temporary protective measure (i.e., the seizure of assets or inventory) from a court before the matter is referred to the arbitration.

Tunisia gives effect to some provisions of the *Convention on the Recognition and Enforcement of Foreign Arbitral Awards* (the "New York Convention") – to which it is a signatory.

---

[348] The *Tunisian Arbitration Code* was adopted by the *law n° 93-42* dated April 26, 1993.

IX. Non-Competition Provisions

If the franchise agreement prohibits the franchisee from engaging in certain competitive activities during the term of the agreement, and for a 12-month period after the termination or expiration of the agreement, please comment on the enforceability of non-competition covenants in your country.

Because non-competition clauses are recognized and enforceable under Tunisian law, the franchise agreement may prohibit the franchisee from engaging in certain competitive activities during the term of the contract, and for a 12-month period after the termination or expiration of the contract. Article 118 of the Tunisian Civil Code (*Code des Obligations et des Contrats*) permits restraints on exercising a certain commerce or industry, in a specified location or for a specific duration.

X. Language Requirements

Does the law in your country require that a franchise agreement be translated into the local language in order to be enforceable between the parties?

Tunisian law does not require that a franchise agreement be translated into the local language to be enforceable between the parties. However, it must be translated into the local language, (in principle by a sworn translator in Tunisia), if the franchise agreement is:

- registered before the Tax Office (as mentioned in Section II.B.1. above);
- filed with any administration (as mentioned in Section III above); or
- presented to Tunisian courts for any reason.

XI. Other Significant Matters

Please advise as to whether there are any significant matters not addressed above of which a franchisor should be aware in connection with its entering into a franchise agreement in your country.

Article 15 of the 2009 Law provides that the compulsory minimum terms of the franchise agreement are set by decree. Article 2 of the Decree provides that the franchise agreements must include the rights and obligations of the franchisor and the franchisee, and notably the following information:

- services provided by the franchisor to the franchisee and notably the transfer of know-how, technical expertise, and use of intellectual property rights;
- remunerations required from the franchisee;
- term of the franchise agreement and the conditions of its renewal;
- conditions of use of the trademark or the corporate name;
- conditions of the termination of the franchise agreement;
- conditions of the exclusivity of supply;
- non-competition conditions;
- delineation of the geographical area of the exclusive use of the trademark or the corporate name;
- franchisee's obligation to keep confidential the information disclosed by the franchisor;
- investment plan to be realized by the franchisee;

- mechanisms on the basis of which the advertising expenses are shared;
- communication to the franchisor regarding the sales and the financial situation of the franchisee;
- conditions under which the franchisor or its representatives have access to franchisee's premises;
- possibility of the franchisee to subfranchise with third parties in respect of each geographical area, in case the franchise agreement is exclusive for the entire territory of Tunisia.

Article 4 of the Decree provides also that the franchise agreement shall not contain anticompetitive clauses intended to:

- impose sale or service prices on franchisee;
- fix a minimum turnover to be realized by the franchisee.

Article 16 of the 2009 Law requires that, during the franchise agreement term, the franchisor must provide to the franchisee the necessary commercial and technical assistance and all material information related to the franchise network.

Article 16 of the 2009 Law also requires that the franchisee must provide to the franchisor information relating to the sales realized and its financial situation. It authorizes the franchisor or its representatives to inspect the franchisee's business premises during the typical work or operating hours.

Franchising in Zambia

Mabvuto Sakala

Corpus Legal Practitioners

Lusaka, Zambia

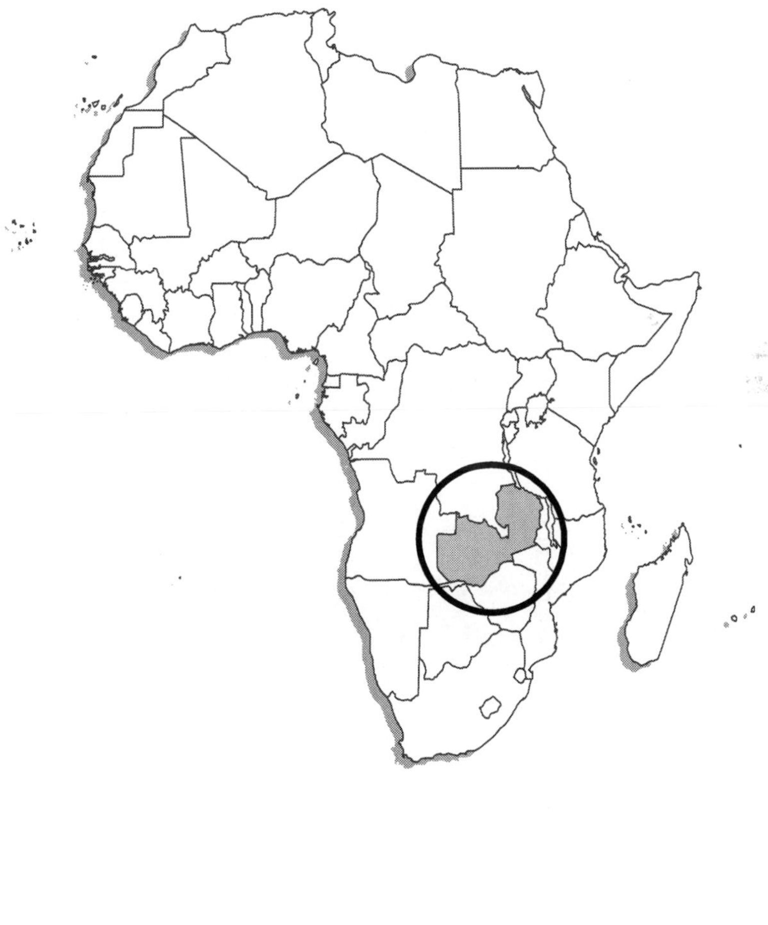

Zambia

I. Introduction

A. Historical Background of Country

During the 1920s and 1930s, advances in mining spurred development and immigration to the territory of Northern Rhodesia. Its name was changed to Zambia upon independence from the United Kingdom in 1964. In the 1980s and 1990s, declining copper prices and a prolonged drought hurt the economy. Elections in 1991 brought an end to one-party rule under Kenneth Kaunda when Frederick Chiluba came into power with the Movement for Multi-party Democracy Party ("MMD"). At the end of his second term of office, Chiluba was succeeded by Levy Mwanawasa who was also a member of MMD. Mwanawasa was re-elected in 2006 in an election that was deemed free and fair. He died in the middle of his second term of office and was subsequently succeed by his Vice President Rupiah Banda, who won a special presidential election in October 2008. In October 2011, Zambia had elections in which the current President Michael Sata emerged victorious. These elections resulted in a transition in government from the MMD to the Patriotic Front ("PF") that for the most part was free, fair, and peaceful.

B. Economy of the Country

Zambia's economy has experienced strong growth in recent years, with real GDP growth in 2005–08 at about 6% per year. Privatization of government-owned copper mines in the 1990s relieved the government from covering mammoth losses generated by the industry and greatly improved the chances for copper mining to return to profitability and spur economic growth. In fact, copper output has increased steadily since 2004 due to higher copper prices and foreign investment. In 2005, Zambia qualified for debt relief under the IMF's Highly Indebted Poor Country Initiative, consisting of approximately US$6 billion in debt relief. The decline in world commodity prices and demand hurt GDP growth in 2009, but a sharp rebound in copper prices and a bumper maize crop have helped Zambia begin to recover. Recently, Zambia was re-classified as a middle-income country by the World Bank and was assigned a B+ sovereign credit by two internationally recognized credit agencies, Standard and Poor's and Fitch.

C. Franchise Legal Overview

Under the Zambian law, there is no specific law that regulates franchise agreements or transactions. The franchise agreement is seen as a contractual agreement between the parties and thus contract law will govern such an agreement.

II. Regulatory Requirements

A. Pre-Sale Disclosure

Please describe any pre-sale franchise disclosure or similar requirements that may apply to franchise transactions.

No pre-sale franchise disclosure or similar requirements apply to franchise transactions under the laws of Zambia.

B. Governmental Approvals, Registrations, Filing Requirements

Please describe any necessary government approvals, registrations, or filing requirements that may apply to franchise transactions.

Zambia does not have any legislation that explicitly regulates franchises.

However, it is advisable to have a franchise agreement approved by the Competition and Consumer Protection Commission (the "Commission"). The Commission is a statutory body created by the *Competition and Consumer Protection Act No. 24 of 2010* (the "CCPA") to review the operations of markets in Zambia and the conditions of competition in these markets. Generally, the Act classifies as anti-competitive any category of agreement, decision or concerted practice that has as its object or effect, the prevention, restriction, or distortion of competition to an appreciable extent in Zambia.

Under the CCPA, any enterprise that enters into an agreement that may have the effect of preventing, distorting, or substantially lessening competition is required to obtain negative clearance from the Commission. Negative clearance is certification by the Commission that otherwise anti-competitive conduct can be allowed under conditions specified by the Commission. In addition, the CCPA provides for the enforceability of certain agreements that may be considered anti-competitive provided the agreements satisfy any of the exemption conditions listed under the Act.

The agreement may be exempted if is likely to contribute to:

(a) maintaining or promoting exports from Zambia;

(b) promoting or maintaining the efficient production, distribution, or provision of goods and services;

(c) promoting technical or economic progress in the production, distribution, or provision of goods and services;

(d) maintaining lower prices, higher quality, or greater choice of goods and services for consumers;

(e) promoting the competitiveness of micro and small business enterprises in Zambia; or

(f) obtaining a benefit for the public which outweighs or would outweigh the lessening in competition that would result, or is likely to result from the competition.

The Commission may grant an exemption subject to such conditions and for such period as it considers appropriate. Should an application for exemption be rejected, the Commission is obliged to give reasons for rejecting an exemption, which reason presumably will be that the agreement does not qualify under any of the instances of exemption enumerated above.

There is no statutory period within which the Commission is required to revert to an applicant. The length of time to obtain approval will generally depend on administrative procedures within the Commission.

If exemption is obtained from the Commission, the terms of the franchise agreement will be rendered legally binding by the execution of the agreement, subject to its authentication if executed outside Zambia.

Further, if the franchise agreement relates to a trade name, services, or goods that are registered with the Patents and Companies Registration Agency ("PACRA"), the franchise agreement will itself be required to be registered with PACRA

Apart from the provisions of the CCPA and the requirement to register a franchise agreement involving a registered trade name, services, or goods, there are no other requirements for a franchise agreement to be registered, recorded, or filed at any public office to render it legally binding.

C. Limits of Fees and Typical Term of Franchise Agreement

Please describe any limits upon the nature and extent of fees and the term of a typical franchise agreement.

As an essentially contractual transaction, the nature and terms of the franchise agreement will be as determined by the parties thereto, conditional on the general requirement that the object of the agreement should not be illegal or against public policy.

Zambia

III. Currency

If all payments under a franchise agreement must be made in immediately available U.S. Dollars, please advise as to any restrictions, reporting requirements, or regulations concerning the exchange, repatriation, or remittance of U.S. Dollars.

Zambia does not have foreign exchange controls. It has a liberal foreign exchange market that operates through commercial banks and bureaux de change. However, *Statutory Instrument No. 33 of 2012* prohibits quoting, paying, demanding payment, or receiving foreign currency as legal tender for goods, services, or any other domestic transaction. A domestic transaction has been defined in *Statutory Instrument No. 78 of 2012* as one involving Zambian based counterparties within Zambia, in contrast to an international transaction, which has been defined as a transaction involving a person or entity who is not resident in Zambia.

Thus, the prohibition of the use of foreign currency as legal tender applies only to those transactions between parties resident in Zambian but does not affect transactions in which one of the parties is not resident in Zambia.

Further, the *Bank of Zambia (Amendment) Act No. 1 of 2013* has now restricted the power of the Bank of Zambia (Central Bank) to only taking measures to monitor balance of payment transactions. In so doing, the Bank of Zambia may, to some extent, have the power to issue directives with respect to the mentioned transactions. Under the amendment, the Bank of Zambia, in promoting the efficient operation of the foreign exchange system, may take measures to monitor:

(a) foreign exchange inflows and outflows remitted;

(b) imports and exports of goods and other inflows and outflows;

(c) international transactions in services;

(d) international transfers to or from non-residents;

(e) profits or dividends received in respect of investments abroad;

(f) borrowing and trade credits from non-residents;

(g) investment in the form of equity and debt securities abroad;

(h) receipts of both principal and interest on loans to non-residents; and

(i) international money transfers into and out of Zambia.

This, to a fairly large extent, limits the powers of the Bank of Zambia to create formal standards, codes of conduct, or rules with regard to the issue of restrictions on dealing in foreign exchange.

IV. Taxes, Tariffs, and Duties

Please do not provide any in-depth comments on tax structuring. However, please provide your general comments on the typical amount of withholding tax that would apply and whether a "gross-up" provision contained in a franchise agreement would be enforceable in your country.

The position of the law in Zambia is that tax is chargeable from a source within or deemed to be within the Republic. Under the *Income Tax Act*, Chapter 323 of the Laws of Zambia, income is deemed to be from within the Republic if it arises from a royalty incurred in the production of income or in the carrying on of a business in the Republic or paid directly or indirectly out of funds derived from within the Republic.

In light of this, a franchisee in Zambia would be liable for withholding tax on royalties at the standard rate of 15% to resident recipients and 20% for payments to non-residents as of the 2013 financial year.

There are no restrictions under Zambia legislation that would prevent the insertion of a standard gross-up tax clause in an agreement; consequently, contracting parties are at liberty to have such a clause in their contract. Such a gross-up provision contained in a franchise agreement would be upheld as a matter of practice.

The tariffs and duties applicable will vary per franchise agreement depending on the subject matter of the tariffs. Zambia is a signatory to the *General Agreement on Tariffs and Trade* ("GATT") and its ancillary agreements. Therefore, its tariffs and duties are largely determined by its commitments under the GATT.

Zambia is a signatory to double taxation agreements with the following countries: Canada, Denmark, Finland, France, Germany, Holland, India, Ireland, Italy, Japan, Kenya, Norway, South Africa, Sweden, Tanzania, Uganda, and the United Kingdom.

In addition, Zambia has double taxation agreements with Mauritius, Yugoslavia, and Zimbabwe. However, to date, these agreements have not been ratified and as such cannot be relied on in Zambian courts.

V. Trademarks

Please advise us as to whether there are any special requirements for granting a valid trademark license, including the use of a registered user agreement or a short trademark license agreement and any required filing of such an agreement with the trademark authorities.

The *Trademarks Act* (the "Act") does not specify any special requirements for granting a trademark license. In this regard, the basic principles of contract law apply. Trademark licensing is, however, a recognized way through which a trademark can be managed and protected in Zambia. Under the Act, a trademark owner can license third parties to do the acts that are covered by the exclusive rights of the trademark in relation to goods, that is, affixing the trademark on the goods, containers, packaging, and labels and using it in advertising, promotional activities, business papers, and documents. The license can be exclusive or non-exclusive.

Any person other than the proprietor of the trademark must apply to the Registrar of Trade Marks to be registered as the user of that trademark in Zambia.

The application for registration of a person as a registered user should be made by the proprietor and the registered user in writing. The application must be accompanied by information verified by statutory declaration relating to the relationship, existing or proposed, between the proprietor and the proposed registered owner, the goods for which registration is proposed, any conditions or restrictions proposed with respect to the characteristics of the goods, and the period of the permitted use if limited in duration.

The Registrar of Trade Marks may register the proposed registered user, after considering the information furnished, and after being satisfied that, in the circumstances, the use of the trademark in relation to the proposed goods by the proposed registered user would not be contrary to the public interest. The Registrar may, however, refuse an application if it appears to him that the grant would facilitate trafficking in the trademark.

VI. Restrictions on Transfer

Please advise as to whether there are any restrictions on (1) a franchisor to restrict transfers in a master franchisee, any interest in a master franchisee, or the assets of the master franchisee or (2) the ability of a master franchisee to control and/or restrict transfers of a subfranchisee's rights under a master franchise agreement, interest in the subfranchisee, or the assets of the subfranchisee.

As per Section II.B. above, any agreements restricting the acquisition of interests as between a franchisor and a master franchisee or any agreements as between a master franchisee and a subfranchisee must be approved by the Commission. The Commission is likely to prohibit an agreement that has the effect of preventing, distorting, or restricting competition or substantially lessening competition in a market for any goods or services unless an exemption for the restrictive agreement is obtained in accordance with the procedure outlined in Section II.B. above.

Regarding the transfer of assets, the parties may determine what restrictions will be placed on the transfer of assets but generally there are no restrictions on the transfer of property. However, the *Property Transfer Tax Act*, Chapter 340 of the Laws of Zambia provides that whenever any property is transferred, there must be charged upon, and collected from, the person transferring such property, a property transfer tax, which rate is currently fixed at 5% of the realized value of the property. The definition of property here comprises any land in Zambia and any shares issued by a company incorporated in Zambia.

Accordingly, any transfer of shares or land whether as between the franchisor and the master franchisee or as between the master franchisee and sub franchisees may be subject to payment of property transfer tax.

VII. Termination

Please advise us as to any laws relating to termination in your country, such as agency laws, required indemnity provisions, notice or "good cause" requirements, or other laws affecting termination of a franchise agreement. Please describe.

Considering their contractual nature, franchise agreements are terminable by expiration of the term or by notice. In instances of change of legislation, the parties may consent to the continuation of the agreement in its executed form unless that change in legislation renders continued performance of the agreement illegal.

The *Interpretation and General Provisions Act*, Chapter 2 of the Laws of Zambia provides that the repeal of any written law will not affect any right, privilege, obligation, or liability acquired, accrued, or incurred under that law. However, where legislation is repealed and amended or replaced, the amending or replacing legislation may specifically provide for the effect of the change in legislation.

VIII. Governing Law, Jurisdiction, and Dispute Resolution

A. Choice of Law of Foreign Jurisdiction

Please confirm whether the choice of law of a foreign jurisdiction would likely to be upheld under the law of the country, except for certain matters such as trademarks, bankruptcy, and competition matters, which we assume would be governed by the law in your country.

Parties are at liberty to choose the governing law of their agreements and there is no legal restriction pertaining to the choice of law by contracting parties. In practice, non-Zambian citizens tend to choose foreign law and it is not uncommon for parties to choose English law due to the fact that Zambia is a common law jurisdiction.

However, if the parties do not agree on which law will prevail, the common law principles dictate that the governing law will be that of the place where the agreement is performed. In determining the governing law, the court may also consider other factors such as intention of the parties, common usage and trade for that particular transaction, prior negotiations between the parties, and the place of conclusion of the contract.

Zambia

B. International Arbitration Dispute Resolution

Please confirm that a court in your country would honor an election of international arbitration dispute resolution, and therefore refuse to hear any disputes arising under a franchise agreement.

Courts in Zambia would honor an election of international arbitration dispute resolution subject to the provisions of the *Arbitration Act No. 19 of 2000* (the "Arbitration Act"). The Arbitration Act recognizes as binding arbitral awards issued under the auspices of the *Convention on the Recognition and Enforcement of Foreign Arbitral Awards* (the "New York Convention"), irrespective of the country in which it was made, upon application in writing to a competent court. In this regard, arbitral awards in Zambia are recognized and enforced under the *Geneva Convention on the Execution of Foreign Arbitral Awards* and the New York Convention.

Recognition or enforcement of a foreign arbitral award may however be refused if, at the request of the party against whom it is invoked, a party furnishes to the competent court where recognition or enforcement is sought, proof of any of the following, non-exclusive facts:

- a party to the arbitration agreement was under some incapacity;
- the agreement is not valid under the law to which the parties have subjected it or, failing any indication thereon, under the law of the country where the award was made;
- the party against whom the award is invoked was not given proper notice of the appointment of an arbitrator or of the arbitral proceedings or was otherwise unable to present its case; or

- the award has not yet become binding on the parties or has been set aside or suspended by a court of the country in which, or under the law of which, that award was made.

IX. Non-Competition Provisions

If the franchise agreement prohibits the master franchisee from engaging in certain competitive activities during the term of the agreement, and for a 12-month period after the termination or expiration of the agreement, please comment on the enforceability of non-competition covenants in your country.

Non-compete covenants are essentially contractual and therefore subject to agreement as between the parties. The law in Zambia recognizes the enforceability of a non-compete clause provided the terms are reasonable. Where the term is considered unreasonable, the courts may be unwilling to enforce them for being unreasonable in restraint of trade. What is reasonable is determined on a case-to-case basis but the court may give consideration to factors such as the term of the covenant and the geographical area to which the covenant extends.

X. Language Requirements

Does the law in your country require that a franchise agreement be translated into the local language in order to be enforceable between the parties?

There is no requirement under Zambian law that makes it a requirement for a franchise agreement to be translated into any local language for the purpose of enforceability as between the parties.

XI. Other Significant Matters

Please advise as to whether there are any significant matters not addressed above of which a franchisor should be aware in connection with its entering into a franchise agreement in your country.

In the event that the franchise agreement is executed outside of Zambia, it will only be enforceable in Zambia if it is authenticated in accordance with the *Authentication of Documents Act.*

Under the *Authentication of Documents Act*, in order for any document executed outside Zambia to be enforceable in Zambia, the document must be authenticated in the manner prescribed. Documents executed in the United Kingdom are sufficiently authenticated if they are executed before a notary public and signed and duly sealed by such notary public. In the case of an execution of documents from any other jurisdiction outside Zambia other than the United Kingdom, the signature and seal of the notary public must be certified by the consular office in Zambia of that foreign jurisdiction.

Thus, a franchise agreement executed outside of the country will have to be authenticated if it is to have legal efficacy in Zambia.

- *Please provide any insight as to any proposed franchise specific legislation that may be under consideration in your jurisdiction.*

There is currently no franchise association in Zambia and there is no franchise-specific legislation being considered currently in the country.

- *Please provide a sample of the franchised brands that operate in your country.*

    - Kentucky Fried Chicken (KFC)

    - Subway

Franchising in Zimbabwe

Nellie R.F. Tiyago-Jinjika

Scanlen & Holderness

Harare, Zimbabwe

Zimbabwe

I. Introduction

A. Historical Background of Country

In 1965, Zimbabwe ceased to be a British colony after the Unilateral Declaration of Independence. Zimbabwe, then known as Rhodesia, remained under the rule of the minority white population. A civil war ensued between the British colonialists and black national freedom fighters in 1965 and eventually ended with the signing of the Lancaster House Agreement in 1979. The agreement facilitated the holding of elections and, on April 18, 1980, Robert Mugabe became the first elected Prime Minister of the new Zimbabwe. General elections held in March 2008 amounted to a censure of the Zimbabwe African National Union – Patriotic Front-led government with the opposition winning a majority of seats in parliament. The Movement for Democratic Change Zimbabwe opposition leader Morgan Tsvangirai won the most votes in the presidential polls, but not enough to win outright. Difficult negotiations over a power-sharing government, in which Mugabe remained president and Tsvangirai became prime minister, were finally settled in February 2009, although the leaders failed to agree upon many key outstanding governmental issues. Since then there have been numerous elections held with the final elections resulting in the ruling party, Zimbabwe African National Union – Patriotic Front (ZANU PF) remaining in power after what has been globally called the "free and fair" elections of Zimbabwe.

B. Economy of the Country

Zimbabwe's economy is growing despite continuing political uncertainty. Following a decade of contraction from 1998 to 2008, Zimbabwe's economy recorded real growth of more than 9% per year in 2010-11, before slowing to 5% in 2012, due in part to a poor harvest and low diamond revenues. The government of Zimbabwe still faces a number of difficult economic problems, including infrastructure and regulatory deficiencies, policy uncertainty, a large external debt burden, and insufficient formal employment. Due to extreme hyperinflation a multi-currency economy was introduced in February 2009 – which allowed currencies such as the Botswana pula, the South Africa rand, and the US dollar to be used locally. This ended hyperinflation and reduced inflation to about 10%.

C. Franchise Legal Overview

Franchise agreements are governed by the laws of Zimbabwe with no specific law that strictly regulates franchising itself. The laws that are applicable to all businesses in Zimbabwe are applied to the business of franchising. Of note are the company laws, indigenization laws, investment laws, competition laws and tax laws.

In Zimbabwe, indigenization laws prescribe that any business conducted in Zimbabwe that meets certain thresholds should be controlled by indigenous people. The laws also prescribe industries which have been reserved to indigenous Zimbabweans and cannot be ventured into without approval.[349]

---

[349] On March 9, 2008, Zimbabwe's President, Robert Mugabe signed the Indigenization and Economic Empowerment Bill into law. The law requires that controlling interest in businesses and business ventures in Zimbabwe revert to indigenous Zimbabweans that were previously disadvantaged before 1980. The act provides for manners in which indigenization may be achieved including points for socio economic projects and community and employee share trust. It further allows the Minister of Indigenization to exercise his discretion when presented with an indigenization plan where there will be a substantial benefit to the Zimbabwean economy. Thresholds have been set for various industries but the general rule is that if a business has a net value of US$500,000 or less, there is no need to indigenize. The threshold for a business in the mining sector is US$1. There are specific sectors of industry that have been reserved for indigenous persons and to enter into these one has to seek the necessary approval from the Zimbabwe Investment Authority and Minister of Indigenization. At the moment the following sectors are reserved: agriculture (primary production of food and cash crops); transportation (passenger buses, taxes and car and car hire services); retail and wholesale trade; barber shops, hairdressing and beauty salons; employment agencies; estate agencies; valet services; grain milling; bakeries; tobacco grading and packaging; tobacco processing; advertising agencies; milk processing and provision of local arts craft, marketing and distribution.

II. Regulatory Requirements

A. Pre-Sale Disclosure

Please describe any pre-sale franchise disclosure or similar requirements that may apply to franchise transactions.

No pre-sale franchise disclosure or similar requirements apply to franchise transactions under the laws of Zimbabwe.

B. Governmental Approvals, Registrations, Filing Requirements

Please describe any necessary government approvals, registrations, or filing requirements that may apply to franchise transactions.

Generally where one is to enter into an agreement that will place an obligation on it to make payments outside Zimbabwe, exchange control regulations as explained in III (Currency) below, must be complied with. Filing requirements as discussed in detail in V (Trademarks) below must also be complied with.

Even though government approval is not specifically required for entering into a franchise agreement, local courts have held that the government has the power to intervene and influence the ambit of a franchise agreement. This has been done before where the Government of Zimbabwe intervened to nationalize the motor industry.[350]

C. Limits of Fees and Typical Term of Franchise Agreement

Please describe any limits upon the nature and extent of fees and the term of a typical franchise agreement.

---

[350] *Acting Minister of Industry and Technology and Another v Tanaka Power (Private) Limited 1990* (2) ZLR 208 Supreme Court.

As there is no specific law governing franchising, parties are free to agree on the terms and conditions of a franchise agreement subject to the laws in Zimbabwe that govern relationships between parties as detailed above.

III. Currency

If all payments under a franchise agreement must be made in immediately available U.S. Dollars, please advise as to any restrictions, reporting requirements, or regulations concerning the exchange, repatriation, or remittance of U.S. Dollars.

Bank regulations require that payments in foreign currency with funds to be remitted outside Zimbabwe must first obtain prior approval of the Reserve Bank of Zimbabwe. In the event that a party binds itself without obtaining prior approval out of ignorance of the law, the approval may be applied for after the fact. Approval is obtained by application made through authorized dealers, which are usually the registered banks who will advise of the requirements at the time of application.

The banking laws also recognize directives from the Governor of the Reserve Bank of Zimbabwe as legally binding on persons conducting business in Zimbabwe. Therefore, one must ensure that there is compliance with the directives as they are published from time to time.

Zimbabwe also subscribes to international anti-money laundering requirements and as such all transactions involving receipt and remittance of money must be conducted through the normal banking channels. Should a bank be suspicious of the activity in an account, they have the power to freeze such account without prior notice to the account holder.

IV. Taxes, Tariffs, and Duties

Please do not provide any in-depth comments on tax structuring. However, please provide your general comments on the typical amount of withholding tax that would apply and whether a "gross-up" provision contained in a franchise agreement would be enforceable in your country.

Below is an overview of the tax applicable to the non-resident Franchisor.

A. Applicable Rate

Dividends may be subject to non-resident sales tax depending on the terms of any double taxation agreements with the country of residence of the recipient.

A non-resident recipient of interest from a source in Zimbabwe may be liable to income tax in Zimbabwe on such interest. Taxable interest also includes interest payable by a person who is ordinarily resident or carries on business in Zimbabwe.

In addition, non-residents may be liable to withholding tax on fees, royalties and remittances to a country outside Zimbabwe. The current applicable withholding tax rate is 10%.

Presently, Zimbabwe has double taxation agreements with the United Kingdom, Germany, Netherlands and South Africa.

B. Gross-up Clauses

Gross-up provisions are practiced and permitted under the laws of Zimbabwe.

V. Trademarks

Please advise us as to whether there are any special requirements for granting a valid trademark license, including the use of a registered user agreement or a short trademark license agreement and any required filing of such an agreement with the trademark authorities.

The registration of marks is governed by the Trade Marks Act 26:04, which prescribes the manner in which marks are to be registered in Zimbabwe. This includes filing of an application with copies of the mark to be registered and payment of the prescribed fee. The mark to be registered is published in the Trademarks Journal, after which it is sealed and registered if no objection to the registration is raised. A mark successfully registered will be protected for a renewable 10 year period.

The proprietor of a registered mark may apply to the Registrar of Trade Marks for registration of another person as a registered user under terms of the Trade Marks Act. A registered use application must be submitted to the Registrar by both the user and the owner, and must state the particulars of the relationship, the goods covered, and the conditions of the use. The following items are required to record a license:

(1) a registered user or license agreement;

(2) forms of authorization from the owner and user (equal to a power of attorney); and

(3) a declaration and statement of case from the owner or the registered user describing the circumstances, terms and conditions of use associated with the license.[351]

Finally, Zimbabwe is the headquarters for ARIPO (African Regional Intellectual Property Organisation). ARIPO has eighteen member states in Africa.[352] Application for registration of one's mark or patent will result in protection in the states chosen by the applicant.

---

[351] See also Edward Fennessy, *supra* note 256 at 181-17.

[352] The following countries are currently members of ARIPO: Botswana, the Gambia, Ghana, Kenya, Lesotho, Malawi, Mozambique, Namibia, Sierra Leone, Liberia, Rwanda, Somalia, Sudan, Swaziland, Tanzania, Uganda, Zambia and Zimbabwe

VI. Restrictions on Transfer

Please advise as to whether there are any restrictions (1) on a franchisor to restrict transfers by a master franchisee, any interest in a master franchisee, or the assets of the master franchisee or (2) the ability of a master franchisee to control and/or restrict transfers of a subfranchisee's rights under a master franchise agreement, interest in the subfranchisee, or the assets of the subfranchisee.

In relation to a Master Franchise and Subfranchise:

A. Assignment

Parties may agree on assignment provisions provided that they comply with the laws of Zimbabwe and are not deemed to be contrary to public policy.

B. Change of Control

Change of control of any Zimbabwean registered entity requires compliance with the indigenization laws and competition laws.

C. Transfer of Assets

Parties may agree on the timing and manner in which assets will be transferred. The valuation formula may be predetermined by the parties. Any funds transferred in connection with asset transfers must be processed through the proper banking channels. Of note are laws in Zimbabwe that prohibit non-Zimbabweans from participating in hire purchase arrangements.[353]

[353] Hire purchase agreements are those that allow a party to purchase property through installments. Ownership of the property does not transfer until all payments are satisfied.

VII. Termination

Please advise us as to any laws relating to termination in your country, such as agency laws, required indemnity provisions, notice or "good cause" requirements, or other laws affecting termination of a franchise agreement. Please describe.

Termination is dependent on the agreement between parties. Where termination is by virtue of breach of contract, it is common to have a notice period provided for in the agreement. Alternatively, an agreement can be worded in such a manner as to automatically terminate upon occurrence or non-occurrence of certain events. Consequences of termination must be in compliance with the laws.

VIII. Governing Law, Jurisdiction, and Dispute Resolution

A. Choice of Law of Foreign Jurisdiction

Please confirm whether the choice of law of a foreign jurisdiction would likely to be upheld under the law of the country, except for certain matters such as trademarks, bankruptcy, and competition matters, which we assume would be governed by the law in your country.

Parties may choose a particular jurisdiction to govern their agreement, including a foreign jurisdiction. The parties must consider which jurisdiction will provide them with effective and timely resolution of any disputes.

B. International Arbitration Dispute Resolution

Please confirm that a court in your country would honor an election of international arbitration dispute resolution, and therefore refuse to hear any disputes arising under a franchise agreement.

Arbitrations in Zimbabwe are governed by the Arbitration Act Chapter 7:15, which was enacted to give effect to domestic and international arbitration agreements. In addition, the Arbitration Act applies, with modifications, the Model Law on International Commercial Arbitration as adopted by the United Nations Commission on International Trade Law on June, 21, 1985.

It is important that parties should have an exhaustive arbitration clause that will detail selection of arbitrators and procedures to be followed during the arbitration to avoid an abuse of the arbitration process. In addition, it must be specifically agreed that the decision of the arbitrator is final and binding on the parties.

Zimbabwe is a signatory to the *Convention on the Recognition and Enforcement of Foreign Arbitral Awards* (the "New York Convention").

IX. Non-Competition Provisions

If the franchise agreement prohibits the master franchisee from engaging in certain competitive activities during the term of the agreement, and for a 12-month period after the termination or expiration of the agreement, please comment on the enforceability of non-competition covenants in your country.

Provisions that prohibit or restrict competition are not allowed under the competition laws of Zimbabwe. The Competition Act Chapter 14:28 aims to promote and maintain competition in the economy of Zimbabwe, to provide for the prevention and control of restrictive practices, to prevent and control of monopoly situations and prohibit unfair trade practices.

A non-compete clause will generally be regarded as a penalty clause which one can challenge both in terms of contract law and competition laws.

X. Language Requirements

Does the law in your country require that a franchise agreement be translated into the local language in order to be enforceable between the parties?

Zimbabwe is an English speaking country with a very high literacy rate. Agreements are valid regardless of the language they may be entered into. It is prudent to have a certified translation of agreements which may from time to time be required by relevant authorities.

XI. Other Significant Matters

Please advise as to whether there are any significant matters not addressed above of which a franchisor should be aware in connection with its entering into a franchise agreement in your country.

There are no other significant matters to be discussed.

Appendices

Appendix A
Form of Questionnaire

Regulatory Requirements

A. Pre-sale Disclosure

Please describe any pre-sale franchise disclosure or similar requirements that may apply to franchise transactions.

B. Government Approvals, Registrations, Filing Requirements

Please describe any necessary government approvals, registrations, or filing requirements that may apply to franchise transactions.

C. Limits on Fees and Typical Term of Franchise Agreement

Please describe any limits upon the nature and extent of fees and the term of a typical franchise agreement.

Currency

If all payments under a franchise agreement must be made in immediately available U.S. Dollars, please advise as to any restrictions, reporting requirements, or regulations concerning the exchange, repatriation or remittance of U.S. Dollars.

Taxes, Tariffs, and Duties

Please do not provide any in-depth comments on tax structuring. However, please provide your general comments on the typical amount of withholding tax that would apply and whether a "gross-up" provision contained in a franchise agreement would be enforceable in your country.

Trademarks

Please advise us as to whether there are any special requirements for granting a valid trademark license, including the use of a registered user agreement or a short trademark license agreement and any required filing of such an agreement with the trademark authorities.

Restrictions on Transfer

Please advise as to whether there are any restrictions on (1) a franchisor to restrict transfers by a master franchisee, any interest in a master franchisee, or the assets of the master franchisee or (2) the ability of a master franchisee to control and/or restrict transfers of a subfranchisee's rights under a master franchise agreement, interest in the subfranchisee, or the assets of the subfranchisee.

Termination

Please advise us as to any laws relating to termination in your country, such as agency laws, required indemnity provisions, notice or "good cause" requirements, or other laws affecting termination of a franchise agreement. Please describe.

Governing Law, Jurisdiction, and Dispute Resolution

A. Choice of Law of Foreign Jurisdiction

Please confirm whether the choice of law of a foreign jurisdiction would likely to be upheld under the law of the country, except for certain matters such as trademarks, bankruptcy and competition matters, which we assume would be governed by the law in your country.

B. International Arbitration Dispute Resolution

Please confirm that a court in your country would honor an election of international arbitration dispute resolution, and therefore refuse to hear any disputes arising under a franchise agreement.

Non-Competition Provisions

If the franchise agreement prohibits the franchisee from engaging in certain competitive activities during the term of the agreement, and for a 12-month period after the termination or expiration of the agreement, please comment on the enforceability of non-competition covenants in your country.

Language Requirements

Does the law in your country require that a franchise agreement be translated into the local language in order to be enforceable between the parties?

Other Significant Matters

Please advise as to whether there are any significant matters not addressed above of which a franchisor should be aware in connection with its entering into a franchise agreement in your country.

Appendix B
Franchise Industry Associations

Egyptian Franchise Development Association

49 Al-Batal Ahmed Abdel Aziz,
Mohandeseen, Giza, Egypt
Telephone: (202) 33464306/ (202) 33021105
Fax: (202) 33458292
Email: info@efda.org.eg
Website: www.efola.org.eg

The Egyptian Franchise Development Association is a non-governmental, non-profit organization that supports and develops the franchise industry in Egypt. The EFDA was founded in 2001 by 16 businessmen, owners, and operators of over 40 renowned international franchise brands.

The association works to develop franchise projects by increasing the awareness of the franchise form of doing business. By providing a database of franchise industry parties, and holding exhibitions, seminars, and conferences, the EFDA establishes partnerships between potential franchisees and interested franchisors worldwide.

Franchising has developed extensively in Egypt over a short time, especially in the fast-food sector. There are currently 40 international franchisees in Egypt at present, 58% of these are food franchises, 88% of which are U.S. food franchises.

Franchise Association of South Africa

Third Floor
H Santos Building
30 Arena Circle
Bruma, South Africa
Telephone: 27 11 615 0359
Fax: 27 11 615 3679

Email: vera.valasis@fasa.co.za; fasa@fasa.co.za
Website: www.fasa.co.za

In 1979, a group of franchise companies operating in South Africa met to form the Franchise Association of South Africa, and establish ethical guidelines for franchise businesses. For nearly 30 years, FASA has continued to develop and expand the business environment for franchising in South Africa. FASA represents franchisors, franchisees, and the professional organizations associated with the franchise industry.

FASA holds the annual "International Franchise Expo" (IFE), the official franchise exhibition in South Africa. The event showcases a wide range of business sectors, and attracts thousands of individuals and organizations interested in the franchising industry.

Franchise Association of Zimbabwe

c/o Zimbabwe National Chamber of Commerce
SMES and Business Development Sub-Committee
Chairman Mr. N. Sibanda
Box 187
Gwanda
Telephone: 263 84 23568/9
Email: nmaghoba@gmail.com
Website: www.zncc.co.zw

Among other functions, the Franchise Association of Zimbabwe, which is operating under the ambit of the Zimbabwe National Chamber of Commerce, brings together franchisors and franchisees from the local, regional, and international market. It is expected in the long run to facilitate the development of competitive local brands and act as a critical mechanism for skills and technological transfer into the country. FAZ is structured as a non-profit-making organization whose goal is to communicate franchise operators' concerns.[354]

Moroccan Franchise Association

Fédération Marocaine de la Franchise (FMF) Angle rue Ain Taoujdate et rue Ain Ifrane Résidence Kacimi
2 éme étage Appt N° 9 Bourgogne - Casablanca
Telephone: 212 77057003/ 21222 48 58 10
Fax: 212 22 48 58 10
Email: fmf@menara.ma; Eee@fmf.ma; omari@fmf.ma (for Miss Btissam Omari)
Site Web: www.fmf.ma

The FMF (Moroccan Federation of Franchise) is chaired by Mr. Abderrahmane Belghiti in Morocco. FMF works to ensure that the conditions for the qualitative development of the franchises are achieved.

Nigerian International Franchise Association

The Executive Secretary
Nigerian International Franchise Association
NOTAP Office
19 Kingsway Road
Ikoyi, Lagos, Nigeria
Telephone: 01 741 5029
Email: nifa@nigerianfranchise.org; info@nigerianfranchise.org
Website: www.nigerianfranchise.org

According to its website, the Nigerian International Franchise Association is a trade association committed to the development and promotion of franchising in Nigeria. Its goals, among many others, are to educate potential investors and entrepreneurs in Nigeria on fundamentals of franchising and its proven track record for success and growth in business; to create a conducive

---

[354] *See* http://allafrica.com/stories/201105120120.html (last visited March 7, 2014).

atmosphere in Nigeria that attracts United States, Canadian, European, and other foreign franchise companies; and to become a central clearinghouse for franchise companies interested in expansion into the Nigerian market.

Appendix C
Quick Reference Guide

	Angola	Botswana	Burundi	Cape Verde	DRC	Egypt	Ethiopia	Ghana	Kenya	Mozambique	Nigeria	Rwanda	South Africa	Tunisia	Zambia	Zimbabwe
Pre-Sale Disclosure Requirement													X	X		
Double Taxation Treaty with United States						X							X	X	X	
Trademark License Registration	X	X			X	X	X	X	X		X	X	X	X	X	X
Central Bank Filing	X		X	X	X	X	X		X	X	X		X	X		X
Signatory to New York Convention		X*				X		X*	X*	X*	X*	X*	X*	X*	X*	X

* with some limitations

44163741R00258

Made in the USA
Charleston, SC
16 July 2015